SAP Lumira®, Discovery Edition

SAP PRESS is a joint initiative of SAP and Rheinwerk Publishing. The know-how offered by SAP specialists combined with the expertise of Rheinwerk Publishing offers the reader expert books in the field. SAP PRESS features first-hand information and expert advice, and provides useful skills for professional decision-making.

SAP PRESS offers a variety of books on technical and business-related topics for the SAP user. For further information, please visit our website: *www.sap-press.com*.

Chang, Hacking, van der A
SAP Lumira, Designer Edition: The Comprehensive Guide (3rd Edition)
2018, approx. 775 pages, hardcover and e-book
www.sap-press.com/4512

Ah-Soon, Brogden, Marks, Orthous, Sinkwitz
SAP BusinessObjects Web Intelligence: The Comprehensive Guide (4th Edition)
2017, 814 pages, hardcover and e-book
www.sap-press.com/4412

Chabert, Forster, Tessier, Vezzosi
SAP Predictive Analytics: The Comprehensive Guide
2018, 491 pages, hardcover and e-book
www.sap-press.com/4491

Ah-Soon, Mazoué, Vezzosi
Universe Design with SAP BusinessObjects BI: The Comprehensive Guide
2014, 729 pages, hardcover and e-book
www.sap-press.com/3412

Xavier Hacking, Martijn van Foeken

SAP Lumira®, Discovery Edition

The Comprehensive Guide

Rheinwerk
Publishing

Editor Meagan White
Acquisitions Editor Hareem Shafi
Copyeditor Kezia Endsley
Cover Design Graham Geary
Photo Credit Shutterstock.com/174676946/© solarseven
Layout Design Vera Brauner
Production Kelly O'Callaghan
Typesetting SatzPro, Krefeld (Germany)
Printed and bound in the United States of America, on paper from sustainable sources

ISBN 978-1-4932-1612-3
© 2018 by Rheinwerk Publishing, Inc., Boston (MA)
1st edition 2018

Library of Congress Cataloging-in-Publication Data
Names: Hacking, Xavier, author. | Van Foeken, Martijn, author.
Title: SAP Lumira discovery : the comprehensive guide / Xavier Hacking,
Martijn van Foeken.
Description: 1st edition. | Bonn ; Boston : Rheinwerk Publishing, 2018. |
Includes index.
Identifiers: LCCN 2017051118 (print) | LCCN 2018000318 (ebook) | ISBN
9781493216130 (ebook) | ISBN 9781493216123 (alk. paper)
Subjects: LCSH: Information visualization--Computer programs. | Data
mining--Computer programs. | SAP Lumira.
Classification: LCC QA76.9.I52 (ebook) | LCC QA76.9.I52 H33 2018 (print) |
DDC 006.3/12--dc23
LC record available at https://lccn.loc.gov/2017051118

Contents at a Glance

PART I   Getting Started

1	Introduction to SAP Lumira, Discovery Edition	31
2	Installing SAP Lumira, Discovery Edition	47
3	SAP Lumira, Discovery Edition Interface	67
4	Creating Your First Story	95

PART II   Data

5	Data Acquisition	113
6	Live Data	167
7	Data Analysis	181
8	Data Manipulation	189

PART III   Data Visualization and Stories

9	Chart Creation	235
10	Crosstabs	255
11	Comparison Charts	271
12	Percentage Charts	281
13	Correlation Charts	289
14	Trend Charts	297
15	Geographic Visualizations	309
16	Filters	317
17	Story Formatting	347
18	Linking Datasets	353

PART IV   Sharing

19	Sharing Stories	365
20	Exporting Data	373
21	Integrating SAP Lumira with SAP BusinessObjects BI Platform	383
22	Using SAP Lumira Content in the BI Launchpad	421
23	SAP Lumira, Discovery Edition on Mobile	437
24	Interoperability with SAP Lumira, Designer Edition	455

Dear Reader,

It has been my delight to work with Xavier Hacking and Martijn van Foeken on this project. Not only are they both experts in their field with an unbelievable work ethic, but they are also talented writers. Editing this book was a dream, and I can't wait to work with them again on future projects as SAP Lumira grows and changes.

As you discover SAP Lumira between these pages, you'll learn how to create visualizations from start to finish. Xavier and Martijn have included an incredible amount of detail on every step in the process and every option available to you—I almost feel that I could sit down at a desk and create one myself! While I'll likely stick to editing in the foreseeable future, I wish you luck with all your data visualization projects!

What did you think about *SAP Lumira, Discovery Edition: The Comprehensive Guide*? Your comments and suggestions are the most useful tools to help us make our books the best they can be. Please feel free to contact me and share any praise or criticism you may have.

Thank you for purchasing a book from SAP PRESS!

Meagan White
Editor, SAP PRESS

meaganw@rheinwerk-publishing.com
www.sap-press.com
Rheinwerk Publishing · Boston, MA

Contents

Foreword 19

Acknowledgments 21

Introduction 23

PART I   Getting Started

1   Introduction to SAP Lumira, Discovery Edition   31

1.1	**Self-Service Business Intelligence**	32
	1.1.1 Data	32
	1.1.2 Visualizations and Stories	33
	1.1.3 Sharing	35
1.2	**SAP Lumira Suite**	36
	1.2.1 SAP Lumira, Discovery Edition	36
	1.2.2 SAP Lumira, Designer Edition	37
	1.2.3 SAP Lumira, Server Edition	38
1.3	**SAP Lumira and SAP's Business Intelligence Portfolio**	38
	1.3.1 SAP's BI Portfolio	39
	1.3.2 Client Portfolio Conversion Strategy	40
	1.3.3 Content Creation and Consumption	42
	1.3.4 Interoperability	44
1.4	**Summary**	45

2   Installing SAP Lumira, Discovery Edition   47

2.1	**License Model and 30-Day Trial**	47
2.2	**System Requirements**	50
2.3	**Downloading SAP Lumira, Discovery Edition**	51
2.4	**Installing SAP Lumira, Discovery Edition**	55
2.5	**Uninstalling SAP Lumira, Discovery Edition**	59

2.6   Updating SAP Lumira, Discovery Edition 61

2.7   Tracing 63

2.8   Summary 66

3   SAP Lumira, Discovery Edition Interface   67

3.1   Home Page 67
    3.1.1   Data Source 68
    3.1.2   Recently Used 68
    3.1.3   Local Documents 69
    3.1.4   SAP BusinessObjects BI Platform 70

3.2   Menu 71
    3.2.1   Home 72
    3.2.2   File 72
    3.2.3   Edit 76
    3.2.4   Data 76
    3.2.5   Help 78
    3.2.6   Preferences 80
    3.2.7   Extensions 84
    3.2.8   Exit 85

3.3   Data View 86

3.4   Design View 87

3.5   Preview 90

3.6   Toolbar 90

3.7   Comparing SAP Lumira 1.x and SAP Lumira 2.x 92

3.8   Summary 94

4   Creating Your First Story   95

4.1   Creating a New Story 96

4.2   Analyzing Data 97

4.3   Data Preparation 99
        4.3.1   Create a Date/Time Hierarchy 100
        4.3.2   Create Measure 102

4.4   Creating a Visualization 104

4.5   Finalizing Your Story 107

4.6   Sharing Your Story 109

4.7   Summary 110

PART II   Data

5   Data Acquisition   113

5.1   Microsoft Excel 114

5.2   Text 117

5.3   Windows Clipboard 121

5.4   SAP BW 124
        5.4.1   Direct Connection to SAP BW 125
        5.4.2   Connection via Managed OLAP Connection on
                  SAP BusinessObjects BI Platform 130
        5.4.3   SAP BW Limitations 132

5.5   SAP HANA 136
        5.5.1   Direct Connection to SAP HANA 137
        5.5.2   Connection via Managed OLAP Connection on
                  SAP BusinessObjects BI Platform 142

5.6   Universe 144

5.7   Query with SQL 149
        5.7.1   Supported SQL Drivers 149
        5.7.2   Installing and Uninstalling a Driver 152
        5.7.3   Creating a Dataset 154

5.8   Dataset Refresh and Edit 158
        5.8.1   Refreshing a Dataset 159

	5.8.2	Editing Connection Parameters	160
	5.8.3	Editing Dataset Acquisition Details	162
5.9	**Summary**		165

6   Live Data   167

6.1	**SAP BW**		168
	6.1.1	Direct Connection to SAP BW	169
	6.1.2	Connection via Managed OLAP Connection on SAP BusinessObjects BI Platform	171
6.2	**SAP HANA**		173
	6.2.1	Direct Connection to SAP HANA	175
	6.2.2	Connection via Managed OLAP Connection on SAP BusinessObjects BI Platform	177
6.3	**Summary**		179

7   Data Analysis   181

7.1	**Data View**	182
7.2	**Grid View**	183
7.3	**Facet View**	185
7.4	**Summary**	188

8   Data Manipulation   189

8.1	**Objects**		190
	8.1.1	Dimensions	190
	8.1.2	Measures	193
8.2	**Hierarchies**		194
	8.2.1	Geographic Hierarchies	194

    8.2.2   Date/Time Hierarchies 201

    8.2.3   Custom Hierarchies 202

8.3   **Calculated Objects** 204

    8.3.1   Calculated Dimension 204

    8.3.2   Formula Syntax and Functions 207

8.4   **Data Actions** 219

8.5   **Merging Datasets** 223

8.6   **Appending Data** 227

8.7   **Configuring Auto-Enrichment** 229

8.8   **Summary** 231

PART III   Data Visualization and Stories

9   Chart Creation

235

9.1   **Chart Canvas** 235

9.2   **Chart Builder** 238

    9.2.1   Using the Chart Builder 238

    9.2.2   Chart Properties 240

9.3   **Visualization Formatting** 245

    9.3.1   Colors Palette 245

    9.3.2   Visualization Properties 246

9.4   **Reference Line** 249

9.5   **Conditional Formatting** 251

9.6   **Summary** 254

10   Crosstabs

255

10.1 **Creating a Crosstab** 255

    10.1.1 Adding a New Crosstab 255

	10.1.2	Formatting	256
10.2	**Analysis Options**		259
	10.2.1	Sorting	260
	10.2.2	Totals	260
	10.2.3	Filtering	262
	10.2.4	Drilling	263
	10.2.5	Swap Axes	264
10.3	**SAP BW and SAP HANA Live Data**		264
	10.3.1	Hierarchy	265
	10.3.2	Attributes	266
	10.3.3	Suppress Zeros in Rows/Columns	266
	10.3.4	Compact Display in Rows/Columns	266
	10.3.5	Add Dynamic Calculation	267
10.4	**Summary**		269

11   Comparison Charts

271

11.1	**Bar Chart**	271
11.2	**Column Chart**	274
11.3	**Marimekko Chart**	274
11.4	**Radar Chart**	276
11.5	**Tag Cloud**	277
11.6	**Heat Map**	278
11.7	**Numeric Point**	279
11.8	**Summary**	280

12   Percentage Charts

281

| **12.1** | **Pie Chart** | 281 |
| **12.2** | **Donut Chart** | 283 |

12.3   Stacked Bar Chart 284

12.4   Stacked Column Chart 286

12.5   Funnel Chart 287

12.6   Summary 288

13   Correlation Charts

289

13.1   Scatter Plot 289

13.2   Scatter Plot for Time Series 291

13.3   Bubble Chart 292

13.4   Bubble Chart for Time Series 294

13.5   Network Chart 294

13.6   Tree 295

13.7   Summary 296

14   Trend Charts

297

14.1   Line Chart 297

14.2   Stacked Area Chart 300

14.3   Waterfall Chart 301

14.4   Box Plot 302

14.5   Parallel Coordinates Chart 303

14.6   Combination Chart 304

14.7   Summary 306

15   Geographic Visualizations 309

15.1   Online versus Offline Maps 309
   15.1.1   Esri Online Map 310
   15.1.2   Offline Map 311
   15.1.3   Customized Online Map 312

15.2   Setting Up a Geo Map 312
   15.2.1   Choropleth 313
   15.2.2   Bubble 313
   15.2.3   Marker 314
   15.2.4   Pie 315

15.3   Summary 316

16   Filters 317

16.1   Filtering Data in Datasets 318

16.2   Filtering Data in Visualizations 320
   16.2.1   Adding Filters 320
   16.2.2   Filtering on Measures 324
   16.2.3   Interacting with Filters 325
   16.2.4   Selecting Data Points 326
   16.2.5   Filtering Using Hierarchies 328
   16.2.6   Ranking 331
   16.2.7   Linked Analysis 334

16.3   Filtering Data in Stories 336
   16.3.1   Applying Filters 336
   16.3.2   Interacting with Filters 338

16.4   Using Controls 338
   16.4.1   Add Controls to the Canvas 339
   16.4.2   Edit Controls 345
   16.4.3   Delete Controls 345

16.5   Summary 346

17   Story Formatting

17.1   **Story Pages** 347

17.2   **Text Boxes** 349

17.3   **Images, Illustrations, and Shapes** 350

17.4   **Background** 351

17.5   **Summary** 352

18   Linking Datasets

18.1   **Linking versus Merging** 353

18.2   **Creating Dataset Links** 356

18.2.1   Define Dataset Links 356

18.2.2   Create Visualization 359

18.2.3   Linking Dataset During Visualization Creation 361

18.3   **Summary** 362

PART IV   Sharing

19   Sharing Stories

19.1   **Local** 365

19.2   **SAP BusinessObjects BI Platform** 368

19.2.1   Saving a Document 369

19.2.2   Opening a Document 371

19.3   **Summary** 372

20   Exporting Data

20.1   Export to PDF 373

20.2   Export Records 375

20.3   Export Datasets 376
        20.3.1   Export as File 376
        20.3.2   Publish to SAP HANA 377

20.4   Summary 382

21   Integrating SAP Lumira with SAP BusinessObjects BI Platform

21.1   Overview 383

21.2   Deployment Scenarios 385

21.3   System Requirements 386

21.4   Installing SAP Lumira, Server Edition 387
        21.4.1   Downloading SAP Lumira, Server Edition 387
        21.4.2   Installation on a Windows Platform 390
        21.4.3   Modifying, Repairing, or Removing the Server 393

21.5   Configuring the SAP BusinessObjects BI Platform 394
        21.5.1   Enable SAP HANA HTTP Connection 394
        21.5.2   Creating an SAP HANA HTTP OLAP Connection 395
        21.5.3   Creating an SAP BW OLAP Connection 397

21.6   Sizing 399
        21.6.1   Users 399
        21.6.2   Quick Sizer 400

21.7   Single Sign-On 404

21.8   Managing Content on the SAP BusinessObjects BI Platform 406
        21.8.1   Authorization 407
        21.8.2   Bookmarks 411
        21.8.3   Auditing 414

21.8.4   Lifecycle Management   416

21.8.5   Managing Extensions   418

21.9   Summary   420

22   Using SAP Lumira Content in the BI Launchpad   421

22.1   Interacting with Stories   422

22.1.1   Opening an SAP Lumira Document   422

22.1.2   Interacting with an SAP Lumira Document   424

22.1.3   Working with Data Sources   425

22.1.4   Saving a Document   426

22.1.5   Refreshing Data   426

22.1.6   Generating OpenDocument Links   428

22.1.7   Using Bookmarks   430

22.2   Sharing and Scheduling   432

22.2.1   Sharing   432

22.2.2   Scheduling   434

22.3   Creating a New Story   435

22.4   Summary   436

23   SAP Lumira, Discovery Edition on Mobile   437

23.1   Supported Devices   437

23.2   Connectivity   438

23.3   Setting Up the Mobile Category   439

23.3.1   Generic Mobile Category   439

23.3.2   Specific Mobile Categories   441

23.4   Native and HTML Modes   443

23.5   Using Content in the Mobile App   445

23.5.1   Running an SAP Lumira Story   446

23.5.2   Collaboration Features   451

23.6   Summary   453

24 Interoperability with SAP Lumira, Designer Edition 455

24.1 Adding Advanced Features 456

24.2 Combining Multiple Stories 459

24.3 Upgrading the Story 462

24.4 Data Enrichment 465

24.5 Limitations 470

    24.5.1 Editing 470

    24.5.2 Data Sources 470

24.6 Summary 470

Appendices 471

A Converting SAP Lumira 1.x Documents to SAP Lumira 2.1 473

B Software Development Kit 483

C The Authors 489

Index 491

Foreword

SAP Lumira 2.0 plays a key role in the SAP analytics portfolio. Its ability to increase end-user adoption for self-service analytics is remarkable. SAP Lumira, discovery edition excels at accessing and analyzing corporate and non-corporate data. As such, it is very successful in onboarding users into the world of insights and analytics. SAP Lumira, discovery edition allows for easy access to SAP HANA, SAP BW (or SAP BW/4HANA), any SQL-driven databases, universes, and .txt/.csv formatted files; as such, it allows data to be transformed and blended into insights.

SAP Lumira, Discovery Edition: The Comprehensive Guide is the ultimate guide for both beginners and advanced users of SAP Lumira, discovery edition. It covers both the functional and technical aspects of the tool to the highest level of detail. It also guides you in the way you should manage, tune, and maintain your analytics environment based around SAP Lumira, discovery edition. Every single aspect of the tool, from connectivity through data wrangling and highly advanced visualizations, is covered in this guide. Especially valuable here is the use of SAP Lumira, discovery edition as part of the SAP BusinessObjects BI platform. Leveraging the SAP BusinessObjects BI platform is the way to scale, govern, and maintain the use of SAP Lumira, discovery edition throughout an enterprise.

This excellent book came to fruition through a collaboration of two SAP Lumira 2.0 experts, Xavier Hacking and Martijn van Foeken. They work for the well-known consulting organization Interdobs in the Netherlands, and are amongst the top authorities on SAP Lumira, discovery edition. They are both recognized leaders in the area of SAP analytics and especially in SAP Lumira 2.0. I have come across them many times the last few years working with customers, presenting at public events, and attending hackathons. Every time they amaze with their practical knowledge, and their mastery of SAP Lumira, discovery edition. In my option, individuals only become real thought leaders when they are ready to share their knowledge and experience. That is exactly what Xavier and Martijn have done when delivering this book.

At SAP, we are very happy with this book. We believe that SAP Lumira, discovery edition can be the ultimate cornerstone for data exploration and visualization in any enterprise. A book like this shows how our vision is correct; SAP Lumira, discovery edition is essential to any enterprise that is serious about providing analytics and insights for all employees, anywhere, and any place. I would also recommend that you pick up *SAP Lumira, Designer Edition: The Comprehensive Guide, 3rd Edition*. This book explains SAP Lumira, designer edition, which is closely related to SAP Lumira, discovery edition through the interoperability mode.

I am personally also very passionate and involved in SAP analytics, publishing insights and best practices. My insights come from a strong belief in the importance that good analytics play in a digitized economy. I love the interoperability with SAP Lumira, designer edition and believe it is a game changer in winning your end users. If you're interested in SAP Lumira 2.0, please feel free to follow me on LinkedIn or Twitter (*http://twitter.com/ivervandezand*) or check out my writing at *http://www.ivervandezand.com*. SAP Lumira 2.0 is a topic I often touch in my articles.

Iver van de Zand
Global Head of Analytics and SAP Leonardo Presales at SAP

Acknowledgments

After writing a couple of books on SAP tooling, it is clear to me that these projects can't be successful without a first-class environment to work in. As the tools become more complex with every release, the books also grow in size and complexity. This requires proper planning, great resources, clear communication, and most essentially, an excellent team.

First of all, I want to thank my co-author Martijn van Foeken for the pleasant teamwork that we had over the past year while creating this book. Martijn brought his impressive SAP BusinessObjects knowledge and experience to the table to make sure this book is as complete and content-rich as possible.

I also want to thank SAP PRESS coordinator and editor Meagan White for all the support and discussions during the writing process.

A special word of thanks goes out to Rob Huisman and Leon Huijsmans of our company Interdobs for—again—doing absolutely everything imaginable to help us reach our goal. Also, René van Es and Sander van Gemert deserve a shout out here, as they made sure that all the SAP servers that we used were up and running, and got updated almost instantly after each new software update.

The SAP BI community on Twitter deserves a mention as well. This is the place where all the news, updates, and experiences regarding SAP Lumira, discovery edition and all the other SAP BI tools are shared and discussed on a daily basis.

Finally, and most importantly, I want to thank my girlfriend, Marieke, for all of her support.

Xavier Hacking

As this is my first ever book, the whole process to get from idea to print was an exciting journey. I'm thankful that I was able to take that journey together with my co-author Xavier Hacking, a well-known and respected member of the SAP analytics community. With his experience gained in other writing projects and his thorough knowledge as subject matter expert, his contribution was crucial. I'm proud and honored he asked me to be his co-author.

I also want to thank Meagan White of SAP PRESS and the team from Interdobs who supported us in every possible and required way during the writing of this book. Rob, Leon: joining Interdobs in 2016 was the best choice I ever made in my professional career. Lots of respect and admiration goes out to you and let's keep up the good work together.

Last but not least, a big thanks goes out to my wife Manja and our children Stijn, Isa, and Roos for their support during the writing process. Having a family that supports each other to reach our goals in life is priceless.

Martijn van Foeken

Introduction

SAP Lumira, discovery edition (originally called Visual Intelligence, later rebranded to SAP BusinessObjects Lumira) was first released in May 2012 and has been placed in the SAP business intelligence product portfolio as the primary tool for self-service data analysis and visualization scenarios. Since its introduction, SAP Lumira, discovery edition has evolved into a tool that supports the growing need of users to immediately explore data on their own, without the involvement of an IT department, and to share insights by creating stories.

Now that SAP has released the SAP Lumira 2.0 product family, it's time to dive into all the details. Let's look at how this book is organized, who it's for, and what resources accompany the book.

Target Group and Prerequisites

This book is intended for anyone who wants to learn more about SAP Lumira, discovery edition. It can be used by experienced data analysts who are familiar with creating datasets and sharing insight using stories, or readers who are new to the business intelligence domain and want to learn all there is to know about this tool. No pre-existing knowledge is required, as the book will explain every aspect of SAP Lumira, discovery edition step-by-step, building up from easy-to-understand overview chapters to chapters that are dedicated to the various steps to create stories and share insights.

Structure of the Book

This book is divided into four parts. Part I: Getting Started, begins with a broad overview of the SAP Lumira, discovery edition tool. In the first chapters, we introduce you to the product, compare it with other SAP products and walk you step-by-step through the installation procedure. Part I of the book concludes with a chapter that helps you to create your first SAP Lumira, discovery edition story.

In Part II: Data, we focus on all data-related topics, from data acquisition to using live data connections and analyzing and manipulating data.

Once you have familiarized yourself with all data-related topics, we go into more depth about how you can create different types of charts in Part III: Data Visualization and Stories. In this part of the book, we also describe how to filter data and focus on how to format your stories.

In the final part of our book, Part IV: Sharing, we tell you all about sharing your stories and data sets. Furthermore, this part describes how SAP Lumira, discovery edition seamlessly integrates with the SAP BusinessObjects BI platform and leverages all existing functionality. Finally, we show you a couple of scenarios that shows the opportunities at hand through the interoperability with SAP Lumira, designer edition.

Now that you have a general sense of the book's layout, the following addresses the topics covered in each individual chapter:

- **Chapter 1: Introduction to SAP Lumira, Discovery Edition**
  We start the book with a high-level introduction to SAP Lumira, discovery edition and give a general overview of the SAP Lumira suite that also includes SAP Lumira, designer edition and the SAP Lumira, server edition. We also provide an overview of the SAP business intelligence front-end portfolio with details regarding the positioning and usage of each tool along with how SAP Lumira, discovery edition fits in the modern self-service business intelligence approach.

- **Chapter 2: Installing SAP Lumira, Discovery Edition**
  This chapter offers a walk through the process of downloading, installing and updating SAP Lumira, discovery edition.

- **Chapter 3: SAP Lumira, Discovery Edition Interface**
  After installing SAP Lumira, discovery edition we take a look at the interface to get familiar with the tool, so you can start creating stories. We discuss the available menu items and toolbar options in both the data and design view. For those of you familiar with SAP Lumira 1.x, a comparison is also included in this chapter.

- **Chapter 4: Creating Your First Story**
  Now that you are familiar with the user interface of SAP Lumira, discovery edition, we guide you through the process of creating your first SAP Lumira story.

- **Chapter 5: Data Acquisition**
  An essential step to create an SAP Lumira story is to add data. Without data, we can't create SAP Lumira stories. This chapter describes the wide range of supported data sources from which data can be acquired, including all their specific options.

- **Chapter 6: Live Data**

  This chapter introduces you to the concept of using live data connectivity to both SAP BW and SAP HANA. We also highlight the main differences between acquired data and live data along with any limitations. Finally, we share insights on how to leverage connections defined on the SAP BusinessObjects BI platform versus using direct connections.

- **Chapter 7: Data Analysis**

  SAP Lumira, discovery edition offers a data view to help you to analyze your dataset. This chapter describes the grid and facet view options to browse through the rows and columns and to display the distinct values and the number of occurrences.

- **Chapter 8: Data Manipulation**

  One of the strengths of a self-service BI tool is that you can execute data manipulation actions without the involvement of your IT department. SAP Lumira, discovery edition offers capabilities to clean your dataset, create objects and generate hierarchies to fully prepare your data.

- **Chapter 9: Chart Creation**

  In this chapter we explain how you can create and setup charts either directly from the canvas or using a more detailed approach via the chart builder. Here we also discuss generic visualization options to format charts and show you how to create reference lines and apply conditional formatting.

- **Chapter 10: Crosstabs**

  One of the most popular visualization methods is the crosstab. We devote this chapter on how to create a crosstab in SAP Lumira, discovery edition and make you familiar with its analysis options.

- **Chapter 11: Comparison Charts**

  SAP Lumira, discovery edition offers a wide range of chart types. In this chapter we start with comparison charts, which are used to visualize the differences between dimension members and multiple measures.

- **Chapter 12: Percentage Charts**

  In this chapter we describe the different types of charts that can visualize relative values of parts as well as their specific settings and formatting options.

- **Chapter 13: Correlation Charts**

  In Chapter 13 we describe correlation charts which visualize the relationship between two or more variables. Examples are for instance the scatter plot and bubble chart.

- **Chapter 14: Trend Charts**

  Here we discuss the final group of charts that can be used to visualize changes in values, mostly time-related. This chapter also contains an overview of the major strengths and weaknesses for each of the charts we discuss.

- **Chapter 15: Geographic Visualizations**

  Besides using crosstabs and charts to visualize data, plotting data on maps to support location intelligence is becoming more popular. In Chapter 15 we describe how to visualize geographic data on a map and create different layers.

- **Chapter 16: Filters**

  By applying filters to datasets, visualizations, pages and stories you can more efficiently communicate information to your users and perform analysis. SAP Lumira, discovery edition offers a wide range of options, from applying filters based on dimensions and measures to using data point selection, ranking, and linked analysis to filter your data. This chapters provides a deep-dive that explains all these options in detail.

- **Chapter 17: Story Formatting**

  This chapters shows you how to create beautiful stories by formatting the story pages and supplementing the data visualizations with text boxes, illustrations, and images.

- **Chapter 18: Linking Datasets**

  With dataset linking you can quickly combine data from different datasets in a single visualization.

- **Chapter 19: Sharing Stories**

  In this chapter we will discuss how to share your SAP Lumira, discovery edition stories with other users. This can be done with local exports, and via the SAP BusinessObjects BI platform.

- **Chapter 20: Exporting Data**

  Besides sharing the complete, interactive stories that we create in SAP Lumira, discovery edition, we have also the option to export to PDF. Furthermore, we can export data to a file or even an SAP HANA view.

- **Chapter 21: Integrating SAP Lumira with SAP BusinessObjects BI Platform**

  This chapter provides all the details to setup an SAP BusinessObjects BI platform for usage with SAP Lumira, discovery edition. We discuss all the details from installing and configuring the SAP BusinessObjects BI platform, to managing the client tool and SAP Lumira content from the SAP BusinessObjects BI Central Management Console.

- **Chapter 22: Using SAP Lumira Content in the BI Launchpad**
  SAP Lumira, discovery edition stories can be run in the web-based SAP Business-Objects BI Launchpad. This means that also users without an installation of the SAP Lumira, discovery edition client tool can make use of the stories. As we will see in this chapter, they can even create stories from scratch!

- **Chapter 23: SAP Lumira, Discovery Edition on Mobile**
  SAP Lumira, discovery edition stories can also be used on mobile devices like an iPad. In this chapter we will go through the details on how to set this up, and we will show you the features of the mobile app.

- **Chapter 24: Interoperability with SAP Lumira, Designer Edition**
  The final chapter of the book introduces you to the world of interoperability. It discusses a number of scenarios where SAP Lumira, discovery edition and SAP Lumira, designer edition extent each other's features.

Additional Resources

This book comes with a number of datasets that can be used to follow along with examples in the book and to create your own stories. These datasets can be downloaded from the book's webpage at *www.sap-press.com/4511*. Each dataset is used in the following chapters:

- Auto_Customer_Analysis.xlsx: Chapters 4, 7, 8, 16
- US States Cities by crime rate.xlsx: Chapter 8
- Crime Rates per US State.xlsx: Chapter 8
- Rotten Tomatos.xlsx: Chapters 5, 9, 10, 11, 12, 13, 14, 15
- Disc Rental Data.xlsx: Chapters 5, 9, 10, 11, 12, 13, 14, 15
- Westcity_Demographics.xlsx: Chapter 18
- Westcity_HealthStatistic_MERGED_date.xlsx: Chapter 18

Let's now jump into Part 1: Getting Started!

PART I
Getting Started

Chapter 1

Introduction to SAP Lumira, Discovery Edition

SAP Lumira, discovery edition is SAP's on-premise solution for self-service business intelligence.

SAP Lumira, discovery edition is a self-service data analysis and visualization tool. It enables you to manipulate, visualize, analyze, and share data. The tool is not only intended for the experienced data analyst, but especially for those who just entered the domain of business intelligence. As you will see in this book, the tool is set up in a consistent way and is easy to learn.

Over the past years, self-service business intelligence (BI) has become more and more a familiar term. BI users no longer accept the situation where new reporting requirements, or even small adjustments to existing solutions, take weeks or months before the IT department can execute them. Users don't want to wait for IT anymore. They want to immediately explore their data on their own and create and change their own reports without delay.

This is also why Microsoft Excel is still such a popular and powerful tool. It allows users to do a form of self-service BI, where they grab data from several sources, mash it up with some Excel formulas or macros, and do their analyses and reporting with it. The drawbacks of this kind of road approach become clear over time: updating the dataset is a hassle and takes a lot of time, it is extremely error-prone, and typically the bigger the workbook gets, the harder it is to understand and keep up with what exactly is going on in it. With each iteration, these reports drift further away from the governed data it once started with.

That is where SAP Lumira, discovery edition comes in. SAP Lumira, discovery edition is completely integrated within the SAP BI ecosystem, and therefore can provide connectivity to governed data sources as SAP BW and SAP HANA, while having the option to add local user data as well. As you will see later in this chapter, users can use SAP Lumira, discovery edition to build their own visualizations and stories with this data. Furthermore, the SAP BusinessObjects BI platform facilitates the storing and sharing of SAP Lumira documents.

Does this all sound a bit fancy for you, as you just want to analyze that dataset you receive via a text file every week? No problem! SAP Lumira, discovery edition can be used in a standalone scenario, without connections to enterprise data warehouses and BI platforms.

In this chapter, we first discuss how SAP Lumira, discovery edition enables self-service business intelligence. Next, we look at the full SAP Lumira suite. Finally, we provide an overview of the other tools in the SAP's business intelligence portfolio and explain how they interrelate.

1.1 Self-Service Business Intelligence

Regardless of your background or technical expertise, SAP Lumira, discovery edition is easy to install, set up, and use as it does not require a complex IT infrastructure.

A typical self-service workflow with SAP Lumira, discovery edition starts by bringing in data from a data source and generating a dataset within SAP Lumira, discovery edition. This dataset can be adjusted, enriched, visualized, and analyzed within the tool to create a story. Finally, a story can be shared with other users directly or via the SAP BusinessObjects BI platform.

1.1.1 Data

SAP Lumira, discovery edition supports a wide range of data sources (Figure 1.1). We can distinguish here the local sources (Microsoft Excel, CSV, text files, clipboard), the SAP systems (SAP BW, SAP HANA, SAP BusinessObjects BI universe), and the relational SQL sources like Microsoft SQL, Oracle, or Apache Hadoop. Access to the local sources and the SAP systems does not require any drivers, this is already built in SAP Lumira, discovery edition. For some of the SQL sources, it is necessary to install a driver.

Data from these data sources can imported, where all the data is acquired into SAP Lumira, discovery edition, or used with a live connection, where the data remains in the data source. This latter, online scenario, is supported for SAP HANA and SAP BW data sources.

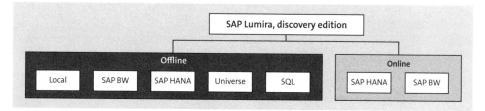

Figure 1.1 SAP Lumira, Discovery Edition Data Sources

Once the data is available in SAP Lumira, discovery edition, it can be processed and refined by the user. When the data is imported, it is for example possible to split fields into multiple columns, add hierarchical relationships, create custom dimensions or calculations, correct errors, and enrich the dataset with data from additional datasets. When using a live data source, a limited set of data actions is available, as the data itself still resides in the underlying database system.

1.1.2 Visualizations and Stories

When the dataset is set up, we can create visualizations to display our data graphically. SAP Lumira, discovery edition contains a wide range of charts and other visualization components, which have in their turn a lot of properties to exactly show the data as you want to. All the well-known charts are included. We have column charts, bar charts, line charts, pie charts, stacked column charts, waterfall charts, heat maps, and so on. In addition, visualizations as tag clouds, funnels, bubble charts, and box plots are included. Of course, a table or a single numeric value is also available. For geographical visualizations, SAP Lumira, discovery edition uses a geo map component that offers ESRI maps.

The visualizations can be set up from the dataset by dragging and dropping the measures and dimensions into the visualizations (Figure 1.2).

Multiple visualizations combined form a story. A story also includes interactive options, for example to enable filtering via input controls (Figure 1.3).

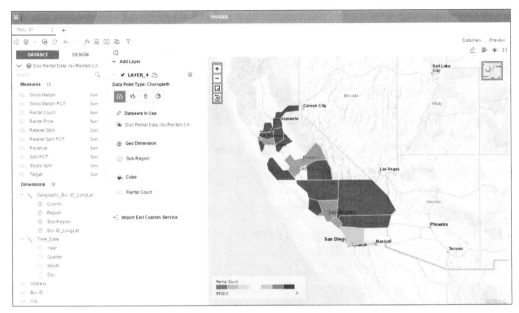

Figure 1.2 Setting Up a Visualization in SAP Lumira, Discovery Edition

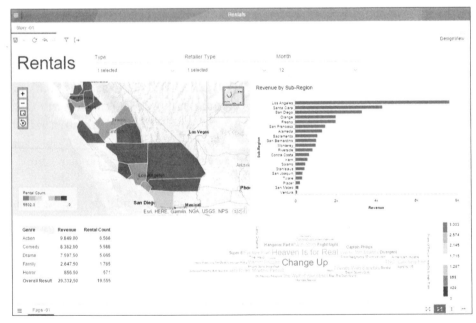

Figure 1.3 SAP Lumira, Discovery Edition Story with Visualizations and Input Controls

1.1.3   Sharing

Finally, when the story is ready, we have the ability to share it with others. The local options are that we can create a PDF export of the story and export datasets to CSV files. We can also simply share the whole SAP Lumira document file itself. The actual sharing must be done manually in these cases, for example by email or via a shared disk drive.

We can also publish the story to the SAP BusinessObjects BI platform, where other users can run it in their browser via the BI Launchpad (Figure 1.4), or via the SAP BusinessObjects Mobile app. If users have the SAP Lumira, discovery edition desktop client installed, they can also open the document from the SAP BusinessObjects BI platform in there.

Figure 1.4 Using an SAP Lumira, Discovery Edition Story on the BI Launchpad

1.2   SAP Lumira Suite

The SAP Lumira suite facilitates users in gaining insights from governed enterprise data sources and personal data. They can then share those insights via interactive visualizations, stories, and advanced analysis applications and dashboards with other users. This is done via desktop browsers and mobile devices.

The SAP Lumira suite consists of three components: SAP Lumira, discovery edition, SAP Lumira, designer edition, and the SAP Lumira, server edition. These components share the same code base, user interface (UI), data sources connectivity artifacts, and the .lumx file type. Let's have a quick look at the characteristics of the different components and where they supplement each other.

1.2.1   SAP Lumira, Discovery Edition

SAP Lumira, discovery edition is a standalone desktop application, aimed at business users who want to create their own reports for data analysis and share the results (Figure 1.5). As we saw in Section 1.1, SAP Lumira, discovery edition facilitates the complete self-service BI approach: Data can be gathered from a range of offline and online data sources, and after setting this up, a story can be created that contains several interactive visualizations. From here on, the data can be analyzed and the story can be shared with other users. This all without any intervention of IT.

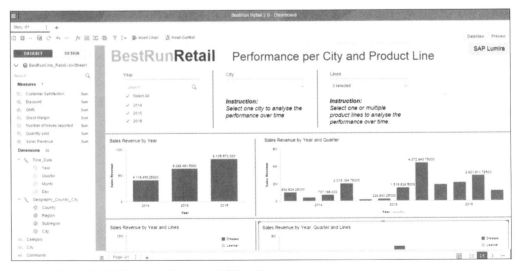

Figure 1.5 SAP Lumira, Discovery Edition Story

Depending on how the SAP Lumira, discovery edition story is saved, users can consume and edit the story either in their installation of the SAP Lumira, discovery edition desktop application, or use the stories on the BI Launchpad, which is the web-based user portal of the SAP BusinessObjects BI platform. In addition, it is possible to run them in the SAP BusinessObjects Mobile app on a mobile device.

1.2.2   SAP Lumira, Designer Edition

SAP Lumira, designer edition is also a standalone desktop application and is aimed at professional designers of advanced analysis applications and dashboards (Figure 1.6). Previously, this tool was known as SAP BusinessObjects Design Studio (and, briefly, SAP BusinessObjects Lumira Designer or SAP Lumira Designer). It continues where SAP Lumira, discovery edition stops. It offers full control over the look and feel of the application, and with its scripting capabilities it is possible to include very advanced user interactions.

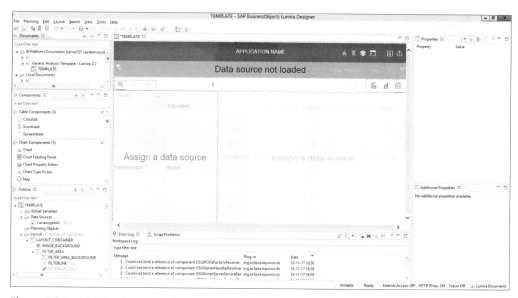

Figure 1.6 Lumira Designer Application

SAP Lumira, designer edition is meant to build standardized, governed analysis applications that can be rolled out to a large user community. In addition to the analysis applications, planning applications based on SAP BW's integrated planning and SAP Business Planning and Consolidation (SAP BPC) can also be created.

The SAP Lumira, designer edition desktop application is only used by the designers. The users consume the applications on the BI Launchpad on their desktop browser, or via the SAP BusinessObjects Mobile app on a mobile device.

As SAP Lumira, discovery edition and SAP Lumira, designer edition share the same code base and artifacts, a business user could create an SAP Lumira, discovery edition story and share it with IT to extend its functionality with SAP Lumira, designer edition.

SAP Lumira, Designer Edition

For more information on SAP Lumira, designer edition, check out *SAP Lumira, Designer Edition: The Comprehensive Guide* (SAP PRESS, 2018).

1.2.3   SAP Lumira, Server Edition

SAP Lumira, server edition is an add-on for the SAP BusinessObjects BI platform. It enables the hosting and integration of SAP Lumira, discovery edition stories and SAP Lumira, designer edition applications on the SAP BusinessObjects BI platform. This means that users can run their stories and applications via their desktop browsers and mobile devices, but also make use of the typical SAP BusinessObjects BI platform features as scheduling, document sharing, and authorization.

SAP Lumira, discovery edition is even available as a web-based application in the BI Launchpad, where users can create their stories from scratch when they are based on live SAP HANA or SAP BW data sources (Figure 1.7).

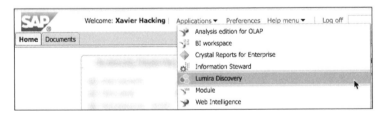

Figure 1.7 SAP Lumira, Discovery Edition Application in BI Launchpad

1.3   SAP Lumira and SAP's Business Intelligence Portfolio

In this section, we provide you with a general overview of SAP's business intelligence portfolio, so you can see how SAP Lumira fits into its overall strategy.

1.3.1   SAP's BI Portfolio

Since the acquisition of BusinessObjects by SAP in 2007, the SAP business intelligence frontend portfolio has changed dramatically. Before the acquisition, there were only a few options in the SAP BW toolset to present data from the SAP BW system to the end user. With SAP BEx Analyzer, you could create workbooks in Microsoft Excel, and with SAP BEx Web Analyzer, you could run SAP BEx queries in a web-based environment. SAP BEx Web Application Designer allowed you to develop interactive web applications based on SAP BW InfoProviders and SAP BEx queries.

The SAP BusinessObjects BI portfolio added a set of new tools and brought in a complete business intelligence enterprise environment. This web-based platform integrates the SAP BusinessObjects BI tools and, with the BI Launchpad, offers a single place for end users to create, store, and execute their reports. The following tools were included:

- SAP Crystal Reports
- SAP BusinessObjects Web Intelligence
- SAP BusinessObjects Dashboards (formerly known as Xcelsius)
- SAP BusinessObjects Analysis, edition for Microsoft Office
- SAP BusinessObjects Analysis, edition for OLAP
- SAP BusinessObjects Explorer

However, SAP didn't stop with the BusinessObjects acquisition—it continued to broaden its analytical product suite. In 2012, two major new tools were introduced: SAP Lumira (at that time named SAP Visual Intelligence) and SAP BusinessObjects Design Studio (at that time named SAP BusinessObjects Analysis, edition for Application Design). As we already saw in this chapter, these tools are now part of the same product suite as SAP Lumira, discovery edition and SAP Lumira, designer edition.

In 2015, SAP started offering a cloud-based, software-as-a-service BI solution, called SAP Analytics Cloud (formerly SAP BusinessObjects Cloud and SAP Cloud for Analytics). The idea behind this solution is that it features reporting, analytical, predictive, and planning features in a single environment, and it is hosted and serviced by SAP on the SAP Cloud Platform (in contrast to all the other tools that run on-premise). In 2016, SAP broadened its cloud offering by acquiring Roambi, which is a mobile BI solution that allows easy reporting on all possible (mobile) devices.

1.3.2   Client Portfolio Conversion Strategy

With the releases of the initial versions of SAP BusinessObjects Design Studio and SAP Lumira, SAP also started to slim down the number of tools in its BI portfolio. The strategy is to go from twelve tools back to just four, which all use the same platform and offer deep interoperability features.

The SAP Lumira suite plays an essential role in this convergence strategy, as the discovery edition and designer edition both cover the functionality of all the tools from both the discovery and analysis and the dashboards and applications areas, which make up half of the total toolset. As Table 1.1 shows, SAP Lumira 1.x, SAP Business-Objects Explorer, SAP BusinessObjects Analysis for OLAP, SAP BusinessObjects Design Studio, SAP BusinessObjects Dashboards, and SAP BEx Web are converged into the SAP Lumira suite.

In the office integration area, we see that only SAP Analysis for Microsoft Office remains. SAP BusinessObjects Live Office and the SAP BEx Analyzer will disappear.

Finally, the reporting area loses SAP BusinessObjects Desktop Intelligence, which functionally should be fully covered by SAP BusinessObjects Web Intelligence. SAP Crystal Reports also remains. For these two tools, SAP BusinessObjects Live Office remains for embedding report parts into Microsoft Office documents.

Tool Area	Current Toolset	Converged Toolset
Discovery, analysis, dashboards, and applications	■ SAP Lumira ■ SAP BusinessObjects Explorer ■ SAP BusinessObjects Analysis, edition for online analytical processing (Analysis OLAP) ■ SAP BusinessObjects Design Studio ■ SAP BEx Web Application Designer ■ SAP BusinessObjects Dashboards	■ SAP Lumira 2.0 (both discovery edition and designer edition)

Table 1.1   Convergence of SAP Business Intelligence Tools

Tool Area	Current Toolset	Converged Toolset
Office integration	■ SAP Analysis for Microsoft Office ■ SAP BusinessObjects Live Office ■ SAP BEx Analyzer	■ SAP Analysis for Microsoft Office
Reporting	■ SAP Crystal Reports ■ SAP BusinessObjects Web Intelligence ■ SAP BusinessObjects Desktop Intelligence	■ SAP Crystal Reports ■ SAP BusinessObjects Web Intelligence

Table 1.1 Convergence of SAP Business Intelligence Tools (Cont.)

This move has lots of advantages. For SAP, as a software vendor, it will be easier to provide support for a limited toolset and focus its developments. This is necessary as business needs are changing more rapidly, and SAP should be able to react faster and apply new features more often.

For the customers, the complexity of tool selection will decrease. The twelve tools had a lot of overlap in functionality, and thus also in purpose and application. This made the selection process difficult. Customers can now focus their investments on a limited number of tools.

The convergence strategy doesn't mean that the excluded tools cannot be used anymore. All of them are still supported by SAP, but at some point in time they will get a planned final maintenance date. Also, there has been almost no investment in new functionalities for these tools over the past years, and none should be expected in the future. If there are any future updates, then they most likely will only include bug fixes and compatibility adjustments.

End-of-Maintenance Dates

The end-of-maintenance for each SAP tool can be found in the SAP Knowledge Base Articles: *http://support.sap.com/en/my-support/knowledge-base.html*.

1.3.3   Content Creation and Consumption

As you may already have noticed in the previous section, not all tools are used by end users. Table 1.2 shows this distinction, where the very fixed reporting outputs (e.g., the SAP Crystal Reports documents and the dashboards from SAP Lumira, designer edition) are completely created by developers from the IT department. The business users work with the other tools to create their own reports and make custom analyses on their own. SAP Analytics Cloud is a special case here, as it combines reporting and analytical features, and it is designed to be used by IT and business users.

	Data Discovery and Applications	Office Integration	Reporting
IT	<ul><li>SAP Lumira, designer edition</li><li>SAP Roambi Analytics</li><li>SAP Analytics Cloud</li></ul>	None	<ul><li>SAP Crystal Reports</li><li>SAP Analytics Cloud</li></ul>
Business Users	<ul><li>SAP Lumira, discovery edition</li><li>SAP Analytics Cloud</li></ul>	SAP Analysis for Microsoft Office	<ul><li>SAP BusinessObjects Web Intelligence</li><li>SAP Analytics Cloud</li></ul>

Table 1.2 Content Creators by Category

SAP determines four levels of business users: executive, senior management, business analysis, and individual contributors. In Table 1.3, the products that present more aggregated data in a fixed way are toward the top of the table, and the products that provide more detailed and ad hoc reporting solutions are on the bottom. The broad scope of the SAP Lumira suite is clearly highlighted here.

	Data Discovery and Applications	Office Integration	Reporting
Executives	■ SAP Lumira, designer edition ■ SAP Roambi Analytics ■ SAP Analytics Cloud	None	None
Senior Management	■ SAP Lumira, designer edition ■ SAP Roambi Analytics ■ SAP Analytics Cloud	SAP Analysis for Microsoft Office	■ SAP Business-Objects Web Intelligence ■ SAP Analytics Cloud
Business Analysts	■ SAP Lumira, discovery edition ■ SAP Lumira, designer edition ■ SAP Analytics Cloud	SAP Analysis for Microsoft Office	None
Individual Contributors	■ SAP Lumira, discovery edition ■ SAP Lumira, designer edition ■ SAP Analytics Cloud	SAP Analysis for Microsoft Office	■ SAP Crystal Reports ■ SAP Business-Objects Web Intelligence ■ SAP Analytics Cloud

Table 1.3 Content Consumption by Category

Table 1.4 shows the various options for content consumption environments and the SAP BusinessObjects BI tools. The options are a desktop computer with a local installation of the tool, a web-based version of the report through the BI Launchpad, and a mobile device. As you can see, almost all the solutions offer reports that are accessible through mobile devices with SAP BusinessObjects Mobile, which is available for iOS and Android devices.

	Data Discovery and Applications	Office Integration	Reporting
Desktop	SAP Lumira, discovery edition	SAP Analysis for Microsoft Office	■ SAP Crystal Reports ■ SAP Business-Objects Web Intelligence
Web-based	■ SAP Lumira, discovery edition ■ SAP Lumira, designer edition ■ SAP Analytics Cloud	None	■ SAP Crystal Reports ■ SAP Business-Objects Web Intelligence ■ SAP Analytics Cloud
Mobile	■ SAP Lumira, discovery edition ■ SAP Lumira, designer edition ■ SAP Roambi Analytics ■ SAP Analytics Cloud	None	■ SAP Crystal Reports ■ SAP Business-Objects Web Intelligence ■ SAP Analytics Cloud

Table 1.4 Content Consumption Environment by Category

1.3.4   Interoperability

The convergence of the SAP BI portfolio toward a limited number of tools also provides more options for interoperability. This means that reports and applications created with different tools still can work together smoothly, and in a way can extend the boundaries of a tool. This offers a hassle-free user experience, where the user can jump from one tool to the other.

As you will see in Chapter 24, SAP Lumira, discovery edition and SAP Lumira, designer edition work extremely closely together, as they share the same code base, the same set of visualizations and connectivity artifacts, and the same .lumx file type. This last characteristic means that documents that were created in SAP Lumira, discovery edition, can be opened and edited in SAP Lumira, designer edition.

1

All the other tools also have options to be connected with each other. For example, a user could start his or her analysis in an interactive SAP BusinessObjects Web Intelligence report, and from there open an SAP Crystal Reports document that shows all the details of the selections made in the SAP BusinessObjects Web Intelligence report, and is pixel-perfectly formatted for further distribution. It is even possible to connect SAP Analysis for Microsoft Office to an SAP Analytics Cloud data model.

1.4   Summary

This chapter provided a high-level introduction to SAP Lumira, discovery edition. We had a look at the broader SAP Lumira suite that also includes SAP Lumira, designer edition and the server add-on for the SAP BusinessObjects BI platform. We described how SAP Lumira, discovery edition fits in a modern self-service business intelligence approach. Finally, we gave an overview of the full SAP BI frontend portfolio and the typical positioning and usage of each tool.

In the next chapter, we install and set up SAP Lumira, discovery edition so you are fully prepared to create your first stories.

Chapter 2

Installing SAP Lumira, Discovery Edition

The first step to get started with SAP Lumira, discovery edition is to download the installation file and start the Installation Manager. This chapter covers the steps to prepare your system and install the software.

Now that you have a first impression of SAP Lumira, discovery edition and how it fits into the analytics portfolio and strategy of SAP, it's time to get started. But before we explain how to download and install SAP Lumira, discovery edition, covered in Section 2.3 and Section 2.4, we briefly describe the two types of licenses available.

After selecting the right license, it's important to ensure that your operating system and hardware specifications are compliant with the prerequisites for installing SAP Lumira, discovery edition. In Section 2.5 we quickly show you how to uninstall (if necessary) and update SAP Lumira, discovery edition to the latest available version by applying Service Packs and patches (Section 2.6).

If you run into any error while working with SAP Lumira, discovery edition you can enable tracing to generate log files. These trace files and logs will help you find the root cause and can be shared with SAP when you log an incident in the SAP Support Portal. Section 2.7 explains how you can use a simple batch file to enable tracing and collect these logs files for further investigation.

2.1 License Model and 30-Day Trial

The license model for SAP Lumira, discovery edition is quite simple, with only two options listed in Table 2.1.

Standard Edition	Desktop Edition
Access to Microsoft Excel files, CSV files, databases, and SAP HANA.	Includes all features and capabilities from standard edition.
Transform and manipulate data.	
Visualize data with charts and maps.	
Create and share storyboards.	
No connectivity to SAP ERP and SAP BW.	SAP ERP and SAP BW connectivity.
No maintenance available.	Covered by SAP Enterprise Support or SAP Standard Support.
Must be repurchased to receive major version upgrades.	Free upgrades to the next major version under the support agreement.
Cannot log in to the SAP BusinessObjects BI platform.	Fully integrated with the SAP BusinessObjects BI platform.

Table 2.1 SAP Lumira, Discovery Edition License Options

Based on your requirements, mainly depending on data source connectivity and distribution of SAP Lumira documents, you can decide which SAP Lumira, discovery edition license you need.

Standard edition licenses can be purchased directly from the SAP Store (*https://www.sapstore.com*). For the pricing of the desktop edition, you should contact your SAP account manager.

Before deciding whether or not to purchase licenses for SAP Lumira, discovery edition, you can try the software for free during a 30-day trial period to explore the capabilities.

Browse to *https://saplumira.com* and click on **Try it Free** (Figure 2.1) in the upper-right corner. Make sure your browser is not blocking any popups.

To download the software for a 30-day trial period, please submit your email address, select your country, and select whether you work on a PC or Mac. Optionally, select the checkbox to confirm you want to receive news and updates from SAP and click on **Download** (Figure 2.2).

Figure 2.1 Try SAP Lumira, Discovery Edition for Free

Figure 2.2 Download 30-Day Trial

The download of the file *SAP_LUMIRA_DISCOVERY_2.1_SETUP.exe* will start after clicking on **Download Now**, as shown in Figure 2.3. Please note that if you need to open SAP Lumira 1.x documents in SAP Lumira 2.1, you need to download SAP Lumira 1.31.8 or higher first and follow the conversion instructions described in Appendix A.

Figure 2.3 Download SAP Lumira, Discovery Edition

When the file is downloaded successfully, double-click to start the installation process described in Section 2.4. An email will be sent with some links to get you started (Figure 2.4).

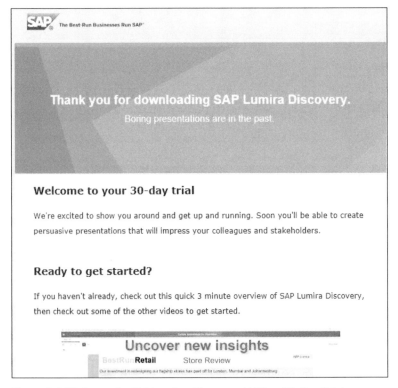

Figure 2.4 Welcome to SAP Lumira, Discovery Edition 30-Day Trial

2.2   System Requirements

To be able to install SAP Lumira, discovery edition, you need to meet the following prerequisites:

- The operating system must be 64-bit. In comparison to SAP Lumira 1.3x, there is no 32-bit version of the installer available.
- Your account needs to have Administrator rights on your operating system.

2

- The drive on which you install SAP Lumira, discovery edition needs to have at least 1 GB of free space.

- The drive that is hosting the user application folder (for example, on Windows 10, this folder is *C:\Users\<user>\Documents\SAP Lumira Documents*) must have at least 2.5 GB of free space available. This folder is used to store local documents.

- The drive that contains the temporary folder (for example, on Windows 10, this folder is *C:\Users\<user>\AppData\Local\Temp*) requires 200 MB of free space.

- Local HTTP port 6401 needs to be available.

- One port in the range of 4520 and 4539 must be available.

- Microsoft redistributable runtime VS 2015 DLL(X64) is installed. If this is not the case, this component will be automatically installed.

These prerequisites will be checked by the SAP Lumira, discovery edition installation wizard.

Product Availability Matrix (PAM)

For a list of all supported platforms and information about configurations, please check the latest version of the PAM available on the SAP Support Portal at *https:// apps.support.sap.com/sap/support/pam*.

2.3   Downloading SAP Lumira, Discovery Edition

The SAP Lumira, discovery edition desktop installation file can be downloaded from the SAP Software Download Center on the SAP Support Portal (*https://launchpad.support.sap.com/#/softwarecenter*). To begin the download, perform the following steps:

1. Use your web browser to go to the SAP Software Download Center on the SAP Support Portal at *https://launchpad.support.sap.com/#/softwarecenter*.

2. Please provide your S-user account ID, with sufficient privileges to download the software, to log in to the SAP ONE Support Launchpad. If you don't know your S-user account ID, contact your SAP Administrator or SAP Support.

3. Click **By Alphabetical Index (A-Z)** under **Installations & Upgrades** to navigate in the alphabetical list of available products (Figure 2.5).

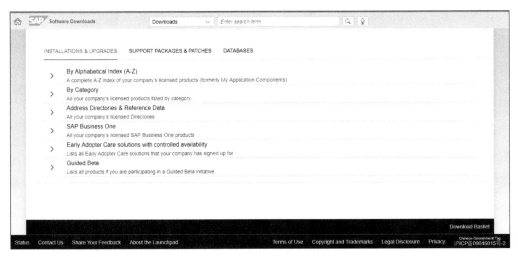

Figure 2.5 Installations and Upgrades

4. Click on **L** to browse to the SAP Lumira download area (Figure 2.6).

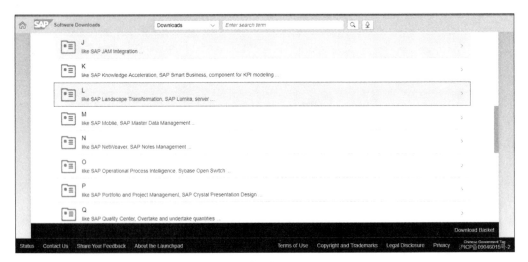

Figure 2.6 Browse to the Lumira Download Area

5. Select the **SAP Lumira** folder to view all available versions of the software (Figure 2.7).

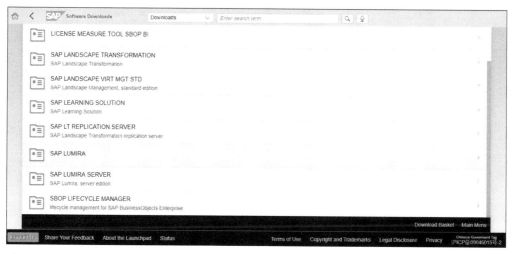

Figure 2.7 SAP Lumira Folder

6. Select **SAP Lumira** in the screen in Figure 2.8. **SAP Lumira Desktop** refers to all available versions of SAP Lumira 1.x.

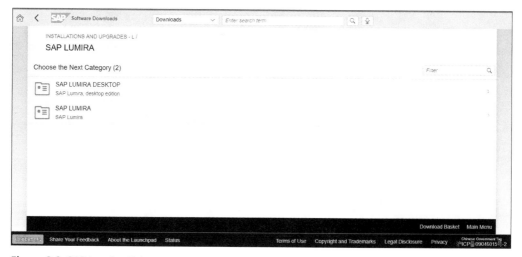

Figure 2.8 SAP Lumira Category

7. Click on the **SAP Lumira 2.1** (Figure 2.9).

Figure 2.9 SAP Lumira 2.1 Folder

8. Click on **Installation and Upgrade** (Figure 2.10).

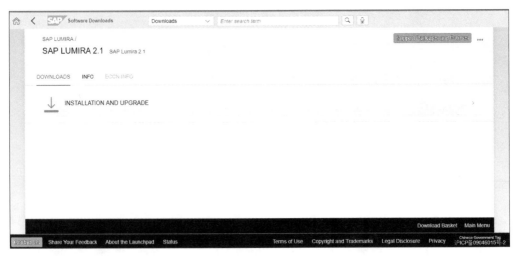

Figure 2.10 Installation and Upgrade Folder

9. Click on the name of the installation file, in this example **51052698**, to start downloading the ZIP file (Figure 2.11).

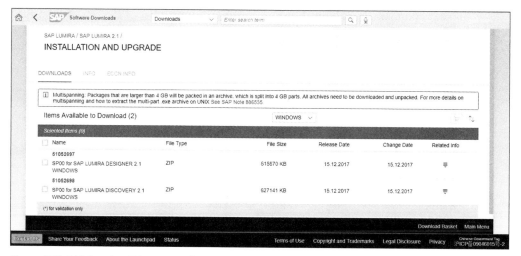

Figure 2.11 SAP Lumira, Discovery Edition Installation File

10. After the download is complete, unpack the installation file.

11. In the next section, we walk you through the installation process of the SAP Lumira, discovery edition client.

2.4 Installing SAP Lumira, Discovery Edition

Once we downloaded and unpacked the SAP Lumira, discovery edition installation file, it's time to launch the SAP Lumira, discovery edition Installation Manager. The Installation Manager will guide you through the five installation steps shown at the top, marking the installation process. To install SAP Lumira, discovery edition please follow these steps:

1. Browse to the location where you unpacked the installation file.

2. Double-click on the **51052698 · DATA_UNITS** folder.

3. Open the **SAP_LUMIRA_DISCOVERY_21_SP00** folder.

4. Double-click on the *SAPLumiraDiscoverySetup.exe* file to launch the Installation Manager. The self-extracting archive will unpack all the necessary installation files.

   During the launch of the SAP Lumira, discovery edition Installation Manager, the installer performs system checks to verify if all the prerequisites listed in Section 2.2 are met.

If a prerequisite is not met, a dialog will appear with a list of the missing components. You can click on an item for detailed information on the action required. To be able to continue with the installation, you have to resolve the issues related to the prerequisites first.

5. Step 1 of the Installation Manager (Figure 2.12), **Define Properties**, allows you to change the setup language by selecting one of the available languages.

6. Furthermore, you can change the destination folder where SAP Lumira, discovery edition will be installed. By default, the destination folder is *C:\Program Files\SAP BusinessObjects Lumira\Lumira Discovery*. If necessary, you can change the destination by either browsing to a different path through the folder icon or entering it manually.

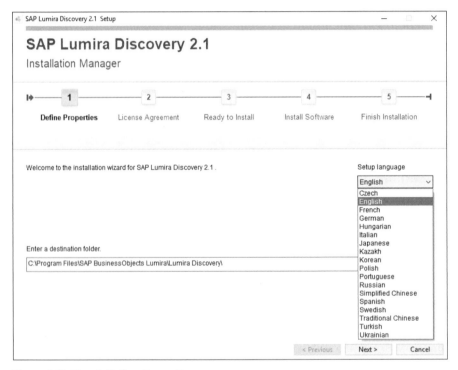

Figure 2.12 Step 1: Define Properties

7. Choose **Next** to proceed to Step 2 (Figure 2.13) of the Installation Manager: accepting the **License Agreement**.

8. Accept the license agreement and click **Next**.

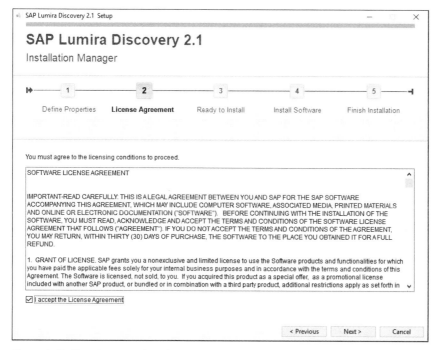

Figure 2.13 Step 2: Accepting the License Agreement

9. Click **Next** in Step 3, **Ready to Install** (Figure 2.14) to start the installation of SAP Lumira, discovery edition.

Figure 2.14 Step 3: Ready to Install

10. A progress bar is displayed while the SAP Lumira, discovery edition Installation Manager proceeds with Step 4, the installation of the SAP Lumira, discovery edition software (Figure 2.15).

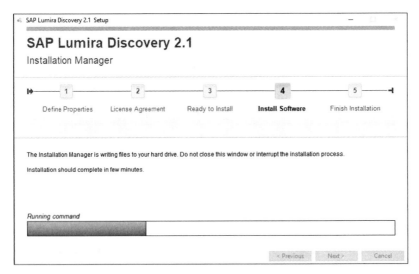

Figure 2.15 Step 4: Install Software

11. When the installation is complete, click **Finish** (Figure 2.16) and by default the Installation Manager will launch SAP Lumira, discovery edition.

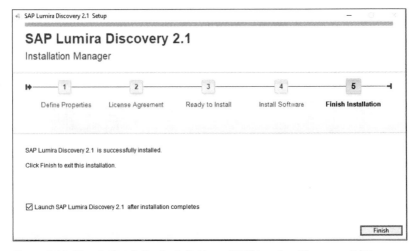

Figure 2.16 Step 5: Finish the Installation of SAP Lumira, Discovery Edition

> **Installation Logs**
>
> If you encounter any issues during the installation of SAP Lumira, discovery edition, please check the log files created during the installation process. The log files can be found in the installation folder, for instance: *C:\Program Files\SAP BusinessObjects Lumira\Lumira Discovery\InstallData\logs*.

12. If you want to uninstall SAP Lumira, discovery edition, please follow the steps in the next section.

2.5   Uninstalling SAP Lumira, Discovery Edition

Uninstalling SAP Lumira, discovery edition will remove all the installation files but will keep the SAP Lumira Documents folder that contains your Lumira documents, including the samples.

Follow these steps to uninstall SAP Lumira, discovery edition:

1. Choose **Start · Control Panel · Programs · Programs and Features**.
2. Locate SAP Lumira, discovery edition in your list of installed programs.
3. Right-click **SAP Lumira Discovery 2.1** and select **Uninstall** to open the SAP Lumira, discovery edition Installation Manager, as shown in Figure 2.17.

Figure 2.17 Step 1: Confirm Uninstall

4. Click **Next**. A progress bar is displayed while the SAP Lumira, discovery edition Installation Manager uninstalls SAP Lumira, discovery edition (Figure 2.18).

Figure 2.18 Step 2: Uninstall Software

5. Once SAP Lumira, discovery edition is uninstalled, click on **Finish** to close the SAP Lumira, discovery edition Installation Manager (Figure 2.19).

Figure 2.19 Step 3: Finish Uninstallation

In the next section, we walk you through the process of updating the SAP Lumira, discovery edition client.

2.6   Updating SAP Lumira, Discovery Edition

SAP releases updates for SAP Lumira, discovery edition on a regular basis. According to the maintenance statement of SAP, a new minor release will become available every six months. In between, SAP delivers support packages about every 8-10 weeks that contain product enhancements and defects corrections. It's recommended to always upgrade to the latest available version if possible.

Compatible Versions

If you save and distribute SAP Lumira documents on the SAP BusinessObjects BI platform (Chapter 21), please ensure that the server add-on and the client are on the same version. When this is not the case, some functionality might not work properly.

Instead of checking the SAP Support Portal on a regular basis whether an update has been released, SAP Lumira, discovery edition can execute this check during startup. In the **Preferences** menu (Figure 2.20), you can determine if and how often checks need to be executed.

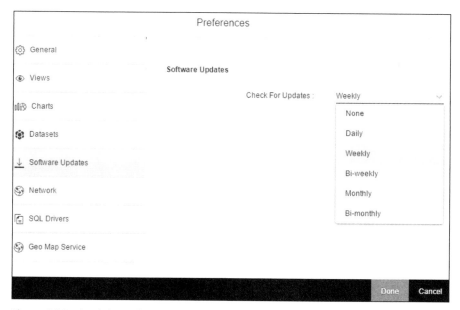

Figure 2.20 Check for Software Updates

Check for Updates

As of the writing of this book, the feature that checks for updates was not implemented, although it was available through the software updates menu as part of the preferences. We expect SAP to reintroduce this feature, which was available in Lumira 1.3x, in one of the upcoming releases.

The steps to check and download the latest update of the software via SAP Software Download Center on the SAP Support Portal are similar to what is described in Section 2.3. The only difference is to select **Support Packages & Patches** when browsing to the installation file, as shown in Figure 2.21.

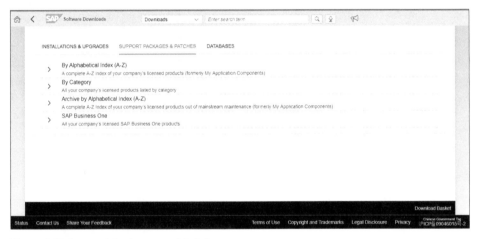

Figure 2.21 Support Packages and Patches

Maintenance Strategy and Release Schedule

For more information on the maintenance strategy and product support of SAP Lumira 2.0, please visit *http://bit.ly/2ALo4P2*.

For more information on the SAP Lumira 2.0 release schedule, please visit *https://launchpad.support.sap.com/#/notes/2465894*.

2.7   Tracing

To troubleshoot issues, it can be very useful to enable tracing and collect log files from SAP Lumira, discovery edition. The default mechanism for other SAP Business-Objects BI products, based on the *BO_trace.ini* file, is also used for SAP Lumira, discovery edition. The *BO_trace.ini* file is used to configure the tracing and is located in *C:\Program Files\SAP BusinessObjects Lumira\Lumira Discovery\Desktop*.

To change the tracing settings, open the file for editing, modify the settings, and save it. The parameters as well as their default and possible values are described within the *BO_trace.ini* file as comment lines.

Instead of changing the settings within the *BO_trace.ini* file manually, SAP has created a batch file called *enabletracingv2_Discovery.bat*. This batch file, available as an attachment in SAP KBA 2220451 (Creating High Level SAP Lumira Desktop Trace Log Files, Lumira 1.x and Lumira 2.x), can be used to:

- Enable/disable SAP Lumira Desktop tracing.
- Enable SAP Java Connector tracing (used for tracing SAP BW, SAP ERP, and SAP Java connector issues).
- Gather the most recent set of generated log files.

In the following steps, we show you how to use this batch file to enable tracing and collect log files from SAP Lumira, discovery edition:

1. Browse to the SAP Support Portal (*https://support.sap.com/en/index.html*) and search for SAP KBA **2220451**.
2. Click on **Attachments** and select *enabletracingv2_Discovery.zip* to download the file (Figure 2.22). The file *enabletracingv2.zip* can be used in combination with SAP Lumira 1.x.

Figure 2.22 SAP Note 2220451: Download Batch File

3. Before we can enable the tracing we have to close SAP Lumira, discovery edition. Without a restart, the trace logs with the proper level of detail will not be generated.

4. Run the batch file. If you are not logged in as an administrator on your OS, you will be prompted to re-launch the script (Figure 2.23).

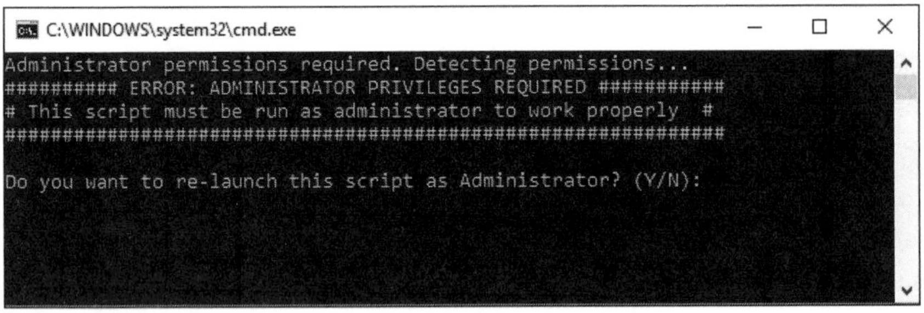

Figure 2.23 Re-Launch Script as Administrator

5. When the script is relaunched with administrator privileges, you will be presented with the options shown in Figure 2.24. Some basic information regarding file locations and trace status is displayed at the top.

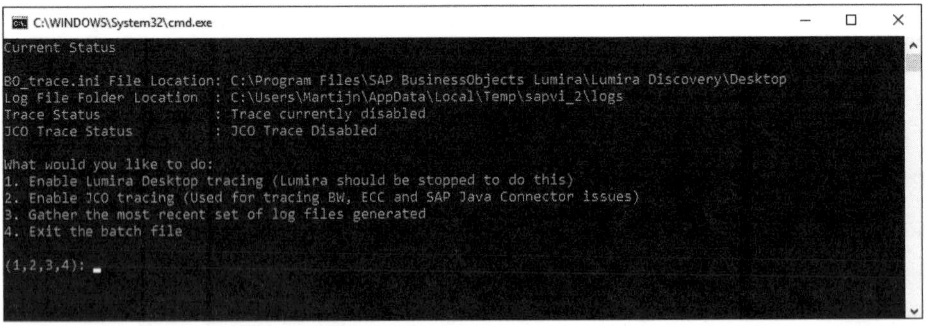

Figure 2.24 SAP Lumira, Discovery Edition Tracing Options

6. To enable SAP Lumira, discovery edition tracing, select option 1. The script will create a backup of the *BO_trace.ini* file and will enable tracing set as high (Figure 2.25). Press any key to continue to the main menu of the script. If you are troubleshooting issues related to SAP Java Connector, also enable SAP Java Connector tracing with option 2.

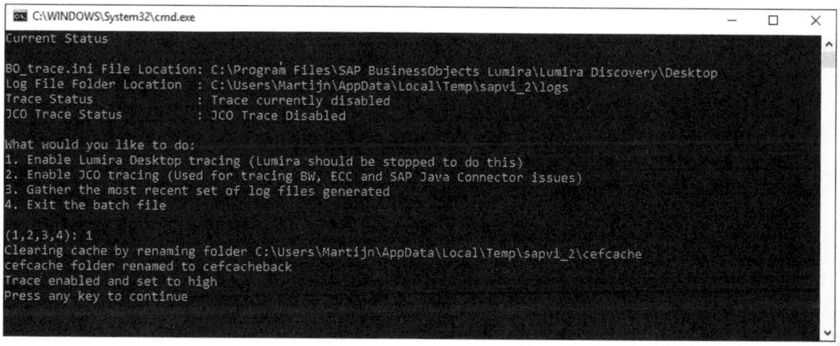

Figure 2.25 Enable SAP Lumira, Discovery Edition Tracing

7. Open SAP Lumira, discovery edition and execute the workflow for which you want to collect trace logs.

8. Once this is finalized, you can gather the generated log files by selecting option 3. The collected log files are copied to the following location: *C:\Users\<USER>\App-Data\Local\Temp\sapvi_2\logs\RecentLogs* and the folder opens in Windows Explorer (Figure 2.26). Furthermore, a summary of the copy actions is provided in the script dialog (Figure 2.27).

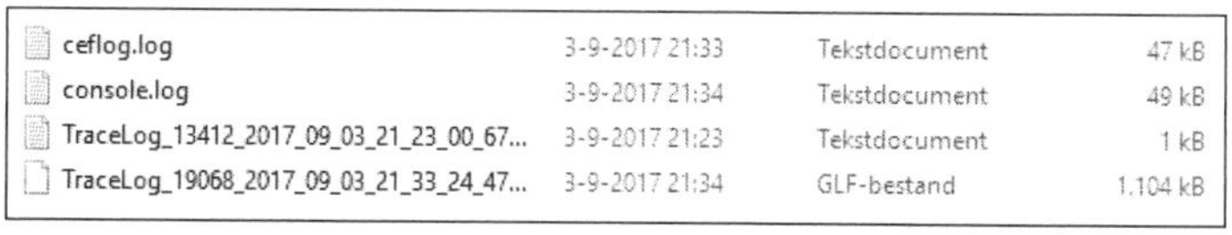

Figure 2.26 Log Files

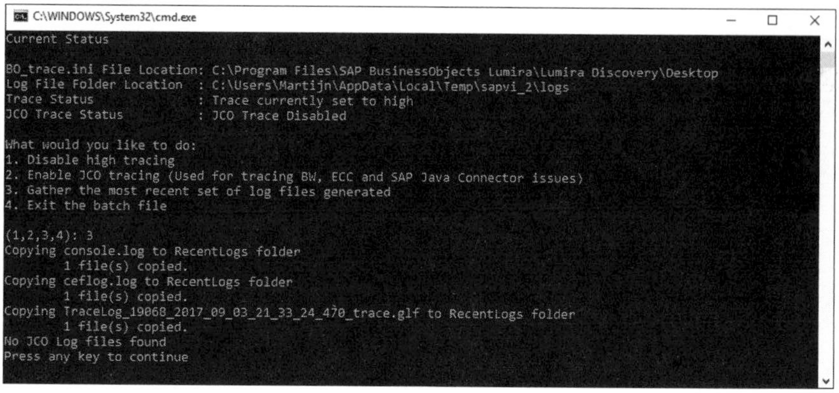

Figure 2.27 Overview of Copied Log Files

9. Before you exit the batch file (option 4), you can disable the tracing and the script will revert the *BO_trace.ini* file back to the previous state by replacing it with the backup.

10. For more information and for the latest version of the batch file, please visit SAP KBA 2220451 via *https://launchpad.support.sap.com/#/notes/2220451*.

2.8   Summary

In this chapter we walked you through the simple process of downloading, installing, and updating SAP Lumira, discovery edition. Furthermore, we explained the differences between the standard and desktop edition license and provided you with tips and tricks regarding tracing if you bump into any unexpected issues when executing a specific workflow.

The next chapter will get you started on the completely revisited user interface, compared to SAP Lumira 1.x.

Chapter 3

SAP Lumira, Discovery Edition Interface

Before you start building SAP Lumira stories, you should know your way around SAP Lumira, discovery edition. This chapter walks you through the SAP Lumira, discovery edition interface and shows you how you can interact with the tool.

The SAP Lumira, discovery edition user interface has gotten a complete overhaul. If you used SAP Lumira 1.x in the past, you will probably recognize a lot of the concepts and features from SAP Lumira 1.x in SAP Lumira, discovery edition. But as you will see in this chapter, they are not always in the same place. There is no need to be worried; the user interface and way of working in SAP Lumira, discovery edition is definitely an improvement over the way Lumira 1.x was set up.

In this chapter, we go through the full user interface of SAP Lumira, discovery edition, to familiarize you with all the menus, views, and options, so that you are fully prepared to build your own SAP Lumira stories.

3.1   Home Page

Let's start with the first thing that you see after starting SAP Lumira, discovery edition: the home page (Figure 3.1). From this home page you can, for example, connect to a data source and create a new document, or open existing SAP Lumira documents.

Figure 3.1 SAP Lumira, Discovery Edition Home Page

3.1.1   Data Source

Creating a new SAP Lumira document always starts by connecting to a data source. No data source, no document. From the **Data Source** list, we can choose the five most common used data sources: SAP BW, SAP HANA, SAP BusinessObjects BI universe (UNX), Microsoft Excel, and Query with SQL. For SAP BW and SAP HANA, we need to decide to use either live data or import the data into SAP Lumira, discovery edition. For all other data sources, the data will be imported.

After expanding the list (**Show All**), all available data sources are shown in tiles, and grouped by **Databases**, **Files**, and **Extensions**. Within the **Files** category, we now also see the options to **Copy data from Clipboard** and import data from a **Text** file. The **Extensions** category will remain empty until you install a custom data source.

3.1.2   Recently Used

In the **Recently Used** list, you will find the five data sources that were most recently used for importing data to your local SAP Lumira documents.

After clicking **Show All**, you will see all the data sources that are used in your locally stored documents (Figure 3.2). Here you can see in which documents a data source is used and edit the connection to the data source file (i.e., choose a different file or its location). With the dropdown box, you can filter on data source type. If you hover over the data sources, some connection details are displayed; for example, the used user name and client number for an SAP BW data source, or the location of a local file.

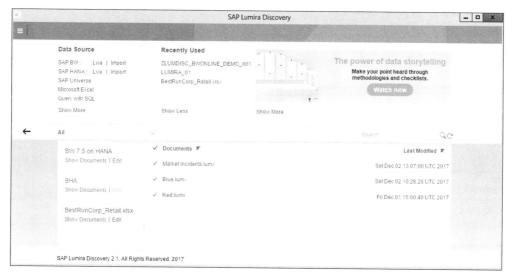

Figure 3.2 Manage Data Sources

3.1.3   Local Documents

In the **Local Document** tab, your locally stored SAP Lumira documents are shown, sorted on the modification date/time. You can open a document by clicking the tile. If you hover over the tile, a recycle bin appears, which lets you quickly delete a document.

Below your own documents, a few sample documents are available. These can be used to try out SAP Lumira, discovery edition, and to make things easy, they include some sample data for you to play around with.

There is a search option to do a text search on all the local documents. The **Refresh** button will refresh the list of local documents and their used data sources. You can for example add a new *.lumx* file to your SAP Lumira documents folder using

Windows Explorer. After you click the **Refresh** button, this document will show up in SAP Lumira, discovery edition.

Finally, you can switch between the default tile view and a list view. Especially when you have a lot of documents, the list view can be easier to navigate (Figure 3.3).

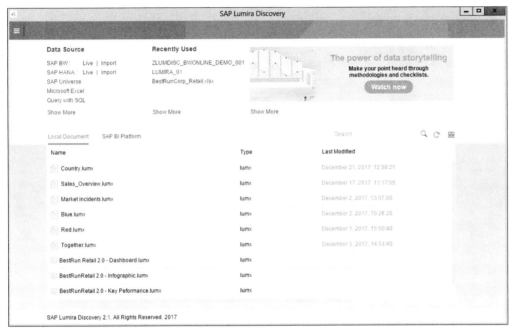

Figure 3.3 Local Documents List View

3.1.4   SAP BusinessObjects BI Platform

In the **SAP BusinessObjects BI Platform** tab, the SAP Lumira documents that you have access to on an SAP BusinessObjects BI platform environment can be shown. To see these remote documents, you obviously need to log in to an SAP BusinessObjects BI platform first.

After successfully logging on, your favorites and public folders are visible and can be browsed, just as on the BI Launchpad, so there is no tile or list view here (Figure 3.4). By double-clicking you can open a document. There is an option to **Refresh** the folders and a button to **Log out**.

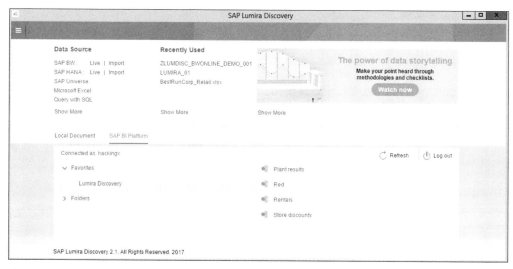

Figure 3.4 Browsing the SAP BusinessObjects BI Platform

3.2 Menu

The menu bar is accessible through the triple bar menu in the top-left corner of the application (Figure 3.5). We discuss each of these menus and their items in this section.

Figure 3.5 SAP Lumira, Discovery Edition Menu

3.2.1   Home

You can use the **Home** option to go back to the home page. If you haven't saved your story yet, you'll be asked to do so in a popup window. In SAP Lumira, discovery edition, we can only work in a single SAP Lumira document at once. So, when there is a need to go back to the home page to open a different document or create a new one, it is necessary to close the active document first. Actually, this option is the same as the **Close** option in the **File** menu. Another option is to hover the mouse cursor over the document title and click the X. The keyboard shortcut for **Close** is Ctrl+F4, or you can also use Ctrl+W.

3.2.2   File

The **File** menu is about document handling. Here you can import and save an SAP Lumira document and export and publish data (Figure 3.6). Depending on where you are in SAP Lumira, discovery edition, some options are available or hidden.

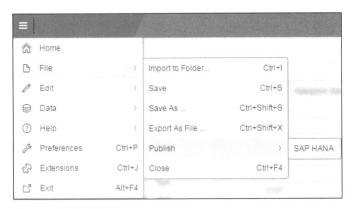

Figure 3.6 File Menu

Import to Folder...

You can import an SAP Lumira document file (.lumx) to your local documents. When you use this option, a copy of the .lumx file will be stored in the following (default) directory: *C:\Users\<ACCOUNT>\Documents\SAP Lumira Documents*.

You can also manually add the SAP Lumira document to this folder and press the **Refresh** button on the home page.

The keyboard shortcut for the **Import to Folder...** option is Ctrl+I.

Save, Save As …

To keep the SAP Lumira document that you have created and store the changes that you have made, you can use the **Save** option. In case of a new document that hasn't been saved earlier, a popup window will appear (Figure 3.7). Here you can choose between storing the document locally or on the SAP BusinessObjects BI platform. A document has a **Name** and an optional **Description**. Also note that this menu has an option to **Save without data**. In that case, only the document structure and components are stored, and the data automatically will be loaded when opening the document. This is in many cases the preferred way to store SAP Lumira documents, as the document may contain data that shouldn't be available for all the users who have access to the document. The keyboard shortcut for this command is $\boxed{\text{Ctrl}}+\boxed{\text{S}}$.

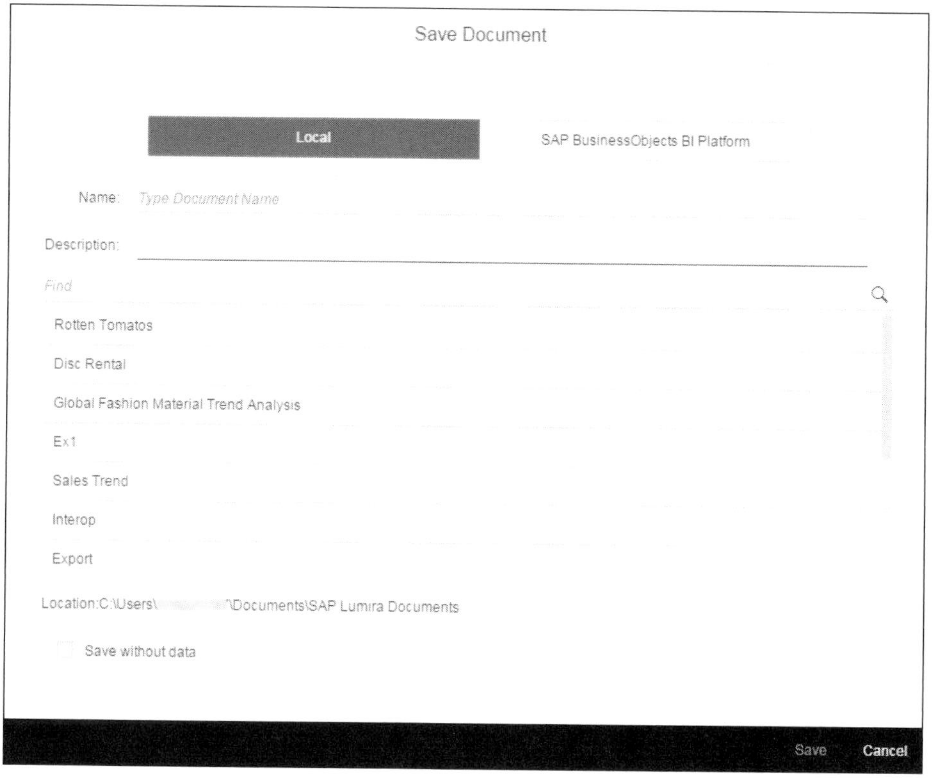

Figure 3.7 Save a Document

> **Save Without Data**
>
> SAP BusinessObjects BI platform administrators can enforce this option, to ensure that no documents containing data are stored on the BI platform. See Chapter 21 on how to set this up.

If you don't want to overwrite your original file, you should use **Save As** .... With this option, the popup window, as shown in Figure 3.7, will always appear. The keyboard shortcut for this option is $\boxed{\texttt{Ctrl}}+\boxed{\texttt{Shift}}+\boxed{\texttt{S}}$.

Save and **Save As** ... are only available when you are working in an SAP Lumira document, not in the home page.

Export As File ...

With **Export As File** ... we can export complete datasets from SAP Lumira, discovery edition to a local file. The output format can be a Microsoft Excel or a CSV (comma-separated values) file. This option is only available in the **DataView** tab, and it will export the active dataset. The keyboard shortcut is $\boxed{\texttt{Ctrl}}+\boxed{\texttt{Shift}}+\boxed{\texttt{X}}$.

Publish

You can publish complete datasets from SAP Lumira, discovery edition to SAP HANA. When you use the **Publish** option, you first need to log on to an SAP HANA environment, either directly via the **SAP HANA** tab, or by using one of the available OLAP connections on the **SAP BI Platform** (Figure 3.8).

Figure 3.8 Publish to SAP HANA Login

Next you can select a package or create a new one, as well as create a new vie̶w̶ replace an existing view (Figure 3.9).

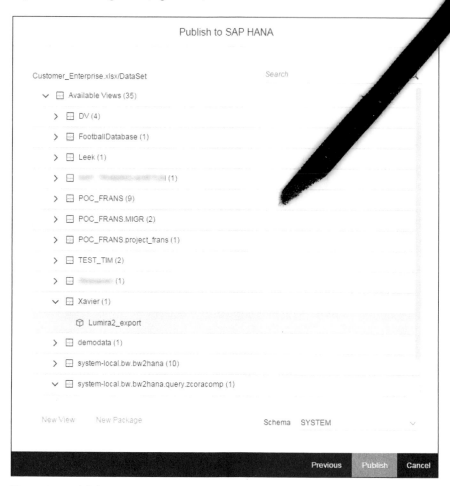

Figure 3.9 Publish to SAP HANA—Create View and Publish

This **Publish to SAP HANA** feature can be very useful, for example if you want to use some locally managed data in an SAP HANA online discovery scenario. You can perform some manual manipulations on an offline dataset (replace values, create groupings, etc.), upload this dataset to an SAP HANA view, and use this view again in a new SAP Lumira, discovery edition scenario where you link data from several views, including the one that you maintain manually.

The keyboard shortcut for **Publish to HANA** is Ctrl + Shift + X .

Limitations

In case you want to publish time hierarchies to an SAP HANA view, you need to take the following into account:

- The maximum calendar range is 50 years.
- The SAP HANA calendar system table has to be available, and it must be a Gregorian calendar.

Close

To close the document that you are working on, you can select the **Close** option or use the keyboard shortcut [Ctrl]+[F4]. If you made changes to the document since the last time that you saved it, a popup will appear asking if you want to save these changes in the current document.

3.2.3   Edit

The **Edit** menu has only two, but very important, features: **Undo** and **Redo**.

You can use **Undo** to reverse an action you performed. For example, if you by accident changed the position of a chart in your story page, or worse, deleted something, you can go back a step. Most actions can be undone, but whenever you change the underlying data, for example by refreshing or appending data to the dataset, the undo history will be cleared. You can do a maximum of three undo actions in a row.

If you used **Undo**, but you still want to apply the change, you can use **Redo** to reverse the undo action. Just as with the undo actions, you can do a maximum of three redo actions in a row.

You should forget about using these two menu item manually from the menu bar. Make sure you learn the keyboard shortcuts, as they will save you a lot of time (and annoyances). For **Undo**, the shortcut is [Ctrl]+[Z] and for **Redo**, it is [Ctrl]+[Y].

3.2.4   Data

The **Data** menu is all about data sources. Here you can add a new data source, and edit, combine, and refresh an existing data source (Figure 3.10). These functions are only available when an SAP Lumira document is opened. Combining data sources using merge or append is covered in detail in Chapter 8.

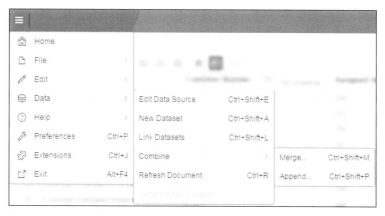

Figure 3.10 Data Menu

Note

The **Generate Full Dataset** option is not yet available in SAP Lumira, discovery edition.

Edit Data Source

The **Edit Data Source** option allows you to make changes to the initial setup of the data source. The displayed window depends on the data source type. You can add or remove columns or fields, change values for input parameters or variables, and adjust filters. In case of a query with a SQL data source, you can edit the SQL query. When a data model change has taken place (for example, a column was removed or added), the **Data Mapping** menu appears so you can resolve the changes. The keyboard shortcut for **Edit Data Source** is Ctrl + Shift + E .

New Dataset

Use the **New Dataset** option to add a dataset to an SAP Lumira document. You will get the same menus and workflows as when you create a new document from scratch and add the first dataset. This is discussed in detail in Chapter 5. The keyboard shortcut for **New Dataset** is Ctrl + Shift + A .

Link Datasets

With **the Link Datasets** option, you can combine data from multiple datasets and use the combined output in a visualization. To link, or blend as it is called sometimes, datasets, at least one common dimension is required between the datasets. Unlike data merging, with data linking there are no changes made to the datasets themselves; the joining of the datasets takes place only in the visualization. Data linking is discussed in detail in Chapter 18. The keyboard shortcut for the **Link Datasets** command is `Ctrl`+`Shift`+`L`.

Combine

The **Combine** menu gives the option to **Merge…** and **Append…** data. In case of merging, fields from two datasets can be combined into a single dataset, based on a common dimension. This can be done as a left outer join, where the primary dataset is supplemented with new fields for all its records that have a common value with the secondary dataset. Also, an inner join can be used, where the result set will consist of only the records that could find a match. More on data merging in Chapter 8. The keyboard shortcut is `Ctrl`+`Shift`+`M`.

With the **Appending…** option, you can add data to your existing dataset. In this case, no additional fields are added, only additional data at the end of the current set of records. This can be useful if you need to add new values to your document each week. Appending is further discussed in Chapter 8. The keyboard shortcut is `Ctrl`+`Shift`+`P`.

Refresh Document

The **Refresh Document** command will refresh all the data sources that are used in your SAP Lumira document. This can be useful if the data in the underlying data source(s) (file, database) has changed, and you want your document to reflect those changes.

When any of the data sources contains prompts, these can be adjusted before the data is refreshed. The keyboard shortcut to refresh a document is `Ctrl`+`R`.

3.2.5   Help

The **Help** menu provides a number of support related options, and this is the place to activate your installation of SAP Lumira, discovery edition.

Help

The **Help** option will start your browser and direct you to the online SAP Help pages for SAP Lumira, discovery edition. You can also use the keyboard shortcut `F1`.

Enter Keycode

In the **Enter Keycode** menu, you can enter your SAP Lumira, discovery edition product license keycode and activate your version of SAP Lumira, discovery edition. If you already activated the tool, it shows the type of active license (Figure 3.11).

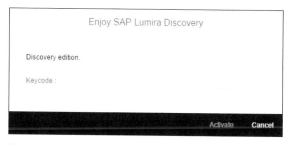

Figure 3.11 SAP Lumira, Discovery Edition Keycode

Get Support...

The **Get Support...** option starts your browser and redirects you to the SAP Support Portal. Here you can report incidents and browse the SAP Notes archive.

About Discovery

You can use the **About Discovery** option to check the release and version number of the SAP Lumira, discovery edition installation that you are running (Figure 3.12).

Figure 3.12 SAP Lumira, Discovery Edition About Menu

3.2.6   Preferences

In the **Preferences** menu, you can manage your setup of SAP Lumira, discovery edition, and change the default settings. The keyboard shortcut to display the **Preferences** menu is ⌈Ctrl⌉+⌈P⌉.

General

With the **Language** setting, you can switch the language of the SAP Lumira, discovery edition user interface. The following languages are available: English, German, Spanish, French, Italian, Hungarian, Polish, Portuguese, Swedish Turkish, Czech, Russian, Ukrainian, Chinese, Japanese, and Korean.

The **Auto Recovery** setting determines if, and how often, a recovery file of your active document is made. If this option is enabled, in case of a crash, the next time you start SAP Lumira, discovery edition the recovery file is located and you can continue with this file if you want to. As this option is set to inactive by default, it is recommended to check this and activate the setting. In addition, the menu option shows the location of the recovered documents.

With the **Default View** option, you can switch between the **Grid** or **Canvas** mode to open documents in by default, where **Grid** opens the **DataView** tab and **Canvas** the **DesignView** tab.

Show Data Protection Disclaimer

The **Show Data Protection Disclaimer** is the popup warning that you see when starting SAP Lumira, discovery edition (Figure 3.13). You can activate or hide it with this setting. If you check the **Don't show again** checkbox in the popup itself, this setting will also change to disabled.

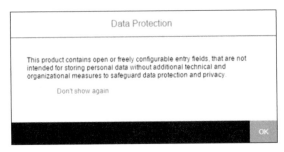

Figure 3.13 Data Protection Popup

Views

In the **Views** menu, you can determine for each offline data source type individually which default view should be selected. This can be the **Grid** view or the **Facets** view. Note that this only applies if you choose **Grid** as the **Default View** in the **General** menu.

Charts

In the **Charts** menu, you can select the default chart color palettes for dimensions and measures. You can choose from a number of **Standard Palettes** or create a custom one (**User Defined Palette**). In this menu you can also select the **Default Export Type** for data export of chart components. This can be **Aggregated** or **Detailed**. In the **Aggregated** option, only data values that are included in the visualization will be exported. In the **Detailed** option, all the data values from the dataset can be exported. More on exporting data can be found in Chapter 20.

Datasets

The **Datasets** menu gives you the option to show or hide the dataset statistics in the status bar (for example, the number of total rows and columns). Also, you can disable the default dataset enrichments here (Figure 3.14). During the acquisition of a dataset, a number of processes are run to detect and add potential metadata to the dataset:

- SAP Lumira, discovery edition creates measures from columns that contain numerical values. By default, they are aggregated with the SUM aggregation function.
- Columns with geographical values as country, region, sub-region, or city names are marked, so that you can use them to create a geographical hierarchy.
- Columns that contain date- or time-related values are marked as such and can be used to create a date/time hierarchy.

If you disable this feature, you will lose all this metadata and have to set up the measures and dimensions by yourself. On the other hand, this detection process can be time consuming, especially in the case of large datasets. There is also an option to enable dataset enrichments if the dataset contains more than 30 million cells. This option is available only if the second option is activated. For more details on the data manipulation options, check out Chapter 8.

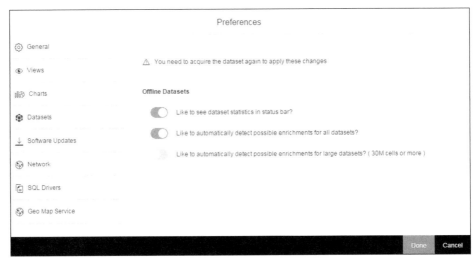

Figure 3.14 Datasets Preferences

Software Updates

In the **Software Updates** menu, you can change the frequency of update checks for new versions of SAP Lumira, discovery edition.

Check for Updates

As of the writing of this book, the feature that checks for updates was not implemented, although it was available through the software updates menu as part of the preferences. We expect SAP to reintroduce this feature, which was available in SAP Lumira 1.3x, in one of the upcoming releases.

See Chapter 3 for other ways to update SAP Lumira, discovery edition.

Network

In the **Network** menu, you can set up the proxy server settings in case this is required for your setup. With the **SAP BI Platform** option, you can enter your standard SAP BI platform environment URL that you want to connect to. You can **Enable RESTfull Logon** and log on **Via Secure Logon Client** here (see Chapter 21 for more information).

SQL Drivers

The **SQL Drivers** menu gives an overview of all SQL drivers that can be used with SAP Lumira, discovery edition for data acquisition with the **Query with SQL** data source type. It shows which of those drivers are installed and active, and this is also the place to install the drivers (Figure 3.15).

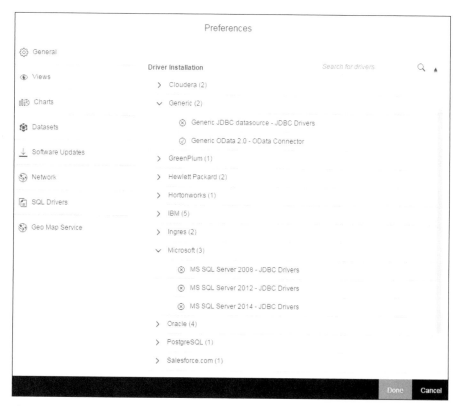

Figure 3.15 SQL Drivers Preferences

Geo Map Service

The geo map chart components use the Esri ArcGIS Online service to provide the base maps, which are included in the SAP Lumira, discovery edition license (default account). In case you are using Esri on-premise, or you have an account for the Esri Map Service, you can enter these credentials here (Figure 3.16).

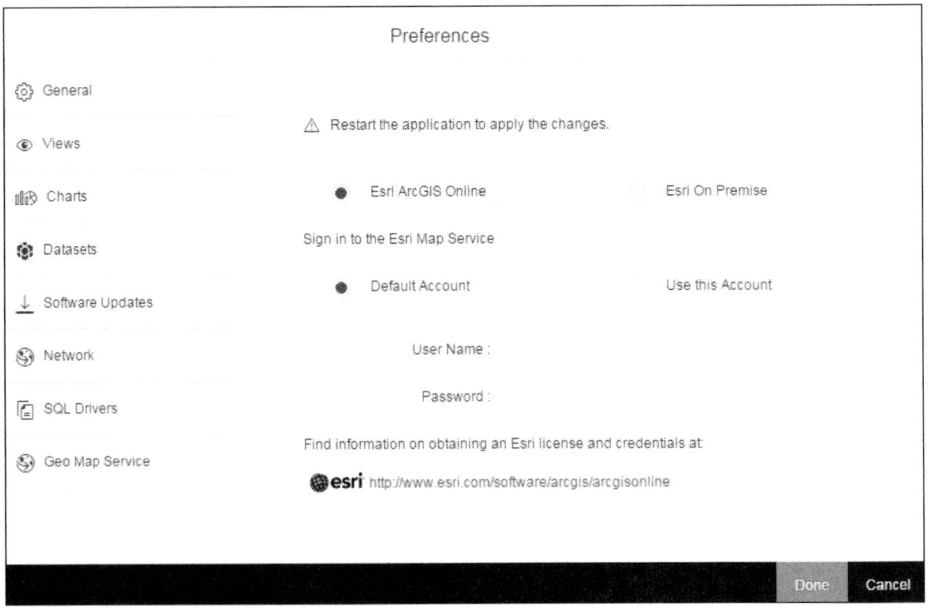

Figure 3.16 Geo Map Service Preferences

3.2.7   Extensions

In the Extension Manager you can manage SAP Lumira, discovery edition add-ons (Figure 3.17). These are third-party plugins that extend the functionalities of SAP Lumira, discovery edition. The two types of extensions are Data Access extensions and Visualization extensions.

The Data Access extensions provide you with the ability to import data from data sources that are not included in the list of default data sources. This could be a connector to, for example, a cloud-based solution or a new data file type.

The Visualization extensions provide additional data visualization options that you can use in your SAP Lumira, discovery edition stories, like advanced geo maps or a specific chart type.

You can develop extensions yourself by using the SAP Lumira SDK (see Appendix B) or install an extension developed by one of the SAP partner companies. The SAP Lumira, discovery edition installation includes a few sample extensions, which can be found in the following directory: *C:\Program Files\SAP BusinessObjects Lumira\ Lumira Discovery\Desktop\samples\extensions\charts*.

In the Extension Manager, you can add extensions by clicking **install** on the top-right corner (Figure 3.17) and selecting the ZIP file of the extension. After installing an extension, a restart is required to activate the extension. Here you can also delete and upgrade previously installed extensions.

Figure 3.17 Extension Manager

SAP App Center

Third-party extensions for SAP Lumira, discovery edition can be found in the SAP App center: *http://bit.ly/2p8z4UE*.

3.2.8   Exit

Exit closes SAP Lumira, discovery edition. If you made some changes to a document since the last time you saved it, a popup window will show up, asking you if you want to save the document. The keyboard shortcut for **Exit** is $\boxed{\text{Alt}}$+$\boxed{\text{F4}}$. You can of course also click the **Close** button in the upper-right corner of the SAP Lumira, designer edition window.

3.3   Data View

The data view is the place to display your acquired dataset and manipulate its data (Figure 3.18). This view is only available when you use offline data.

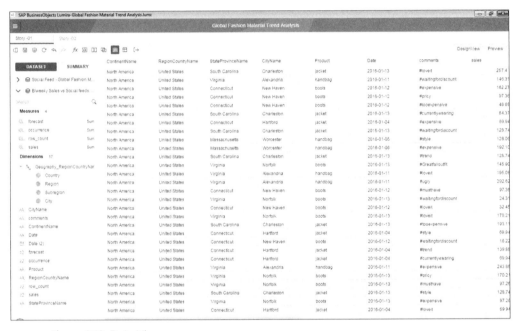

Figure 3.18 Data View

In the data view, we have the following two main areas:

- **Side pane**

  The side pane on the left of the screen contains two tabs, as follows:

  - The **Dataset** tab displays all the data sources that are available in the SAP Lumira document. You can expand a data source and see its measures and dimensions. By default, you'll find here the dimensions and measures that have been detected during the data acquisition, but you can alter these and add objects. These data manipulation features are discussed in Chapter 8.

- The **Summary** tab shows a summary of the values of a selected dimension. It counts the number of records for each value and sorts them accordingly.

■ **Data**

The largest part of the screen is filled with the actual data that is available in the dataset. This can be shown either as a grid or in the facet view. In Chapter 7, we dive into data analysis and show you how to use these views to get to know your data.

Above these two core areas the toolbar is shown. The toolbar commands are described in Section 3.6.

3.4   Design View

The design view is the place where we can build stories from our dataset(s), by creating charts and adding other types of design objects (Figure 3.19). An SAP Lumira document consists of one or more stories, where each story can have multiple pages and each page can have multiple visualizations.

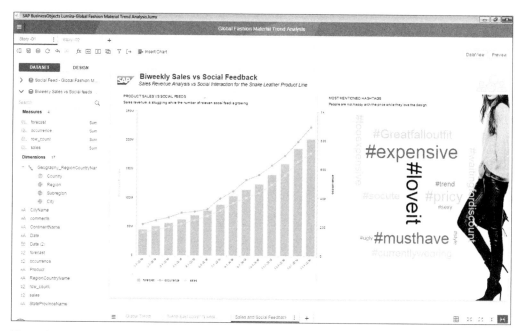

Figure 3.19 Design View

In the design view, we find the following two main areas:

- **Side pane**

  Just as in the data view, the side pane contains two tabs: **Dataset** and **Design**. The **Dataset** tab offers the same features in the design view as in the data view. In addition, we can drag and drop measures and dimensions from this tab to charts in the canvas.

  From the **Design** tab, you can add text objects, images, icons, shapes, adjust the background color or background image of the page, and change the properties of a chart (Figure 3.20). These options are discussed in Chapter 9 on chart creation and in Chapter 17 on story formatting.

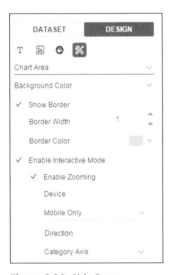

Figure 3.20 Side Pane

- **Canvas**

  The biggest part of the screen is reserved for the canvas. Here you create your SAP Lumira, discovery edition stories by adding charts, filters, input controls, and other design objects.

Also in the design view, a toolbar is shown above the side pane and the canvas. The toolbar commands are described in Section 3.6.

Above this toolbar the stories of the document are displayed in tabs (Figure 3.21). Here you can add a new story with the **+** icon and remove or rename a story via the more options icon (the three dots).

Figure 3.21 Story Bar

Below the canvas, the pages of the selected story are displayed. Again, with the **+** icon you can add a new page. With the popup menu you can duplicate, rename, move the position of the page in the order of pages, and delete the page.

Also from the **Settings** option, you can change the size of the canvas (Figure 3.22) and apply this to the current page or to all pages in the story. You can enter a custom size or choose from three predefined settings:

- Standard (4:3): 1361:1020 pixels
- Extended (16:9): 1361:765 pixels
- BI Launchpad (20:7): 1860:651 pixels

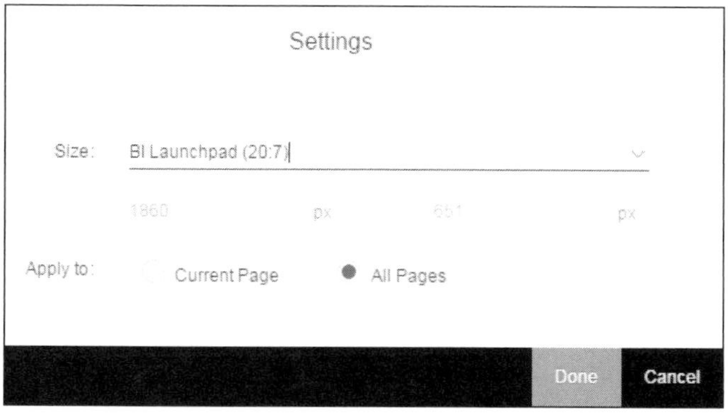

Figure 3.22 Page Settings

In the bottom-right corner, the grid icon lets you show or hide gridlines on the canvas. This grid is useful to align and position charts and other objects. Next to that, there are four options to adjust the size of the displayed page. This can help you see the whole page at once or zoom in to get a more detailed view. The options are:

- **Fit to Content**
- **Actual Size**
- **Fit to Height**
- **Fit to Width**

3.5   Preview

In the **Preview**, you can see how the story would look and what the interacting options are when published (Figure 3.23).

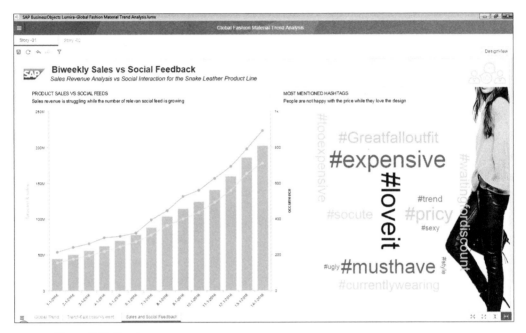

Figure 3.23 Preview

3.6   Toolbar

The SAP Lumira, discovery edition toolbar contains a number of most used commands that you can also find in the menu or at other places in the tool. However, using them from the toolbar is easier and probably a lot faster. You can use a toolbar command by simply clicking the button. The exact commands that you see in the toolbar depend on the view that you are in and the type of data source (offline or online).

Table 3.1 lists all the toolbar buttons that are common in the design view and data view, with a short description of their commands.

Toolbar Button	Command Description
◁▯	Show or hide the side pane.
🖫	Save the current SAP Lumira document.
⌄	Save, or Save As... the current SAP Lumira document.
⬚	Create a new dataset.
↻	Refresh the document (in case of offline data sources).
✎	Edit prompt values (in case of live data sources).
↶	Undo an operation.
↷	Redo an operation.
fx	Create a dimension or measure calculation.
⊞	Merge datasets.
🀫	Append datasets.
🗇	Link datasets.

Table 3.1 Common Toolbar Buttons

Figure 3.24 shows the toolbar in the design view.

Figure 3.24 Design View Toolbar

Table 3.2 lists all the toolbar buttons that are specific to the design view with a short description of their commands.

Toolbar Button	Command Description
▽	Show or hide the filter bar.
[→	Export the story to PDF.
▤ Insert Chart	Insert a new chart.
⬕ Insert Control	Insert control to quickly filter data.

Table 3.2 Design View Toolbar Buttons

Figure 3.25 shows the toolbar in the data view.

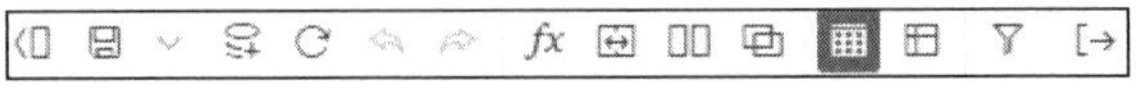

Figure 3.25 Data View Toolbar

Table 3.3 lists all the toolbar buttons that are specific to the data view with a short description of their commands.

Toolbar Button	Command Description
	Show the dataset in grid view.
	Show the dataset in facet view.
	Show or hide the filter bar.
	Export the dataset as a CSV or Microsoft Excel file.

Table 3.3 Data View Toolbar Buttons

Figure 3.26 shows the toolbar in the preview.

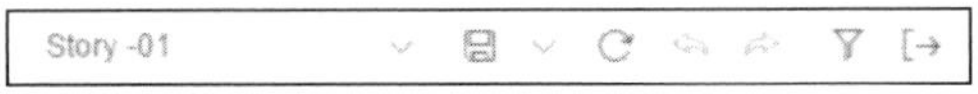

Figure 3.26 Preview Toolbar

3.7 Comparing SAP Lumira 1.x and SAP Lumira 2.x

If you worked with SAP Lumira 1.x, you have seen in the previous sections that the user interface of SAP Lumira, discovery edition is completely different. The most apparent difference is that SAP Lumira, discovery edition combines all the data visualization options in a single view, while SAP Lumira 1.x used several rooms:

- **Prepare**
  This room is comparable to the data view, where you can review and manipulate the datasets.
- **Visualize**
  Here you had to create all the charts (Figure 3.27). The charts were stored as separate objects.

Figure 3.27 SAP Lumira 1.x Visualize Room

- **Compose**

  You could create a story in this room, using the visualizations that you built in the **Visualize** room, supplemented with other objects like text objects, pictures, and input controls (Figure 3.28).

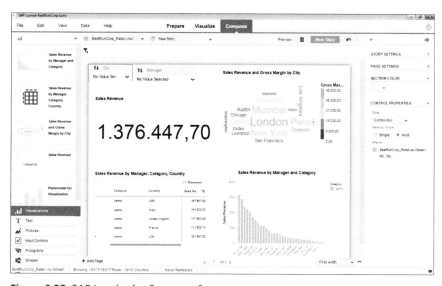

Figure 3.28 SAP Lumira 1.x Compose Room

- **Share**

    This room was removed in SAP Lumira version 1.31, and its features were moved to the **File** menu.

These different rooms led to a lot of switching forward and backward. Also, if you changed a chart in the **Visualize** room, the changes weren't reflected in the story in the **Compose** room. It was necessary to remove the visualization from the story and add it again.

3.8   Summary

In this chapter, we looked at the interface of SAP Lumira, discovery edition, to get familiar with the tool and get ready to create SAP Lumira, discovery edition stories. We discussed the available menu options, the **DataView** and **DesignView** tabs and their toolbars and options, and ended the chapter with a comparison of SAP Lumira, discovery edition and SAP Lumira 1.x.

In the next chapter, you are going to put this knowledge to use by creating your first SAP Lumira, discovery edition story.

Chapter 4
Creating Your First Story

The goal of visualizing data is to clearly and efficiently communicate information to users. Through the concept of stories, SAP Lumira, discovery edition offers capabilities that combine aesthetic form and function to provide insights in complex datasets in an intuitive way.

Now that you are familiar with the user interface of SAP Lumira, discovery edition, it's time to start creating your first SAP Lumira story.

SAP Lumira, discovery edition uses the concept of creating stories to clearly and efficiently communicate information to users. It helps you turn raw data into relevant information using visualizations like charts, text elements, and images.

Before inserting charts onto the canvas, the first step of creating an SAP Lumira story is connecting to a data source and importing a dataset. SAP Lumira, discovery edition is able to connect to a wide range of commonly used data sources. Importing data means that the dataset is retrieved from the data source, stored internally in the in-memory database, and saved in the SAP Lumira document. For SAP HANA and SAP BW, however, SAP Lumira, discovery edition offers a live connection where the dataset remains in the data source and calculations are delegated.

After importing a dataset, we briefly touch on the different ways SAP Lumira, discovery edition offers to analyze the elements, structure, and values using the data view. Switching between the grid and the facet view enables you to gain a better understanding to which extent the data can help you find answers to your business questions.

Enrichment and manipulation actions are often required to create meaningful dimensions and measures out of the raw dataset. In this chapter we use two examples—creating a hierarchy and creating a measure—to provide you with quick insight into how easily these data enrichment and manipulation actions can be performed. You learn more about data manipulation in Chapter 8.

This chapter concludes with step-by-step instructions on how to add charts to the canvas, enrich the story with text, and use the available options to share your story with other users.

> **Note**
>
> The source files used for the exercises in this chapter are available for downloading via *www.sap-press.com/4511*.

4.1   Creating a New Story

You can start creating a new SAP Lumira story by either importing a dataset or creating a live connection to SAP BW or SAP HANA. To do so, follow these steps:

1. Open the **Data Source** dialog box via the **Welcome** page, as shown in Figure 4.1, by selecting one of the following options:

    – For SAP BW or SAP HANA, click on **Live** or **Import**.

    – Select one of the listed data sources:

       • **SAP Universe**

       • **Microsoft Excel**

       • **Query with SQL**

    – Click **Show More** to view all available data sources as tiles in the bottom pane.

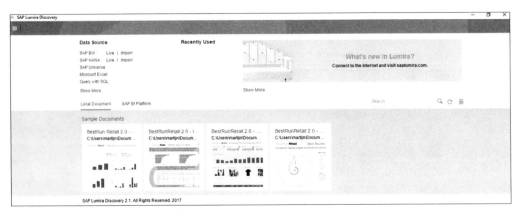

Figure 4.1 Data Source Selection

2. The **Data Source** dialog box options that are displayed depend on the data source type selected. In Chapters 5 and 6, each data source type is described in more detail. In this example, you **Import** a dataset from a Microsoft Excel file, which contains information on car owners and their preferences.

3. Select **Microsoft Excel** as the data source. Browse to the file and click on **Open**.

4. The **Microsoft Excel** data acquisition dialog, as shown in Figure 4.2, offers different options that can be applied before acquiring the dataset, like which columns should be acquired. More details about the available options are described in Chapter 5. For now, keep the default options and click **Visualize**.

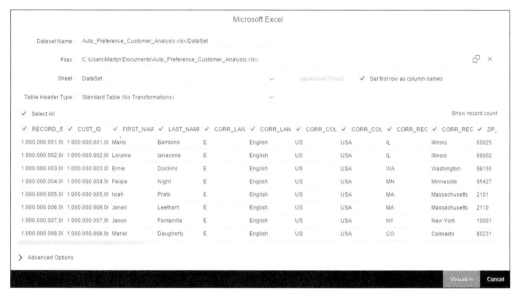

Figure 4.2 Acquire a Microsoft Excel Dataset

Congratulations! You just created your first SAP Lumira document by acquiring a Microsoft Excel-based dataset. Before inserting charts to the canvas and creating your first story with the acquired data, let's start with analyzing the dataset.

4.2   Analyzing Data

Before you can start asking meaningful questions and try to find the answers by visualizing the data in charts, you have to understand the elements and the structure of your dataset. SAP Lumira, discovery edition offers easy-to-use capabilities to view and analyze the dataset by clicking on data view in the upper-right corner of the screen.

The data view, as shown in Figure 4.3, displays all acquired dimensions in a grid. The grid lists all acquired records and allows horizontal and vertical scrolling to view each row and column. Selecting a column header by right-clicking displays a context menu that offers capabilities like sorting and grouping. The functions available depend on the data type of the column.

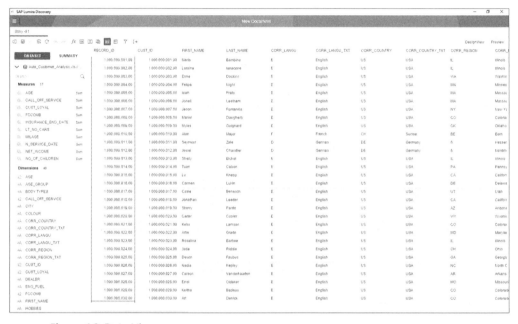

Figure 4.3 Data View

Another way of looking at the acquired dataset is via the facet view. The facet view aggregates all single values in each column and displays, by default, the number of occurrences on the right side of the column. Via **Occurrences • Show Measures**, you can change this to display any other available measure in the dataset for sorting purposes.

As shown in Figure 4.4, right-clicking on a data value in the facet view shows the associated values in the different columns.

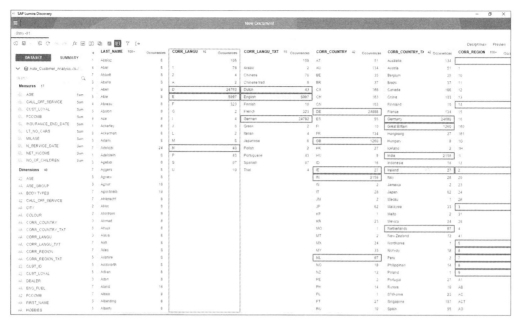

Figure 4.4 Relationship in Facet View

In the side pane on the left of your screen there is an option to switch to a summary view. The data summary displays the actual values and a number based on the se-lected measure of aggregation per column. The summary view also offers search and sorting capabilities, both ascending and descending, to find top and bottom values.

Chapter 7 contains a description of all available features of the grid and facet view.

4.3   Data Preparation

Now that you have a clear understanding of the different dimensions, measures, and the associated values using the data view, the next step is preparing the data. Being able to manipulate and enrich data without a dependency on the IT organization is key for self-service BI.

Among others, SAP Lumira, discovery edition can perform the following data prepa-ration actions:

- Convert to a different data type
- Replace, edit, and group values
- Create geographic, date/time, and custom hierarchies

- Merge, append, and link datasets
- Create calculated measures and dimensions

In Chapter 8, you can find a complete overview and the details of all available options to manipulate and enrich datasets. In this chapter, we limit to two actions—creating a date/time hierarchy and creating a measure with a change of the aggregation type.

4.3.1   Create a Date/Time Hierarchy

Let's start by enriching our dataset with a date/time hierarchy. This type of hierarchy uses existing date columns in your dataset to create different time periods, which allows you to roll up and visualize data. A prerequisite to creating a date/time hierarchy is to have at least one dimension of the data type date.

Please follow these steps to convert a dimension into a date data type and create a date/time hierarchy:

1. Scroll down in the left pane **DATASET** and right-click on **REG_DATE**. As you can see by the icon in front of the dimension, the current data type of **REG_DATE** is **Text**.

2. Select **Convert to · Date/Time** (Figure 4.5).

Figure 4.5 Convert to Date/Time

3. The **Source Data Format** of **REG_DATE** is automatically detected as "mm/dd/yyyy" (Figure 4.6).

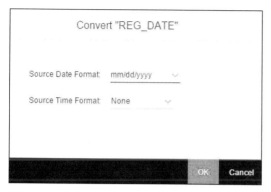

Figure 4.6 Select Source Date/Time Format

4. Leave the **Source Time Format** as **None** and click **OK**.

5. Right-click on the created column **REG_DATE (2)** of data type date/time and select **Hierarchy • Date/Time** (Figure 4.7).

Figure 4.7 Create Date/Time Hierarchy

6. Under dimensions, a date/time hierarchy is created that consists of four levels, which can be used for visualization purposes (Figure 4.8). Each level consists of the concatenated values of the levels above. Scroll to the far right and toggle between the facet and grid mode to view the created dimensions and their values.

Figure 4.8 Date/Time Hierarchy in Facet View

4.3.2   Create Measure

The final data preparation step before you start creating your first story is to create a measure based on **NET_INCOME**. This measure was already created when we acquired the dataset, but with a default aggregation type of **SUM**. As you are interested in learning something more about the average **NET_INCOME** per **AGE_GROUP**, please use the following steps to create a measure and change the aggregation type.

1. Type "NET" in the search field in the left **DATASET** pane.
2. Right-click on **NET_INCOME** under **Dimensions** and select **Create Measure** (Figure 4.9).
3. Select **NET_INCOME (2)** under **Measures** and right-click to rename the measure to **NET_INCOME_AVG**.
4. Right-click again on **NET_INCOME_AVG** and select **Change Aggregation • Average** (Figure 4.10).

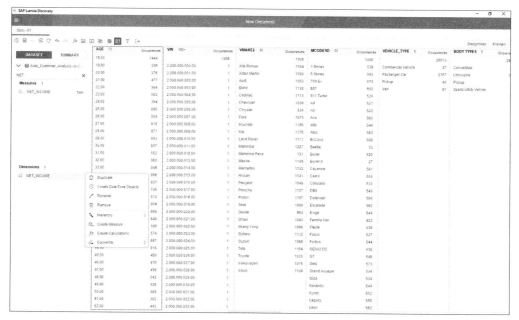

Figure 4.9 Create Measure

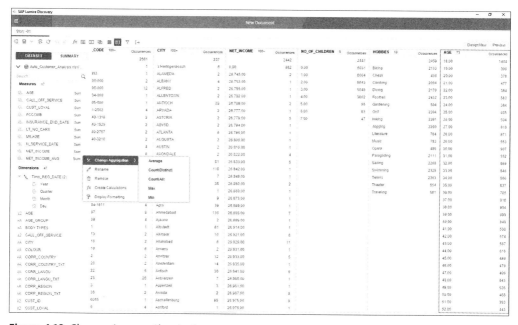

Figure 4.10 Change Aggregation to Average

The aggregation type for the created measure **NET_INCOME_AVG** has now changed to **Average**.

4.4   Creating a Visualization

Once you finalize the initial data preparation steps, it's time to create your first visualization. Switch to design view in the upper-right corner to add measures and dimensions to the default chart. This can be done by either dragging and dropping available objects from the left **DATASET** pane onto the chart, or by selecting **Maximize**, as shown in Figure 4.11.

Figure 4.11 Design View

Let's assume you are interested in learning more about the average net income per age group. Please follow these steps to create this visualization:

1. Select **NET_INCOME_AVG** and drag and drop the measure onto the chart.

2. Repeat the same step for the dimension **AGE_GROUP**.

3. Right-click on the chart and select **Change Chart Type**, as shown in Figure 4.12. The chart picker allows you to change the chart type. Each available chart is categorized, where **Basic** displays the most common used charts. Part III focuses on the use cases and characteristics of each chart category and individual chart type.

Figure 4.12 Change Chart Type

4. Select **Line** to switch to a line chart. As shown in Figure 4.13, the chart displays little variance in **NET_INCOME_AVG** between each **AGE_GROUP**.

Figure 4.13 Line Chart of NET_INCOME_AVG by AGE_GROUP

5. Maximize the chart by right-clicking and choosing **Maximize**. The feeder panel is displayed and it offers more capabilities to add measures and dimensions to the axis, color, and trellis.

6. Hover over **Color** and click on **+**.

7. Select **BODY TYPES**. As shown in Figure 4.14, the chart shows that there is much more variance in the **NET_INCOME_AVG** per **AGE_GROUP** when taking the **BODY TYPES** of the cars into consideration.

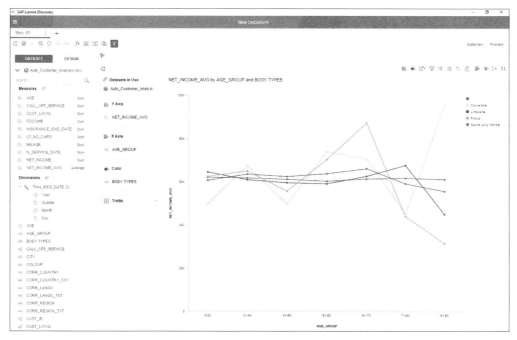

Figure 4.14 Line Chart Visualization

8. Click on **Minimize** in the upper-right corner to return to the canvas.

4.5   Finalizing Your Story

Now that you have returned to the canvas, you can simply add multiple charts, text, and images to enhance your story.

Let's start with adding a second chart to the canvas by following these steps:

1. Click on **Insert Chart** in the toolbar or right-click on the canvas and select **Insert Chart**.

2. Select **Tile (Square) · Heat Map**.

3. Add the following objects to the heat map, as shown in Figure 4.15:

   – MILAGE

   – HOBBIES

   – AGE_GROUP

Make sure you change the aggregation type of **MILAGE** to **Average**. You can maximize the chart to rearrange the added dimensions using the feeder panel.

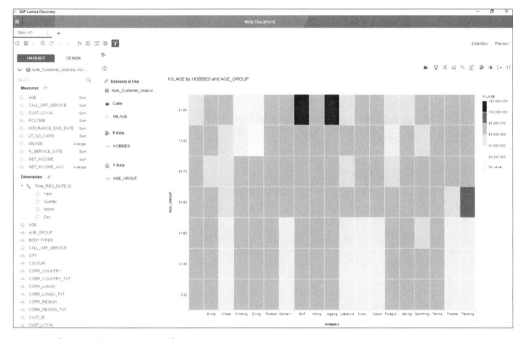

Figure 4.15 Heat Map Chart

4. SAP Lumira, discovery edition offers a grid that helps you more precisely resize and place charts on the canvas. Toggle the grid by clicking on the icon in the bottom-right corner, as shown in Figure 4.16.

5. Re-arrange and resize the two charts using the grid. Keep enough space at the top of the canvas so you can insert a title.

6. Click on **Design** in the left pane.

7. Select **Title** and drag and drop the text field onto the canvas. Place it above the two existing charts. You can resize the text field by selecting the border.

8. Double-click on **Title** and change the text to "My First Story". You can change the **Text Type**, **Size**, **Font Color**, etc., as shown in Figure 4.16, via the context menu, which is available when right-clicking within the text field.

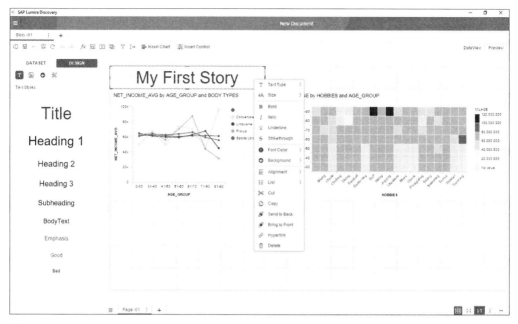

Figure 4.16 Insert a Text Field Onto the Canvas

9. Finally, switch to preview mode in the upper-right corner to view the different elements of your story.

Within an SAP Lumira document, you can add multiple pages and even multiple stories to combine all necessary visualizations within a certain business line to turn raw data into information.

4.6   Sharing Your Story

Now that you finalized your first SAP Lumira story, let's focus on the available options to save the document and share the information with other users. In SAP Lumira, discovery edition, you can save the document locally or publish it to the SAP BusinessObjects BI platform. By publishing the document, users can access and open the document from the BI Launchpad.

More details on the integration of SAP Lumira, discovery edition with the SAP BusinessObjects BI platform and the BI Launchpad can be found in Chapter 21 and Chapter 22.

For now, follow these steps to save the document to your local machine:

1. Open the menu in the upper-left corner and click on **File • Save As** or use the keyboard shortcut `Ctrl`+`Shift`+`S`.
2. Enter a **Name**, optionally a **Description**, and then click on **Save**.

The document will be saved in the default folder displayed at the bottom, as shown in Figure 4.17.

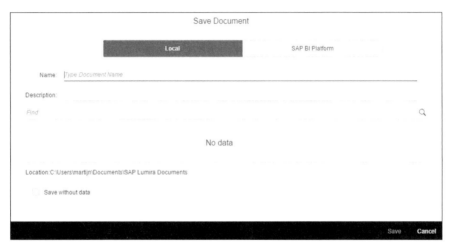

Figure 4.17 Save SAP Lumira Document

Another option to share the information is to publish the dataset to SAP HANA or export records in CSV or Microsoft Excel format, even from individual visualizations.

Chapter 19 explains in more detail how stories can be shared with users via the SAP BusinessObjects BI platform. Chapter 20 describes all available options related to publishing and exporting data.

4.7   Summary

In this chapter you learned how to create your first SAP Lumira story based on a Microsoft Excel dataset. As you have experienced, SAP Lumira, discovery edition offers extensive options to analyze and enrich your dataset and create visualizations. This chapter concludes Part I, which taught you the basics of SAP Lumira, discovery edition. Part II focusses on all data related topics, from acquisition to live connectivity and analyzing and manipulating data.

PART II
Data

Chapter 5
Data Acquisition

To create an SAP Lumira, discovery edition story, you first need to acquire data. With data acquisition, you retrieve data from one of the supported data sources.

Data acquisition is the first step that you need to take care of when you want to create a new SAP Lumira, discovery edition story. You need to bring data into the application, otherwise you can't create any visualizations and perform any analysis. SAP Lumira, discovery edition supports the import of data from a wide range of sources.

Data acquisition is done offline: the dataset is retrieved from one of the data sources, handled in an internal, in-memory way, and saved in the SAP Lumira document. You will see that the data source can be either a locally stored file or a database. Once a dataset has been acquired, you can refresh it and retrieve the most recent dataset or change the setup of the data acquisition.

> **Limitations**
>
> As all the acquired data is included in the SAP Lumira document, the size of the dataset will have impact on the performance of SAP Lumira, discovery edition. The maximum number of cells that can be acquired is determined by the capacity of your computer. If you are running a 64-bit Windows environment, a warning will be showed at 30 million cells. For a 32-bit Windows environment, this warning appears at 15 million cells.
>
> You can configure SAP Lumira, discovery edition to use more memory (RAM) by increasing the -Xmx2048m and -XX:MaxPermSize=256M parameters in the configuration file that you can find at *C:\Program Files\SAP BusinessObjects Lumira\Lumira Discovery\Desktop\SAPLumiraDiscovery.ini*.

> **Datasets Properties for Data Enrichment and Performance**
>
> By default, SAP Lumira, discovery edition automatically detects if data is suitable for metadata enrichment. For example, a country may be interpreted as a geographical object, which enables it for usage in a geographical hierarchy. For large datasets, this enrichment can take quite some time. To prevent performance issues from happening, there is also a property setting to disable this feature for very large datasets. This setting is disabled by default.

SAP Lumira, discovery edition also supports live data sources for SAP BW and SAP HANA. This works in a different way, as the data is not imported into the SAP Lumira document, but remains in the SAP BW or SAP HANA system. Connecting to live data sources is discussed in Chapter 6. Offline and online data sources impact the data manipulation features that SAP Lumira, discovery edition offers in a document. Chapter 8 discusses the differences.

This chapter describes the supported data sources for data acquisition, starting with data imports from local sources (Microsoft Excel, CSV, text files, or the Windows clipboard), then the SAP systems (SAP BW, SAP HANA, and SAP BusinessObjects BI Universe), and finally SQL sources. We conclude the chapter with the options to refresh and edit the dataset.

5.1   Microsoft Excel

Microsoft Excel spreadsheets are wildly popular, and this won't change for a long time. These spreadsheets are a simple, convenient way to store, present, and analyze data, as there is no need to set up a complicated database infrastructure to create and use them. Of course, problems arise as soon spreadsheets need to be up-scaled, to include more and more data, and to be used by more than a single user.

SAP Lumira, discovery edition can acquire data from one or multiple Microsoft Excel files. Supported versions are Microsoft Excel 2007 (.xls file extension), 2010, 2013, and 2016 (.xslx file extension). SAP Lumira, discovery edition can retrieve data from one sheet or all sheets of a spreadsheet. Also, the range of rows and columns that need to be imported can be defined.

If you want to acquire data from multiple files, then the rows from all files are appended in the same dataset. A new column named **Source file** is added to the dataset, which states the title of the source file for each record. The first file that you add is used as a reference template for the column definitions. This means that the header is taken from this file if you use the **Set first row as column names** option.

It is important that the other files have the same setup as the initial file. If another file has fewer columns, or the data types of its columns do not match the ones from the initial file, SAP Lumira, discovery edition will not allow the file to be imported. In case another file has more columns, the extra columns are not added to the dataset.

To create a new dataset from one or multiple Microsoft Excel files, follow these steps:

1. Select **Microsoft Excel** from the **Data Source** menu on the home page of SAP Lumira, discovery edition. If you want to add a data source to an SAP Lumira document, use the **New Dataset** option in the **Data** menu (see Chapter 3).

2. Select your Microsoft Excel file or files in the **Open** dialog.

3. Click **Open** to close the dialog window. A new popup window is shown. Here we see a preview of the dataset and further information and settings for this acquisition (Figure 5.1). If you added multiple files, the additional **Source file** column is added at the end. The **Sheet** dropdown menu contains only sheets from the initial Microsoft Excel file.

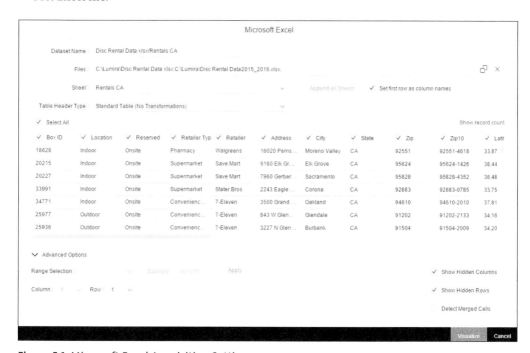

Figure 5.1 Microsoft Excel Acquisition Settings

4. Change the **Dataset Name**.

5. To add more files, use the **Add Files** button to open the **Open** dialog window again and browse for additional files. To remove files, you can delete the file location in the **Files** box or click the **Clear Data** button to remove all files.

6. If your Microsoft Excel file contains multiple sheets, select the correct sheet in the **Sheet** dropdown menu.

7. Select the **Append all sheets** option to include all the data from all the sheets. An additional column **Source sheet** is added to the dataset.

8. Select **Set first row as column names** to use the values that are in the first row as the labels for each column in SAP Lumira, discovery edition. If you disable this option, the column names are displayed as **Column_<n>**, where **<n>** is the number of the column.

9. Depending on the setup of the data in the spreadsheet, select the correct **Table Header Type**. In most cases, a **Standard Table (No Transformations)** is used. In such a table, all the values are organized in rows (Figure 5.2, left table). A cross table uses headers in both the columns and rows to organize the values (Figure 5.2, right table).

Year	Genre	Revenue			Drama	Action	Comedy
2015	Drama	16831		**2015**	16831	256	72384
2016	Drama	35812		**2016**	35812	458	78625
2017	Drama	64832		**2017**	64832	394	68133
2015	Action	256					
2016	Action	458					
2017	Action	394					
2015	Comedy	72384					
2016	Comedy	78625					
2017	Comedy	68133					

Figure 5.2 Standard Table and Cross Table

10. Click **Show Record Count** to display the total number of columns and records in the dataset.

11. Deselect the columns that you don't want to import. You can check **Use Select All** to include all the columns again.

12. Below the preview table, click **Advanced Options**. Here you can enable or disable the retrieval of data from hidden columns and rows (**Show Hidden Columns** or **Show Hidden Rows**).

13. Select **Detect Merged Cells**. With this option, all cells of a merged cell are filled with the value of the merged cell. If you don't check this option, only the first cell is filled with the value.

14. In case you selected **Standard Table (No Transformations)** as the **Table Header Type**, you can alter the **Range Selection** to a **Custom Range**. Enter the coordinates of the top-left and bottom-right cells that contain the data that needs to be acquired (for example, B2:K76) and click **Apply**. In addition, you can change the number of rows that need to be used as the header.

15. If you choose **Cross Table** as the **Table Header Type**, you can change the number of **Columns** and **Rows** that must be used as headers (Figure 5.3).

Figure 5.3 Microsoft Excel Advanced Data Acquisition Settings for Cross Table

16. Click **Visualize** to finish the data acquisition and import the data into your SAP Lumira document.

5.2 Text

The simplest form of data storage is using a text file. You can simply create and manipulate such a file in a text editor like Notepad. SAP Lumira, discovery edition can acquire data from a range of text file types:

- Comma-separated values (.csv)
- Text (.txt)
- Log files (.log)
- Print distributor files (.prn)
- Tab-separated values (.tsv)

The data in these text files must be stored in one of the following two *separation* formats. This is necessary to understand where a value ends and a new value starts.

- Delimited by a character, usually a comma (,) or semicolon (;).
  SAP Lumira, discovery edition can use any character as a delimiter. The only stipulation is that the delimiter character is the same for the whole dataset. Figure 5.4 shows an example of a dataset where the values are separated by a semicolon.
- Columns with a fixed width.

Figure 5.4 Dataset with Comma-Separated Values

In the case of acquiring multiple text files, the same rules apply as when acquiring multiple Microsoft Excel files. The rows from all the files are appended to the same dataset. A new column named **Source file** is added to the dataset, which states the title of the source file for each record.

The first file that's added is used as a reference template for the column definitions. The header is taken from this file if you use the **Set first row as column names** option. If a sequenced file has fewer columns, or the data types of its columns do not match the ones from the initial file, SAP Lumira, discovery edition will not import the file. When a sequenced file has more columns, the additional columns are not added to the dataset.

To create a new dataset from one or multiple text files, follow these steps:

1. Click **Show All** in the **Data Source** menu on the home page of SAP Lumira, discovery edition to display all available data sources.
2. From the **Files** section, select **Text**.
3. Browse to your text file or files, select them, and click **Open**.

4. A new window appears with several settings and a preview of the data from the file that you just selected. In case you used multiple text files, a **Source file** column is added. Here you can check the source of a row of data (Figure 5.5).

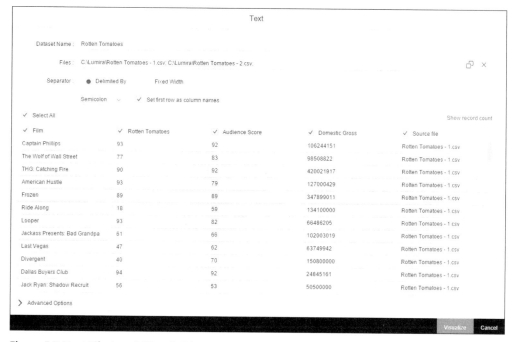

Text

Dataset Name :	Rotten Tomatoes			

Files :   C:\Lumira\Rotten Tomatoes - 1.csv; C:\Lumira\Rotten Tomatoes - 2.csv;

Separator   ● Delimited By   Fixed Width

Semicolon   ∨   ✓ Set first row as column names

✓ Select All   Show record count

✓ Film	✓ Rotten Tomatoes	✓ Audience Score	✓ Domestic Gross	✓ Source file
Captain Phillips	93	92	106244151	Rotten Tomatoes - 1.csv
The Wolf of Wall Street	77	83	98508822	Rotten Tomatoes - 1.csv
THG: Catching Fire	90	92	420021917	Rotten Tomatoes - 1.csv
American Hustle	93	79	127000429	Rotten Tomatoes - 1.csv
Frozen	89	89	347899011	Rotten Tomatoes - 1.csv
Ride Along	18	59	134100000	Rotten Tomatoes - 1.csv
Looper	93	82	66486205	Rotten Tomatoes - 1.csv
Jackass Presents: Bad Grandpa	61	66	102003019	Rotten Tomatoes - 1.csv
Last Vegas	47	62	63749942	Rotten Tomatoes - 1.csv
Divergent	40	70	150800000	Rotten Tomatoes - 1.csv
Dallas Buyers Club	94	92	24845161	Rotten Tomatoes - 1.csv
Jack Ryan: Shadow Recruit	56	53	50500000	Rotten Tomatoes - 1.csv

❯ Advanced Options

Visualize   Cancel

Figure 5.5 Text File Acquisition Settings

5. Change the **Dataset Name**.

6. To add more files, use the **Add Files** button to open the **Open** dialog window again and browse for additional files. To remove files, you can delete the file location in the **Files** box or click the **Clear Data** button to remove all files.

7. For the **Separator**, choose between the following two options, depending on the setup of your text file(s):

   - **Delimited By**: The columns of the dataset are separated by a character. In most cases, SAP Lumira, discovery edition detects this character, but you can alter this manually. You can choose between **Comma**, **Tab**, **Semicolon**, and **Space**, or enter a custom character by using the **Other** option.

   - **Fixed Width**: The columns are detected with a fixed width of characters. Also this is detected by SAP Lumira, discovery edition, but you can adjust the definition with the **Break Column** parameter in the **Advanced Options**.

8. Select **Set first row as column names** to use the values that are in the first row as the labels for each column in SAP Lumira, discovery edition. If you disable this option, the column names are displayed as **Column_<n>**, where **<n>** is the number of the column.

9. Click **Show Record Count** to display the total number of columns and records in the dataset.

10. Deselect the columns that you don't want to import. You can check **Use Select All** to include all the columns again.

11. Below the preview table, click **Advanced Options**. Here we can adjust the following parameters, as shown in Figure 5.6:

   – **Number Format**: In case SAP Lumira, discovery edition didn't recognize the format of the numbers in the dataset, you can select a number format here.

   – **Date Format**: From the dropdown box, you can select the date format that corresponds with the dates in the text file. Table 5.1 lists the details of the different date formatting tokens.

   – **Break Column**: This option is only available when you are using a fixed width separator. You can define the number of characters per columns. For example, 5,5,9,9,9 will define two columns of five characters and three columns of nine characters. After entering the columns' widths, click **Apply** to refresh the dataset and update the previewed data with the adjusted column widths.

   – **Trim leading spaces**: Checking this option will remove all leading spaces from numbers and values in the dataset. For example, the value " USA" has a leading space, but will appear as "USA" in the dataset.

Figure 5.6 Advanced Options for Text

12. Finally, click **Visualize** to finish the data acquisition and import the data into your SAP Lumira document.

Token	Description
d	Day number without leading zeros
dd	Day number in two digits, with an optional leading zero
EEEE	Full day name (Monday, Tuesday, Wednesday, etc.)
M	Month number without leading zeros
MM	Month number in two digits, with an optional leading zero
MMM	Abbreviated month name (Jan, Feb, March, etc.)
MMMM	Full month name (January, February, March, etc.)
yy	Last two numbers of a year
yyyy	Full year number

Table 5.1 Date Format Tokens

5.3   Windows Clipboard

Next to local files, SAP Lumira, discovery edition can create a dataset from data that has been copied to the Windows clipboard `Ctrl`+`C`. This data may come from a file like a Microsoft Excel spreadsheet, or from any other source (i.e., a website or an email). The acquisition process is for the most part similar to that of a text file, as described in the previous section.

To create a new dataset from data that is copied to the Windows clipboard, follow these steps:

1. Copy the data that you want to acquire to the clipboard. In most cases, you can use the keyboard shortcut `Ctrl`+`C` for this.

2. In SAP Lumira, discovery edition, go to the home page and click **Show All** in the **Data Source** menu to display all available data sources.

3. From the **Files** section, select **Copy from Clipboard**.

4. The data on your clipboard is automatically copied into the text editor of SAP Lumira, discovery edition (Figure 5.7). In this text editor you can manually make changes to the text.

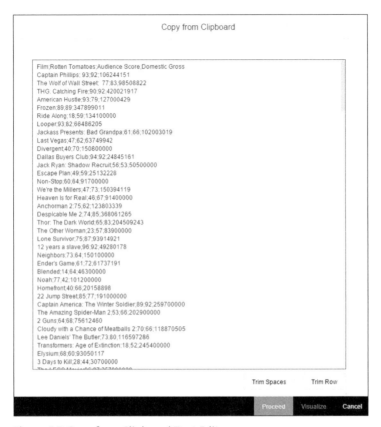

Figure 5.7 Copy from Clipboard Text Editor

5. In case the dataset on your clipboard is unusable by SAP Lumira, discovery edition, for example when it lacks any structure, an error is thrown (Figure 5.8). In case you cannot manually adjust the data, remove the incorrect data (select it with the mouse cursor, or use keyboard shortcut [Ctrl]+[A] to select everything), and press [Delete] (or [Del]), depending on your keyboard) to delete it. Copy the correct data to your clipboard and paste [Ctrl]+[V] it into the text editor.

Figure 5.8 Clipboard Data Error

6. Click **Trim Spaces** to remove any spaces and tabs at the beginning and end of each row of data.

7. Click **Trim Row** to remove empty rows.

8. When you are happy with the data, click **Proceed** to use the content of the text editor as the source for the new dataset.

9. The next screen (Figure 5.9) looks very familiar; it contains the same options as the text file acquisition settings (Section 5.3). As you can see, there is no option to import multiple clipboards, like it was possible to import multiple text files in one go. Don't worry, you can just go back to the text editor by clicking **Previous** and paste multiple snippets of your data in the text editor.

10. Make the necessary adjustments in the **Copy from Clipboard** acquisition settings and finally click **Visualize** to import the data into an SAP Lumira document.

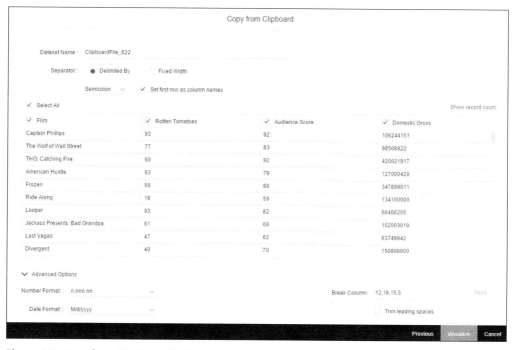

Figure 5.9 Copy from Clipboard Settings

123

5.4   SAP BW

SAP Lumira, discovery edition can acquire data from an SAP BW environment via an SAP BEx query or an InfoProvider. This way you can leverage all the existing SAP BW data models and query definitions and bring your corporate data into SAP Lumira, discovery edition in a structured and controlled way.

Note that, after downloading data from SAP BW into SAP Lumira, discovery edition, the dataset will be recognized as a flat list of data, comparable to a dataset that was created from a text file. The data can be refreshed and retrieved from the SAP BW source, even with adjusted prompts, but all actions after the acquisition happen solely within SAP Lumira, discovery edition, and are not delegated to the SAP BW system. That also means that, in this scenario, no multi-dimensional OLAP analysis features will be present. You will find these features in the online scenario. See Chapter 6 for more information on SAP BW online.

Connecting to SAP BW for data acquisition can be done in two ways:

- **Direct connection to SAP BW**
  In this scenario, SAP Lumira, discovery edition connects to the SAP BW system via the connections that are defined in the SAP Logon application (also referred to as the SAP GUI). The SAP Logon is locally installed on your Windows environment.

- **Connection via managed OLAP connection on the SAP BusinessObjects BI platform**
  In this scenario, SAP Lumira, discovery edition uses the connections that are defined on the SAP BusinessObjects BI platform to connect to SAP BW.

The major advantage of the second scenario is that with the managed OLAP connection, the SAP Lumira documents can be easily shared between users over the SAP BusinessObjects BI platform, as the managed connection on the SAP BusinessObjects BI platform ensures that the same connectivity details are available for all users. The first scenario uses locally maintained connectivity details, which may be not in sync and easily lead to issues. For the final dataset selection and result, there is no difference between the two options.

The supported SAP BW versions are as follows:

- SAP BW 7.0 with Service Pack 23 and above
- SAP BW 7.01/7.02 with Service Pack 8 and above
- SAP BW 7.30 with Service Pack 03 and above
- SAP BW 7.31/7.4/7.5x (all service packs)

The following sections discuss the two connectivity scenarios and give an overview of the limitations when connecting to SAP BW.

5.4.1   Direct Connection to SAP BW

Before you can use a direct connection to SAP BW, SAP Logon must be installed on your Windows environment and a connection must be defined. The error in Figure 5.10 will pop up if this is not the case. You can download SAP Logon from the SAP support website (*http://support.sap.com/swdc*). The software is stored under **Downloads · Installations & Upgrades · By Alphabetical Index (A-Z) · G · SAP GUI For Windows**.

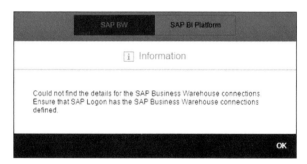

Figure 5.10 Missing SAP Logon Connection Details Error

To create a new dataset from an SAP BW system using a direct connection, follow these steps:

1. Select **SAP BW Import** from the **Data Source** menu on the home page of SAP Lumira, discovery edition. If you want to add a data source to an SAP Lumira document, use the **New Dataset** option in the **Data** menu (see Chapter 3).

2. By default, **SAP BW** is selected as connectivity method. Select the SAP BW **Server** you want to connect to from the dropdown menu (Figure 5.11). If the server is not available in the list, you have to create a connection to this server in SAP Logon first.

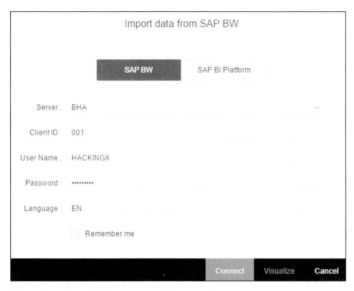

Figure 5.11 Direct Connection to SAP BW

3. Fill in the **Client ID** and your **User Name** and **Password** for the selected SAP BW system. In addition, you can select a **Language** and check whether SAP Lumira, discovery edition should remember your credentials.

4. Click **Connect** to connect to the SAP BW system.

5. In the next dialog window, you can select the SAP BEx query or InfoProvider that you want to import (Figure 5.12). You can switch between the **Roles** or the **InfoAreas View** to browse the SAP BW environment, or you can simply use the search bar to find the required object. Note that you can change the **Presentation Settings** for the SAP BEx queries and the InfoProviders and show not only the **Text** description, but also the **Key**, or both.

6. Click **Next** to advance to the following screen.

7. If you selected an SAP BEx query that contains input variables, the **Variables** window is shown (Figure 5.13). Here you can enter or select the necessary values for each variable. Note that also here, you can show the key, text, or both for the dimension values. Click **OK** to continue.

Figure 5.12 Search and Select an SAP BEx Query or InfoProvider

Figure 5.13 SAP BEx Query Variables

8. Now it is time to select and configure the **Measures** and **Dimensions** that you want
    to bring into SAP Lumira, discovery edition. On the left side of the dialog window
    you see the available **Measures** and **Dimensions**, which you can move to the right
    side to include them in your dataset (Figure 5.14). If you have a lot of measures and
    dimensions, you can use the search bar to quickly find the right object. Looking at
    the dimensions, not only are the dimension values present, but the **Hierarchies**
    and **Attributes** can also be selected. Select the measures and dimensions you want
    to acquire.

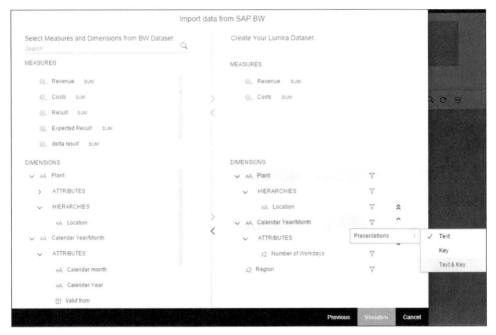

Figure 5.14 Select Measures and Dimensions

9. For the dimensions, you now can define in what **Presentation** manner they
    should be acquired: as **Text**, **Key**, or **Text & Key**. In the last case, two columns will
    be created in the dataset. Select the requested presentation method by selecting
    the dimension and clicking the gear icon.

10. For the dimension hierarchies, you can set the **Level Selection** (Figure 5.15). This
    determines the number of hierarchy levels that will be acquired. You can choose
    the default level defined in the SAP BEx query or define one yourself. For each
    level, a separate column will be created in the dataset. Use the gear icon to set the
    number of levels.

Figure 5.15 Hierarchy Level Selection

11. Before you acquire the data from SAP BW, you can also filter each dimension. The funnel icon activates the **Filter** screen (Figure 5.16). Here we can use several options to filter the values, including selecting values from a list and using wildcards and patterns. Select the filters you want to use and click **Apply**.

Figure 5.16 Dimension Filter

12. Click **Visualize** to acquire the dataset into SAP Lumira, discovery edition and create a new dataset. Figure 5.17 shows the name of the dataset (**Lumira_01_Q01**) and the two acquired **Measures** and fourteen acquired **Dimensions**. For each dimension that we selected in the **Import data from SAP BW** screen, two dimensions are created (**Text** and **Key**). Also, the three hierarchical levels are included as separate dimensions, plus a hierarchical dimension to group them.

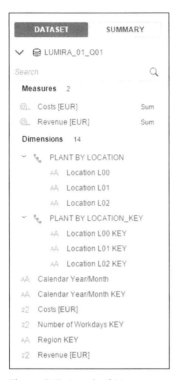

Figure 5.17 Acquired Measures and Dimensions

5.4.2   Connection via Managed OLAP Connection on SAP BusinessObjects BI Platform

The steps to create a data source from an SAP BEx query or InfoProvider are roughly the same when using a connection via a managed OLAP connection on the SAP BusinessObjects BI platform. You first have to log in to the SAP BusinessObjects BI platform; after that, the steps to select a data source and choose the dimensions and measures are exactly the same as in the direct connection scenario.

OLAP Connection

In case there are no OLAP connections for SAP BW present yet, check out Chapter 21, Section 21.5.3, for all the necessary steps to create such an OLAP connection.

To create a new dataset from an SAP BW system via a managed OLAP connection on the SAP BusinessObjects BI platform, follow these steps:

1. Select **SAP BW Import** from the **Data Source** menu on the home page of SAP Lumira, discovery edition. If you want to add a data source to an SAP Lumira document, use the **New Dataset** option in the **Data** menu (see Chapter 3).

2. Select the **SAP BI Platform** connectivity method (Figure 5.18).

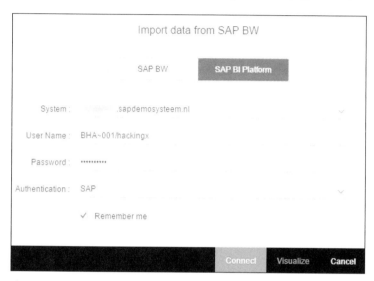

Figure 5.18 Connecting to the SAP BusinessObjects BI Platform

3. Fill in the **System**, your **User Name**, and **Password**. Check **Remember Me** to store your password for the next time that you want to connect.

4. Select the correct **Authentication** method from the dropdown list. If you are using SAP authentication, it may be necessary to fill in your user name in the following format: **<System ID>~<Client>/<User Name>**, for example: *BHA~001/hackingx*.

5. Click **Connect**.

6. An overview of available **OLAP Connections** is shown (Figure 5.19). Only the OLAP connections that point to an SAP BW system are included. Via the **Show Connections** dropdown menu, you can filter the list of OLAP connections on all connections, only connections that point to an SAP BW system, only connections that point to an InfoProvider, or only connections that point to an SAP BEx query or SAP BEx query view. Select the correct OLAP connection and click **Next**.

7. From this step onward, you can continue from Step 5 of Section 5.4.1, as all options to select an SAP BEx query or InfoProvider, and all further import options are similar (Figure 5.12).

Figure 5.19 OLAP Connections on the SAP BusinessObjects BI Platform

5.4.3   SAP BW Limitations

Acquiring data from SAP BW sources comes with a range of limitations and behaviors that are important to know and understand before using this functionality in SAP Lumira, discovery edition. In the following sections, we discuss these limitations in detail.

Dataset Size

As data acquisition from an SAP BW source happens on the lowest detail level of data available (the data is not aggregated), datasets can get very large very quickly. An error will be given stating that the requested result set is too large (Figure 5.20).

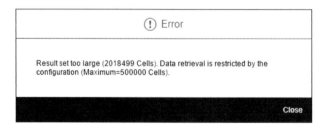

Figure 5.20 Result Set Too Large Error

Before changing the setup of SAP Lumira, discovery edition and your SAP Business-
Objects BI environment, reconsider the acquisition details first: do you really need all the
selected dimensions and measures; do you need all the hierarchy levels; do you need
both key and text values; and is it possible to use more restricted variable prompt values?

To protect the SAP BW environment against extremely heavy query usage that possi-
bly could impact the whole SAP BW system, a safety belt limit is instantiated. This
safety belt limit is used when an SAP BEx query is ran by any of the tools in the SAP
BusinessObjects BI frontend portfolio. Typically, the limit is set between 500,000
and 1,000,000 cells of data (number of rows multiplied by number of columns).

SAP KBA 112715 explains how to adjust this setting in SAP BW. The downside of this is
that the safety limit is then immediately adjusted for all client tools and all users of
the SAP BW system. To override this setting only for the SAP Lumira, discovery edition desktop client, follow these steps:

1. Browse to the *Desktop* folder in the SAP Lumira, discovery edition installation
   folder (typically *C:\Program Files\SAP BusinessObjects Lumira\Lumira Discovery\
   Desktop*).

2. Open *SAPLumiraDiscovery.ini* in a text editor, using administrator rights.

3. Add the following parameters. Make sure that the MAX value is always bigger than
   the DEF value:
   - -DBICS_DA_RESULT_SET_LIMIT_DEF=500000
   - -DBICS_DA_RESULT_SET_LIMIT_MAX=1000000

When you are running an SAP Lumira document on the SAP BusinessObjects BI platform, the same problem may arise. To override the setting on the SAP Business-
Objects BI platform, follow these steps:

1. Log in to the Central Management Console (CMC).

2. Go to **Servers** and select **Lumira Server Services**.

3. Choose the SAP Lumira server and select **Properties** from the context menu.

4. In the **Command Line Parameters**, add the following parameters:
   - -DBICS_DA_RESULT_SET_LIMIT_DEF=500000
   - -DBICS_DA_RESULT_SET_LIMIT_MAX=100000

5. Restart the server.

If there are multiple SAP Lumira servers in your cluster, you have to adjust the
parameters and perform the restart for each of them.

Hierarchies

As you have seen, SAP BEx hierarchies can be acquired, but they are flattened into multi-column, level-based dimensions after acquisition.

Changing SAP BEx hierarchies via hierarchy variables, hierarchy node variables, or key date variables in case of time-dependent hierarchies is not supported.

SAP BEx hierarchies that include link nodes can be acquired, but the context of the data values in the link node is not persisted. This will lead to double-counting when performing aggregations.

> **Link Nodes**
>
> Link nodes are hierarchy nodes that refer to other hierarchy nodes. This way, you can use the same subtree multiple times in the same hierarchy. For more information, see *http://bit.ly/2z0TmSM*.

Structures

Structures (both dimension-based or measure-based) are supported for data acquisition. If they have a hierarchical structure, the hierarchical context is lost.

A dimension structure will be manifested in the acquired dataset as a dimension, where the structure members are the values of that dimension. In addition, a numeric key is generated, which follows the order of the members in the dimension structure.

Measures

For measures that are defined by formulas in the SAP BEx Query Designer, SAP Lumira, discovery edition is unable to determine the aggregation type. Thus, this is set to **None**. You can manually change the aggregation type after the data acquisition (see Chapter 8).

Currencies and Units

Currency and unit symbols assigned to a measure are not supported. Also, mixed currencies and mixed units are not supported. If such metadata is necessary for proper reporting, a workaround would be to add dimensions that show the currency or unit values.

SAP BEx Conditions

SAP Lumira, discovery edition supports SAP BEx conditions that are defined along the rows at the time of the data acquisition. SAP BEx conditions defined along the columns are not supported; they are ignored. After the data acquisition, the whole concept of SAP BEx conditions is not supported.

> **SAP BEx Conditions**
>
> SAP BEx conditions filter the dataset on measure values, example to show a top 10 or only values larger than 1000. SAP BEx conditions defined in the SAP BEx Query Designer. For more information, see *http://bit.ly/ yZd*.

Zero Suppression

Zero suppression defined along the rows is supported at the time of data acquisition. Zero suppression defined along the columns not supported at the time of data acquisition. After the data acquisition, the whole zero suppression concept is not supported.

> **Zero Suppression**
>
> With zero suppression, you can determine whether a row or column that contains zeros, or has zero as a total, should be displayed. Zero suppression is defined in the SAP BEx Query Designer. For more information, see *http://bit.ly/2kZBSS9*.

Prompts

Delegated search in prompts that contain lists of values (LOVs) is supported, except for data, time, hierarchy variable, and hierarchy node variable prompts. The search is based on the selected presentation setting (**Text**, **Key**, or **Text & Key**) and is case-sensitive. When **Text & Key** is selected, the search is executed on the key values first. Only if no key values are found, a delegated search is done on the text values. Note that the use of wildcards is supported. Use * for all and + to represent a single character.

For the manual entry of key values in prompts, only the * wildcard is supported. A value followed by a wildcard (i.e., AB*) does not work though. Pattern matching is supported only when using the = or != operators.

Other SAP BEx Features

A complete overview of all existing BEx features and whether they are supported in SAP Lumira, discovery edition, can be found in the SAP BusinessObjects BI Support Matrix for SAP BW document. This is a spreadsheet that lists all BEx features and all SAP BusinessObjects BI frontend tools and states the level of support between each feature and tool.

You can find the SAP BusinessObjects BI Support Matrix for SAP BW in SAP KBA 1869560.

5.5   SAP HANA

SAP Lumira, discovery edition can acquire data from SAP HANA views. These views are data models, built on top of the physical tables where the data resides in SAP HANA. SAP Lumira, discovery edition supports the acquisition of analytical and calculation views.

Using SAP HANA as a data source looks a lot like using an SAP BW data source. As you saw in the previous section for SAP BW, the data acquisition for SAP HANA also leads to a dataset that acts as a flat list of data. This dataset can be refreshed from the original SAP HANA source and prompts can be changed, but all actions after the data acquisition occur within SAP Lumira, discovery edition. They are not pushed back to the SAP HANA system. For that feature you have to use the online scenario. See Chapter 6 for more information on SAP HANA online.

Connecting to an SAP HANA view for data acquisition can be done in two ways:

- **Direct connection to SAP HANA**
  Here you have to provide all the connection details in SAP Lumira, discovery edition to connect to the SAP HANA system.

- **Connection via managed OLAP connection on the SAP BusinessObjects BI platform**
  SAP Lumira, discovery edition uses the connections that are defined on the SAP BusinessObjects BI platform to connect to SAP HANA.

As was also the case with the SAP BW data acquisition, the second scenario has a big advantage over the first one, in that with the managed OLAP connection, the SAP Lumira documents are easily shared between users via the SAP BusinessObjects BI platform. The managed connection ensures that the same connectivity setup is used for all users. For the dataset selection and result, both scenarios will lead to the same outcome.

The supported SAP HANA versions are as follows:

- SAP HANA SPS 10, Revision 100 and above
- SAP HANA SPS 11, Revision 110 and above
- SAP HANA SPS 12, Revision 120 and above
- SAP HANA 2.0 SPS 01

Product Availability Matrix

The most up-to-date overview of supported source systems can be found in the Product Availability Matrix (PAM) for SAP Lumira. You can find this at *http://support.sap.com/pam*.

Exposing SAP BW Data via SAP HANA Views

In an SAP BW powered by SAP HANA environment, you can import SAP BW models as InfoCubes and DSOs, but also as SAP BEx queries, as analytic views, and as calculation views. For more information on this topic, see *http://bit.ly/2ALo4P2*.

5.5.1   Direct Connection to SAP HANA

To create a new dataset from an SAP HANA system using a direct connection, follow these steps:

1. Select **SAP HANA Import** from the **Data Source** menu on the home page of SAP Lumira, discovery edition. If you want to add a data source to an SAP Lumira document, use the **New Dataset** option in the **Data** menu (see Chapter 3).

2. By default, **SAP HANA** is selected as the connectivity method. Enter the SAP HANA **Server** and **Instance** number (Figure 5.21).

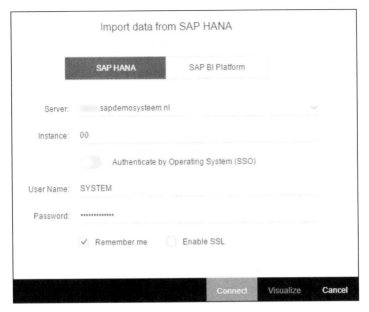

Figure 5.21 Direct Connection to SAP HANA

3. Check **Authenticate by Operation System (SSO)** if you want to log in to the SAP HANA server using single sign-on. If you are not using single sign-on, a user name and password must be provided to authenticate.

4. Enter your **User Name** and **Password** if you don't use single sign-on.

5. Check **Remember Me** to save the password for the next time that you want to log in.

6. Check **Enable SSL** to use a secured connection.

7. Click **Connect** to connect to the SAP HANA system.

8. The list of available SAP HANA views is shown now (Figure 5.22). Only the views accessible to the current SAP HANA account are shown. Use the search option to find a specific view. As you'll see, the list of views is filtered instantly as soon as you start typing.

9. Select the view that you want to use and click **Next**. If you click **Visualize**, the whole view will be acquired, and you can skip the next step where you can make some selections to fine tune the data import.

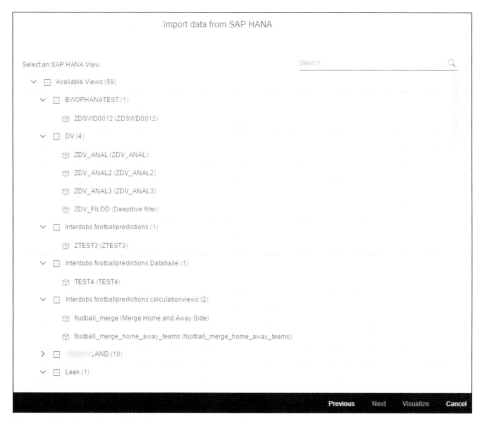

Figure 5.22 Search and Select an SAP HANA View

10. If you selected an SAP HANA view that contains mandatory variables or input parameters, the **Variables** screen is shown (Figure 5.23). Enter the necessary values for each variable or input parameter and click **OK** to continue.

Input Parameters versus Variables

Input parameters are not used to filter data, but are used as input to perform certain calculations. An input parameter could for example be a target currency for a currency conversion. An input parameter is used in such way that it can only have a single value as its input.

A variable, on the other hand, is used to filter an attribute of the view, to limit the dataset. Here it is possible to use single or multiple values, intervals, or ranges of values.

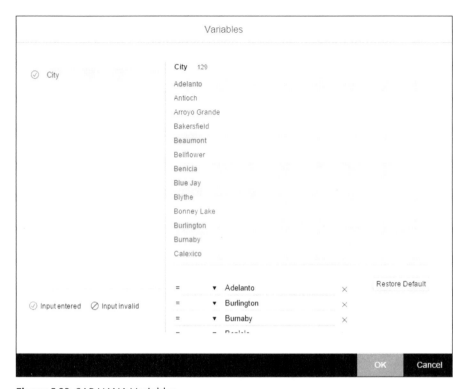

Figure 5.23 SAP HANA Variables

11. On this screen, all the available **Measures** (left) and **Dimensions** (right) are shown (Figure 5.24). You can use the search boxes to quickly search for objects, as the results are instantly adapted to the values that you enter. Use the checkboxes in front of the objects to select the measures and dimensions that you want to acquire. Use the **Show only selected** checkbox to hide all the unselected objects, and only display the selected measures and dimensions.

12. Hover the **Values Preview** column and click the **Click here to see sample values** link to get an idea of the dimension values.

13. Move the mouse cursor a bit to the left and click the funnel icon. Here you can filter the dimension values and further limit the dataset that will be acquired (Figure 5.25).

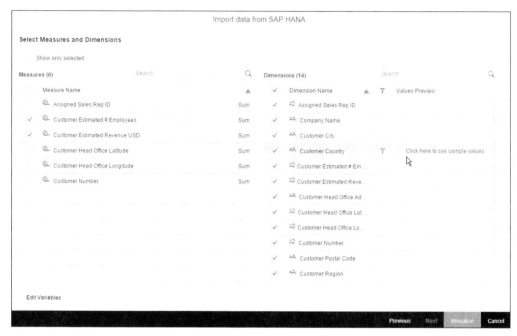

Figure 5.24 Select Measures and Dimensions

Figure 5.25 Dimension Filter

14. Depending on the type of dimension, different filter options are available. For example, if the dimension is numerical, a range can be defined. Activate **View Number of Occurrences** to see how many times each value occurs in the data source and activate **Enable Wildcard Search** for more flexible search options. Add the filter values and click **Apply**.

15. Back in the **Select Measures and Dimensions** window, you'll notice that you can also go back to changing the input parameters and variables, by clicking the **Edit Variables** button in the bottom-left corner (Figure 5.24).

16. Click **OK** to start the data acquisition into SAP Lumira, discovery edition and create a new dataset.

5.5.2   Connection via Managed OLAP Connection on SAP BusinessObjects BI Platform

As in the SAP BW situation, the steps to create a data source from an SAP HANA view via a managed OLAP connection on the SAP BusinessObjects BI platform are almost completely similar. After logging in to the SAP BusinessObjects BI platform, the steps to select a data source and set up the acquisition details are the same as in the direct connection scenario.

> **OLAP Connection**
>
> If there are no OLAP connections for SAP HANA present yet, check out Chapter 21, Section 5.2, for all the necessary steps to create such an OLAP connection.

To create a new dataset from an SAP HANA system via a managed OLAP connection on the SAP BusinessObjects BI platform, follow these steps:

1. Select **SAP HANA Import** from the **Data Source** menu on the home page of SAP Lumira, discovery edition. If you want to add a data source to an SAP Lumira document, use the **New Dataset** option in the **Data** menu (see Chapter 3).

2. Select the **SAP BI Platform** connectivity method (Figure 5.26).

3. Fill in the **System**, your **User Name**, and **Password**. Check **Remember Me** to store your password for the next time that you want to connect.

4. Click **Connect**.

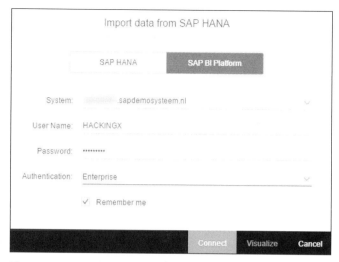

Figure 5.26 Connecting to the SAP BusinessObjects BI Platform

5. An overview of available **OLAP Connections** is shown (Figure 5.19). Only the OLAP connections that point to an SAP HANA system are included. With the **Show Connections** dropdown menu, you can select all connections (default), only connections that point to a system, or only connections that point to a view. Browse or search for the OLAP connection that you want to use (Figure 5.27). Select it and click **Next**.

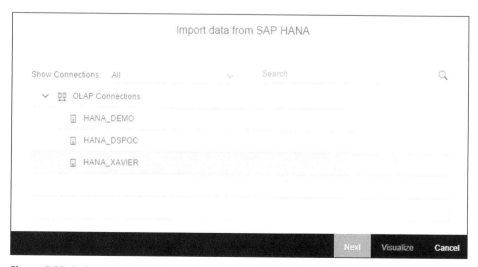

Figure 5.27 SAP HANA OLAP Connections on the SAP BusinessObjects BI Platform

From this step onward, you can continue from Step 8 of Section 5.5.1. All the options to select an SAP HANA view, and all further data acquisition options, are similar.

5.6 Universe

The SAP BusinessObjects BI universe historically has a very important place in the SAP BusinessObjects BI landscape. Originally, it was the layer between data sources and the SAP BusinessObjects frontend tools and had a central position in all developments on the SAP BusinessObjects BI platform. The universe doesn't contain any data itself, but acts as a semantic layer in between.

Nowadays, the main data sources are SAP BW and SAP HANA, which have their own connectors. Nevertheless, for non-SAP data sources, like a Microsoft SQL database or an Oracle database, a universe is still a good way to connect the SAP BusinessObjects BI frontend tools to the data sources. For SAP Lumira, discovery edition, this means that we can access a wide range of data sources, which can be centrally managed on the SAP BusinessObjects BI platform. Also, if you have universes developed on your SAP BusinessObjects BI platform, you can reuse those investments.

Additional Reference

For more details on universes, you can refer to *Universe Design with SAP Business-Objects BI: The Comprehensive Guide* (SAP PRESS, 2014).

As universes are stored on the SAP BusinessObjects BI platform, we need to connect to this environment to acquire data via a universe. To create a new dataset, follow these steps:

1. Select **SAP Universe** from the **Data Source** menu on the home page of SAP Lumira, discovery edition. If you want to add a data source to an SAP Lumira document, use the **New Dataset** option in the **Data** menu (see Chapter 3).

2. Fill in the **System**, your **User Name**, and **Password** (Figure 5.28). Check **Remember Me** to store your password for the next time that you want to connect.

3. Click **Connect**.

4. A list of available universes is shown (Figure 5.29). Browse to the universe that you want to use or use the search function to find the correct universe. Click **Connect** to continue.

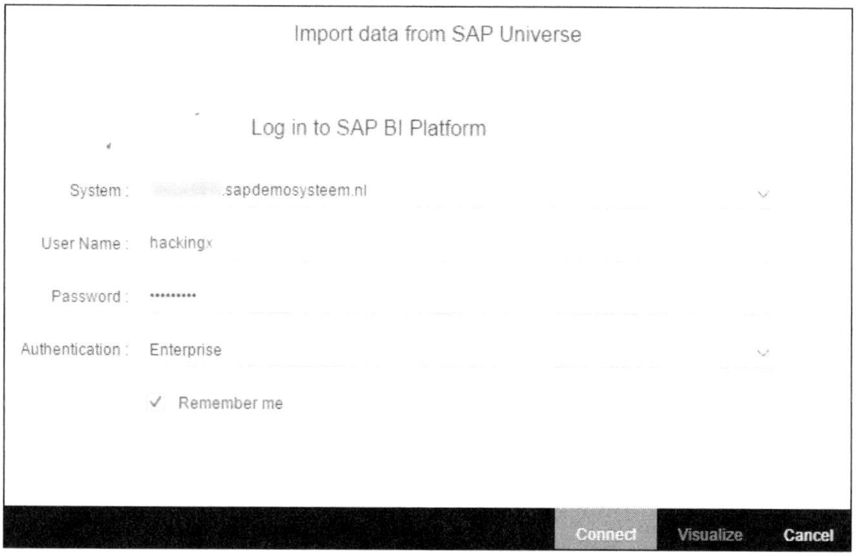

Figure 5.28 Connecting to the SAP BusinessObjects BI Platform

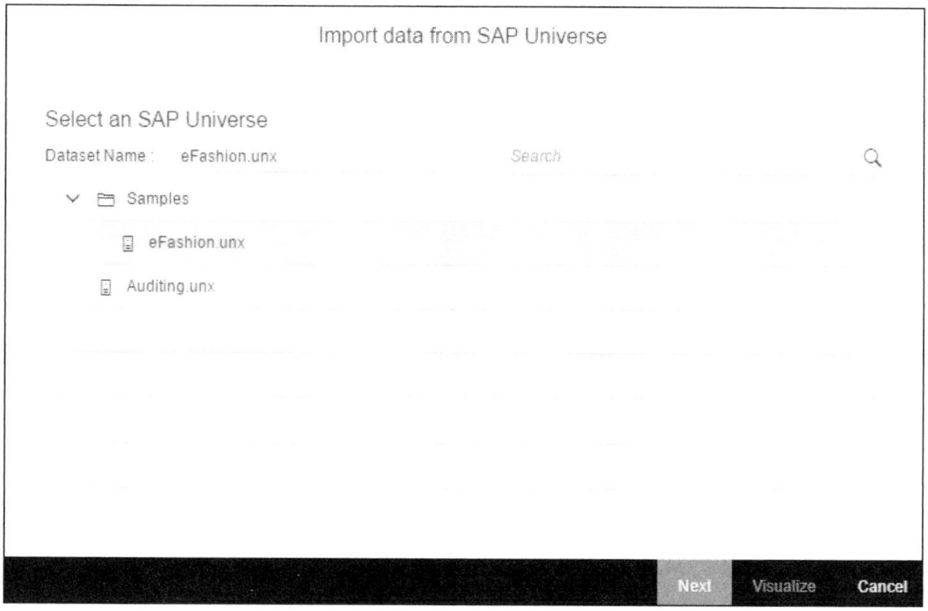

Figure 5.29 Universes on the SAP BusinessObjects BI Platform

5. On the next screen, the universe query panel is shown (Figure 5.30). This is the common interface throughout all SAP BusinessObjects BI tools to access data from a universe. With the universe query panel, you can create a query from the available dimensions and measures in the universe. Here you can determine which objects should be included in your dataset, and you can also create your own prompts. You can combine multiple queries, and it even has the option to manually adjust the generated SQL script. For now, just add the necessary dimensions and measures to the **Results Objects** area.

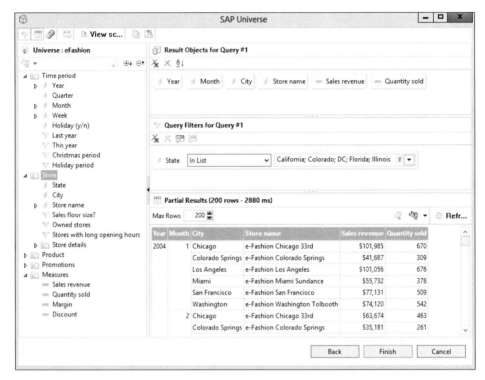

Figure 5.30 Universe Query Panel

Additional Reference

For all details regarding the universe query panel, please refer to *Universe Design with SAP BusinessObjects BI: The Comprehensive Guide* (SAP PRESS, 2014).

6. Click the **Refresh** button to see a preview of the dataset.

7. The universe query panel supports two types of filters: Predefined filters that are defined in the universe (you can recognize these objects from the funnel icon) and custom filters that are created in the universe query panel itself. Drag a dimension into the **Query Filters** area.

8. Select **In List** from the first dropdown menu. In the second dropdown menu, select **List of Values**. Select a number of values from the list in the popup window.

9. Add a second dimension to the **Query Filters** area. Now, select **Prompt** from the second dropdown menu. Click **OK** in the **Edit Prompt** window (Figure 5.31). This will give an input screen in SAP Lumira, discovery edition every time you refresh the dataset. This prompt will also pop up if you refresh the data preview in the universe query panel.

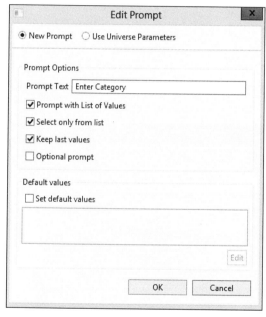

Figure 5.31 Edit Prompt

10. Click **Finish** to continue.

11. Make the selections in the prompt screen and click **Visualize** to start the data acquisition (Figure 5.32).

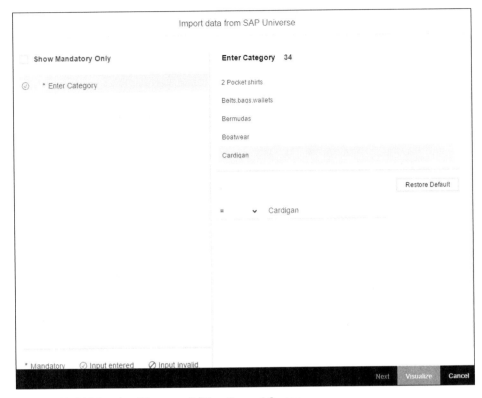

Figure 5.32 SAP Lumira, Discovery Edition Prompt Screen

SAP BusinessObjects BI Universe Limitations

SAP Lumira, discovery edition has a few limitations regarding SAP BusinessObjects BI universes:

- Only relational universes that are created with the Information Design Tool are supported. These universes have an .unx extension. Classic universes, which are created with the Universe Design Tool and have an .unv extension, are not supported.
- Universes based on OLAP data sources are not supported.
- Hierarchical prompts in universe parameter prompts are not supported.
- Multiple flows of SQL are not supported. If a query results in multiple separate SQL statements, the universe must be adjusted before SAP Lumira, discovery edition can acquire data from it.

5.7   Query with SQL

In addition to connecting SAP Lumira, discovery edition to non-SAP data sources via an SAP BusinessObjects BI Universe, it is also an option to make a direct connect to relational databases. In some cases, this requires a specific driver to be installed. This section shows you which database types are supported and how to connect to them.

5.7.1   Supported SQL Drivers

A data access driver is a piece of software, provided by the database vendor, that allows client tools like SAP Lumira, discovery edition to connect to middleware and to access data in the database. SAP Lumira, discovery edition not only includes the drivers to connect to SAP data sources, but also a wide range of drivers to connect to other database types. Table 5.2 lists all supported database middleware, whether the drivers are already included, and the name of the driver file.

Database Middeware	Version	Included?	Driver
Amazon EMR Hive	0.11, 0.13, 2.1	Yes	Simba Driver
Amazon Redshift	–	Yes	RedshiftJDBC4.jar
Apache Hadoop Hive	0.12, 0.13, 0.14, 1.0	Yes	Simba Driver 1.0.25.1033
Apache Hadoop Hive	2.0	Yes	–
Apache Spark	Spark 1.0	Yes	SparkJDBC4.jar Simba Driver 1.0.0.1000
Apache Spark	Spark 2.0	Yes	–
Cloudera Impala	1.0, 2.0	Yes	Simba Driver 1.0.25.1033
Generic JDBC	–	No	–
Generic OData	2.0	Yes	–
Greenplum	4	No	postgresql-9.1-903.jdbc4.jar
HP Vertica	Vertica 6.1, 7.1, 8	No	vertica-jdk5-6.1.2-0.jar vertica-jdbc-7.1.2-0.jar vertica-jdbc-8.0.1-6.jar

Table 5.2 Supported SQL Databases

Database Middeware	Version	Included?	Driver
Hortonworks	Data Platform 2.3	No	Simba Driver- hive-jdbc-0.12.0.jar
IBM	DB2 v10 for LUW DB2 v11 for LUW DB2 for z/OS v12	No	db2jcc4.jar
IBM	IBM Puredata (Netezza) Server 6 IBM Puredata (Netezza) Server 7	No	nzjdbc.jar
IBM	Informix Dynamic Server 11 Informix Dynamic Server 12	No	Ifxjdbc.jar
Ingres	Ingres Database 9,10	No	iijdbc-9.1-3.2.4.jar iijdbc-10.0-4.0.6.jar
Microsoft SQL Server	2008, 2012, 2014	No	sqljdbc4.jar
Microsoft SQL Server	MS Parallel Data Warehouse, 2016	No	sqljdbc4.jar
Oracle	11, 12, Exadata 11, Exadata 12	No	ojdbc6.jar (Oracle 11 and Exadata) ojdbc6.jar or ojdbc7.jar (Oracle 12)
Oracle	12c R2	No	ojdbc8.jar
Oracle	MySQL 5	No	mysql-connector-java-5.1.18-bin.jar
PostgreSQL	9	No	postgresql-9.1-903.jdbc4.jar

Table 5.2 Supported SQL Databases (Cont.)

Database Middeware	Version	Included?	Driver
Salesforce.com	Only supports connecting to the version available at *http://www.salesforce.com*	Yes	–
SAP	SAP HANA Database 1.0 SAP ERP 6 SAP R/3 Release 4 mySAP ERP 2004 SAP MII 14.0 SP 3 or later SAP HANA Vora SAP Vora 1.4 – Simba JDBC	Yes	–
SAP	MaxDB 7.9 SAP HANA Database 2.0	Yes	sapdbc.jar
Sybase	Sybase IQ 15 Sybase IQ 16 SQL Anywhere 12 SQL Anywhere 16 SQL Anywhere 17 Adaptive Server Enterprise 15.7 Adaptive Server Enterprise 16.0	Yes	–
Teradata	14, 15, 16	No	terajdbc4.jar and tdgssconfig.jar

Table 5.2 Supported SQL Databases (Cont.)

5.7.2 Installing and Uninstalling a Driver

As you've seen, SAP Lumira, discovery edition does not include all database drivers by default and therefore cannot connect to all types of databases. If you want to use such a database, you have to install it ourselves. The required drivers are provided as JAR files, and are in most cases available via the website of the database vendor.

To install such a driver, perform the following steps:

1. Make sure you downloaded the JAR file. Check Table 5.2 to see if the name is comparable.

2. Go to the **SQL Drivers** menu in the SAP Lumira, discovery edition **Preferences** menu (see Chapter 3, Section 3.2.6).

3. Navigate to the list of database drivers or use the search option to find the driver that you want to install (Figure 5.33). If a driver is already installed, a green checkmark is shown in front of the name of the database.

Figure 5.33 Installing a SQL Driver

4. If the driver is not installed yet, a red cross icon is displayed in front of the name of the database. Click **Install**.

5. Navigate in the Windows file system to the JAR file and click **Open** (Figure 5.34).

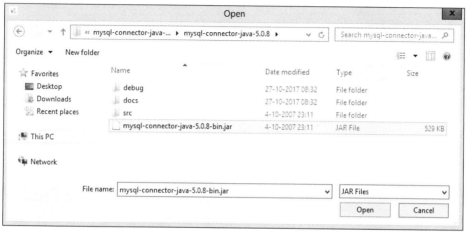

Figure 5.34 Selecting the JAR File

6. Click **Done**.

7. An information box (see Figure 5.35) will pop up to inform you that a restart of SAP Lumira, discovery edition is required to finalize the installation of the driver. Click **OK**, **Exit** SAP Lumira, discovery edition and **Start** SAP Lumira, discovery edition again.

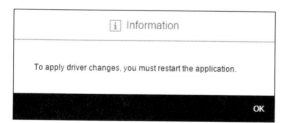

Figure 5.35 Restart SAP Lumira, Discovery Edition

8. The driver is now ready for use.

In some cases, there may be the need to uninstall a driver. For example, if a new version of the driver is available. To uninstall a driver, follow these steps:

1. Go to the **SQL Drivers** menu in the SAP Lumira, discovery edition **Preferences** menu.

2. Navigate to the list of database drivers or use the search option to find the driver that you want to uninstall (Figure 5.36).

3. Click **Uninstall**.

Figure 5.36 Uninstalling a SQL Driver

5.7.3   Creating a Dataset

Now that the necessary driver is installed, you can acquire data from the data source and create a dataset. To create the dataset using Query with SQL, follow these steps:

1. Select **Query with SQL** from the **Data Source** menu on the home page of SAP Lumira, discovery edition. If you want to add a data source to an SAP Lumira document, use the **New Dataset** option in the **Data** menu (see Chapter 3).

2. Select the database type you want to connect to (Figure 5.37). This list displays by default all installed drivers. If you want to see the drivers that are not installed yet, use the dropdown menu to switch between **Installed drivers**, **Uninstalled drivers**, or **All drivers**.

3. Click **Next** to continue.

Figure 5.37 Select a Database Type

4. Fill in your **User Name** and **Password**, the **Server** of the data source and, if necessary, the server port, and the name of the **Database** (Figure 5.38). Check **Remember Me** to store your password for the next time that you want to connect.

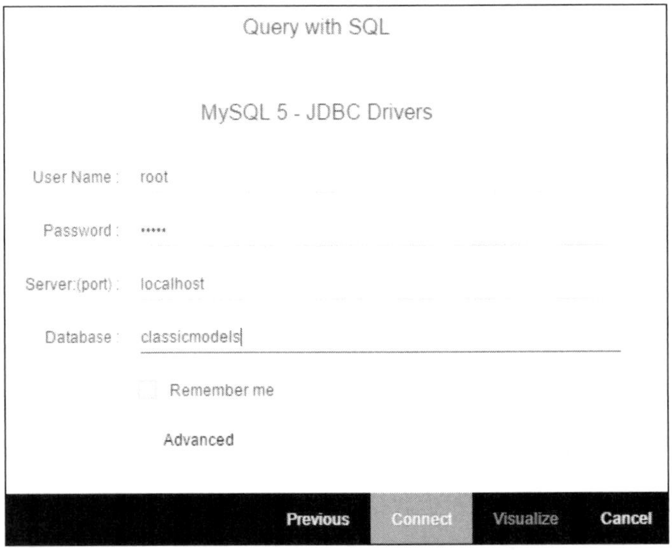

Figure 5.38 Connection Parameters

5. Click **Advanced** to open the **Advanced Parameters** for this connection (Figure 5.39). Here you have some options to adjust the connection settings, as follows:

 – **Connection Pool Mode**: Determines if the connection should be disconnected after each transaction, or should remain open for the amount of time defined in the **Pool Timeout**.

 – **Pool Timeout**: Number of minutes that the connection should be kept open.

 – **Array Fetch Size**: Sets the number of rows that is retrieved from the database with each call. For example, if your query returns 50 rows of data, and the array fetch size is 25, the connection will retrieve the data in two calls of 25 rows each. To deactivate this, enter an array fetch size of one. The data is then retrieved row by row, but this may slow your server's performance. The higher the fetch size, the faster and more efficient the data is retrieved, but take into account that this also has a higher memory footprint.

 – **Array Bind Size**: Sets the size of the bind array before it is transmitted to the database. The bind array is the area in memory where the connection server stores a batch of data to be loaded. Generally, the larger the bind array, the more rows can be loaded in one operation (and the better your performance will be).

 – **Login Timeout**: Number of seconds until a connection attempt times out and is cancelled.

– **Maximum Parallel Queries**: Number of processes that can be executed simultaneously. This way, the database work is divided over multiple processes, which may lead to a higher performance.

– **JDBC Driver Properties**: Specific JDBC driver parameters can be defined here.

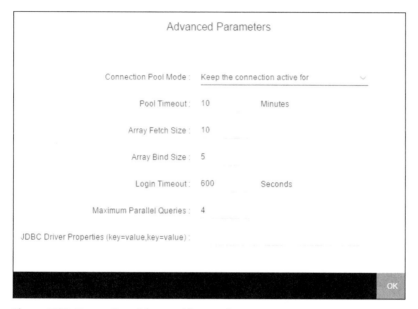

Figure 5.39 Connection Advanced Parameters

6. Click **OK** to close the **Advanced Parameters** screen.

7. Click **Connect** to connect to the database.

8. The SQL Editor is now shown (Figure 5.40). Here you can define which part of the database you want to acquire. On the left, you can browse through the database organization and select a table. Automatically, a SQL statement will appear in the **Query** area that will import the full table. You can adjust this statement, or create a custom statement from scratch. Click the **Preview** button to see a preview of the data.

9. By default, all columns are selected to be acquired. Click **Select All** to toggle between selecting and unselecting all columns. Select the columns you want to import by checking the individual checkmarks for each column.

Figure 5.40 Query with SQL – SQL Editor

10. Click **Show record count** to see the number of selected columns, the number of total columns, and the total number of rows.

11. The **Dataset Name** is by default the name of the table that you selected in the previous step, but you can change this. This value will be used in SAP Lumira, discovery edition to identify the dataset. Adjust the **Dataset Name** to your preference.

12. Click **Visualize** to start the data acquisition.

5.8   Dataset Refresh and Edit

The data source of the dataset(s) that you acquired to build your SAP Lumira, discovery edition stories, can change over time. Its data may be updated, and the connections to access that data may have changed. Let's look at how we can cope with that. In the following sections, we first look at how to refresh the data of a dataset, then how to change the connection settings, and finally how to change the acquisition details that we used.

5.8.1   Refreshing a Dataset

In this chapter we looked at the scenario where data is acquired from a data source and is moved into SAP Lumira, discovery edition. That means that if you build an SAP Lumira story and save that document, the dataset is included in your document. The next time you open the document, you can immediately continue your work, as all the data is present.

However, if the data in the data source changes, you may want to update the dataset in SAP Lumira, discovery edition to stay in sync. When you refresh a dataset, all the data actions that you performed on the dataset are replayed on the newly acquired data (see Chapter 8).

If the data source changes in its structure, this may impact the update of the dataset. If an object is removed, for example a column of a Microsoft Excel spreadsheet is deleted, the dataset is not immediately updated. The **Data Mapping** screen is shown, where you can select how to handle this situation (Figure 5.41). Either the columns will be removed, or the mapping has to be adjusted.

In case additional objects are available, the refresh will proceed without warnings. The additional objects can be added by editing the dataset (Section 5.8.3).

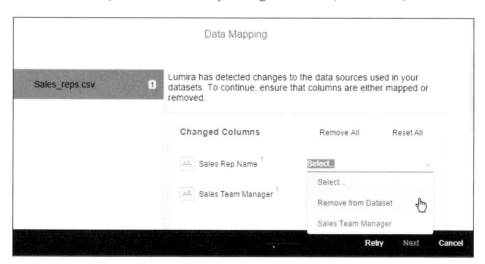

Figure 5.41 Data Mapping Required

To refresh a dataset, follow these steps:

1. Select **Refresh Document** from the **Data** menu in the menu bar. You can also simply click the **Refresh** button in the menu bar or use the keyboard shortcut `Ctrl`+`R`.

2. If your data source requires authentication, and you didn't check the **Remember Me** option when acquiring the dataset, you'll get a dialog box shown in Figure 5.42 for SAP BW. Enter the **User Name** and **Password** and click **Connect**.

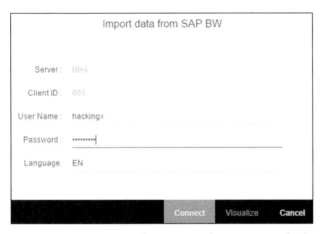

Figure 5.42 Login Prompt for SAP BW After Dataset Refresh

3. If there are any parameters or variables that need to be addressed before refreshing the dataset, the appropriate input options are displayed. This may be the case for SAP BW, SAP HANA, or SAP BusinessObjects BI universe data sources.

4. The data refresh is executed and the SAP Lumira document is updated with the new dataset.

5.8.2   Editing Connection Parameters

In the following cases, the connection to a data source must be adjusted:

- The Microsoft Excel or text file has been renamed and/or moved to a different location.

- The user name and/or password to the data source system has changed.

- The database has been moved to a different server.

In these cases, the connection parameters must be updated to allow a dataset refresh. This can be done with the following steps:

1. Click **Show More** from the **Recently Used** menu on the home page of SAP Lumira, discovery edition. Here all the connections used in SAP Lumira documents are shown (Figure 5.43).

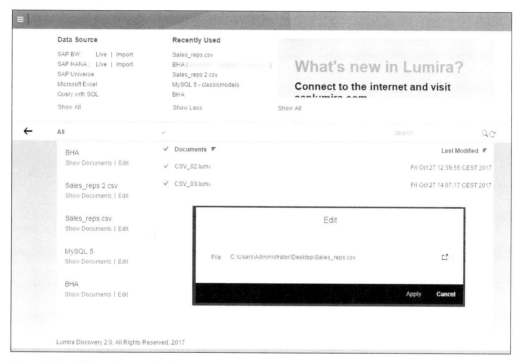

Figure 5.43 Editing Connection Parameters

2. Select a connection and click **Show Documents** to see all the SAP Lumira documents that use this connection.

3. If there are multiple documents that use the same connection, you can select for which of these documents the connection details need to be changed.

4. Now click **Edit** to adjust the parameters of the connection. These parameters depend on the connection type. The popup shown in Figure 5.43 contains the location of a text file data source. Make the adjustments and click **Apply** to confirm the changes on the connection and the selected documents.

5. A **Confirmation** popup will appear (Figure 5.44). Click **OK** to continue.

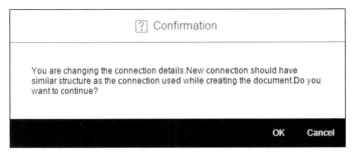

Figure 5.44 Change Connection Confirmation

To conclude this section, a few comments on modifying connections:

- If you used connection parameters that weren't used before, a new connection is added to the list of connections. The selected documents are associated with this new connection.

- If the connection parameters already existed in a different connection, the documents are moved to the existing connection.

- In case no documents use the initial connection anymore, it is removed from the list of connections.

- Adjusting the connection parameters does not change the content of the dataset. For this to happen, the dataset needs to be refreshed first (Section 5.8.1).

- Adjusting the connection parameters does not change the dataset acquisition details (see the next section).

5.8.3   Editing Dataset Acquisition Details

In some cases, there may be the need to make adjustments to the dataset definition, while the data already has been acquired from the data source. For example, you need to include an additional column from an SAP HANA view, or you want to adjust the presentation settings for an SAP BW dimension.

Datasets Based on Clipboard

The only data source type for which it is not possible to do edits is the clipboard. An error message stating that edit is not supported for this data source will be shown.

To edit the dataset acquisition details, follow these steps:

1. Open your SAP Lumira document.

2. Select **Edit Data Source** from the **Data** menu in the menu bar. If your document contains multiple datasets, make sure the dataset that you want to change is selected.

3. The dialog that you'll see now is similar to the ones you used when creating the dataset. Depending on your data source, you'll see one of the following options:

   – For text and Microsoft Excel data sources, you can add or remove any columns from the source file(s). As shown in Figure 5.45, you cannot change the source files or any other setup related parameters.

Figure 5.45 Edit Microsoft Excel Data Source

   – For SAP BW data sources, the **Select Measures and Dimensions from SAP BW Dataset** screen is shown. You can't select a different SAP BEx **query or SAP BW InfoProvider**, but you can add and remove dimensions and measures (Section 5.4.1). Also, you can adjust the presentation settings and apply filters on dimensions.

   – For SAP HANA data sources, the **Select Measures and Dimensions** dialog box is shown. You can't select a different SAP HANA view, but you can add and remove

163

the dimensions and measures (Section 5.5.1). Also, you can **Edit Variables** and apply filters on the dimensions.

– For SAP BusinessObjects BI universes, the universe query panel is shown. Here you can make adjustments to almost everything, except the chosen universe (Section 5.6).

– For Query with SQL data sources, you'll get the SQL Editor (Section 5.7.3). You can't browse the list of tables from the database anymore, but you can change the query and select which columns must be acquired.

4. If you make changes that remove columns from the dataset, the **Data Mapping** window will be shown (Figure 5.46). Here you can determine for each object, what the action should be. You have the option to remove the column from the dataset or remap the column with a different, newly added, object. Make the mapping adjustments and click **Next** to continue.

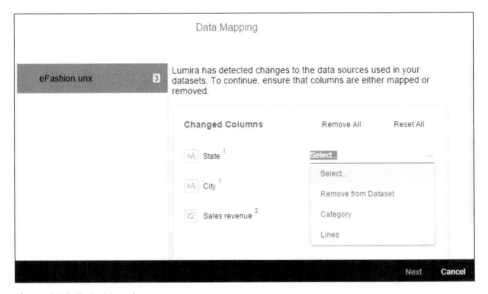

Figure 5.46 Data Mapping

5. The **Remove Column** confirmation screen shows a summary of all the objects that will be removed from the dataset (Figure 5.47). If this is correct, click **Continue** to finalize the changes and update the dataset.

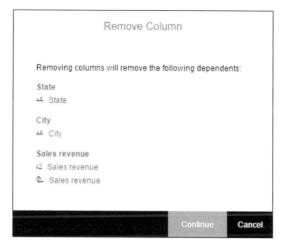

Figure 5.47 Remove Column Confirmation Screen

5.9   Summary

In this chapter, we took a detailed look at the several ways to get data into an SAP Lumira document. This step is essential, as without data, we can't create an SAP Lumira story.

We've seen that SAP Lumira, discovery edition supports a large range of data sources that it can natively access. This included local file types as Microsoft Excel and text files, but also SAP's own data sources SAP BW, SAP HANA, and the SAP Business-Objects BI Universes. In addition to that, SAP Lumira, discovery edition connects directly to a large set of relational databases via the Query with SQL connection type. Almost all the dataset types can be refreshed and edited afterward.

This chapter specifically described the data acquisition options of SAP Lumira, discovery edition. In the next chapter, we dive into the live data connectivity options.

Chapter 6
Live Data

Besides acquiring data to create an SAP Lumira, discovery edition
story, we can also use the live data connectivity. With live connections,
data is not stored in the SAP Lumira document and calculations are
delegated to the data source.

In addition to data acquisition (Chapter 5), SAP Lumira, discovery edition offers the capabilities to use live connections when creating an SAP Lumira, discovery edition story. With this type of connectivity, we can create visualizations and perform analysis without importing or acquiring the dataset into the SAP Lumira document. SAP Lumira, discovery edition supports a live connection to both SAP BW and SAP HANA.

Live data is live: the dataset remains in one of the supported data sources and is not stored as part the SAP Lumira document. This means that when opening an SAP Lumira, discovery edition story based on live connection(s), data is being retrieved directly from the data source(s). Calculations are delegated to the data source and data security defined in SAP BW or SAP HANA is taken into account.

> **Limitations**
>
> Due to the fact that data is not acquired or imported when using live connection(s), data analysis actions using the data view mode or manipulating the dataset (for example split a column) is not supported. Chapter 8 provides a detailed overview about which data manipulation actions can be performed when working with acquired data sources.

This chapter, similarly to data acquisition steps described in Chapter 5, Section 5.4 and Section 5.5, explains how to use a direct or a managed OLAP connection on the SAP BusinessObjects BI platform for live connections to SAP BW and SAP HANA. The main differences between live data and data acquisition is that the latter offers more capabilities through which objects and data, using filtering, are acquired.

6.1   SAP BW

SAP Lumira, discovery edition can connect to an SAP BW environment via an SAP BEx query or an InfoProvider. This allows you to leverage all the existing SAP BW data models and query definitions and bring your corporate data into SAP Lumira, discovery edition in a structured and controlled way.

Connecting to SAP BW for live data can be done in two ways:

- **Direct connection to SAP BW**
  In this scenario SAP Lumira, discovery edition connects to SAP BW system via the connections that are defined in the SAP Logon application (also referred to as the SAP GUI). The SAP Logon is locally installed on your Windows environment.
- **Connection via managed OLAP connection on the SAP BusinessObjects BI platform**
  In this scenario, SAP Lumira, discovery edition uses the OLAP connections that are defined on the SAP BusinessObjects BI platform to connect to SAP BW.

The major advantage of the second scenario is that with the managed OLAP connection, the SAP Lumira documents can be easily shared between users over the SAP BusinessObjects BI platform, as the managed connection on the SAP BusinessObjects BI platform ensures that the same connectivity details are available for all users. The first scenario uses locally maintained connectivity details, which may be not in sync and easily lead to issues. For the result after selecting the SAP BW data source, there is no difference between the two options.

The supported SAP BW versions for live data connections are as follows:

- SAP BW 7.0 with Service Pack 23 and above
- SAP BW 7.01/7.02 with Service Pack 8 and above
- SAP BW 7.30 with Service Pack 03 and above
- SAP BW 7.31/7.4/7.5x (all service packs)

Product Availability Matrix

The most up to date overview of supported source systems can be found in the Product Availability Matrix (PAM) for SAP Lumira. You can find this at *http://support.sap.com/pam*.

6.1.1   Direct Connection to SAP BW

Before you can use a direct connection to SAP BW, SAP Logon must be installed on your Windows environment and a connection must be defined. The following error will pop up if this is not the case: **Could not find the details for the SAP Business Warehouse connection. Ensure that SAP logon has the SAP Business Warehouse connections defined**. You can download it from the SAP Support website (*http://support.sap.com/swdc*). The software is stored under **Downloads · Installations & Upgrades · By Alphabetical Index (A-Z) · G · SAP GUI For Windows**.

> **SAP Logon**
>
> More information on the configuration of SAP Logon connections is available at SAP Help: *http://help.sap.com/*. Search using the keywords "SAP GUI for Windows".

To create a new SAP Lumira document from an SAP BW system using a direct connection, follow these steps:

1. Select **SAP BW Live** from the **Data Source** menu on the home page of SAP Lumira, discovery edition. In case you want to add a data source to an SAP Lumira document, use the **New Dataset** option in the **Data** menu (see Chapter 3).

2. By default, **SAP BW** is selected as the connectivity method. Select the SAP BW **Server** you want to connect to from the dropdown menu (Figure 6.1). If the server is not available in the list, you have to create a connection to this server in SAP Logon first.

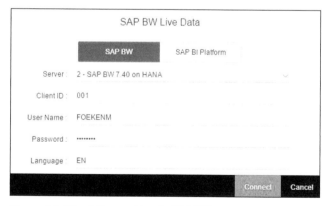

Figure 6.1 Direct Connection to SAP BW

3. Fill in the **Client ID** and your **User Name** and **Password** for the selected SAP BW system. In addition, you can enter a **Language**.

4. Click **Connect** to connect to the SAP BW system.

5. In the next dialog window, select the SAP BEx query or InfoProvider that you want to connect to (Figure 6.2). You can use the search bar to find the required object, or you can simply switch between the **Roles** and the **InfoAreas** tab to browse the SAP BW environment.

6. Click **OK** to advance to the following screen.

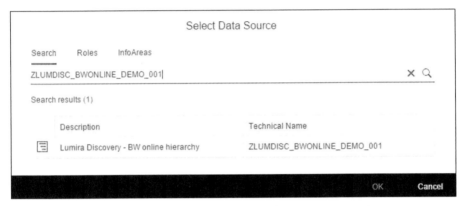

Figure 6.2 Search and Select an SAP BEx Query or InfoProvider

7. If you selected an SAP BEx query that contains prompts, the **PROMPTS** window is shown (Figure 6.3). Here you can enter or select the necessary values for each prompt. Note that you can use the search bar to narrow down the list of prompts. Click **OK** to connect to the selected SAP BEx query and create the SAP Lumira document.

Figure 6.3 SAP BEx Query Prompts

8. Figure 6.4 shows the name of the **Dataset (Lumira Discovery – BW online hierarchy)** and all the available measures and dimensions of the selected SAP BEx query.

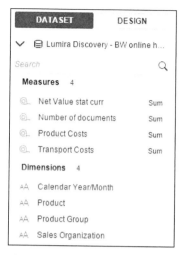

Figure 6.4 Available Dimensions and Measures

6.1.2   Connection via Managed OLAP Connection on SAP BusinessObjects BI Platform

The steps to connect to an SAP BEx query or InfoProvider are roughly the same when using a connection via a managed OLAP connection on the SAP BusinessObjects BI platform. We first have to log in to the SAP BusinessObjects BI platform; after that, the steps are exactly the same as in the direct connection scenario.

OLAP Connection

In case there are no OLAP connections for SAP BW present yet, check out Chapter 21, Section 21.5.3, for all the necessary steps to create such an OLAP connection.

To connect to an SAP BW system via a managed OLAP connection on the SAP BusinessObjects BI platform, follow these steps:

1. Select **SAP BW Live** from the **Data Source** menu on the home page of SAP Lumira, discovery edition. In case you want to add a data source to an SAP Lumira document, use the **New Dataset** option in the **Data** menu (see Chapter 3).

2. Select the **SAP BI Platform** connectivity method (Figure 6.5).

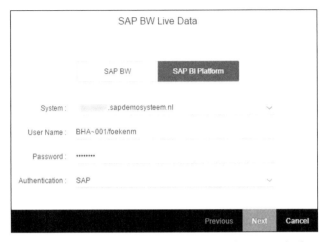

Figure 6.5 Connecting to the SAP BusinessObjects BI Platform

3. Fill in the **System**, your **User Name**, and **Password.**

4. Select the correct **Authentication** method from the dropdown list. If you are using SAP authentication, it may be necessary to fill in your user name in the following format: *<System ID>~<Client>/<User Name>*. For example: *BHA~001/foekenm.*

5. Click **Next**.

6. An overview of available **OLAP Connections** is shown (Figure 6.6).

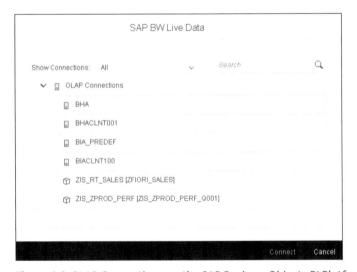

Figure 6.6 OLAP Connections on the SAP BusinessObjects BI Platform

Only the OLAP connections that reference to an SAP BW system are included. Via the **Show Connections** dropdown menu, you can filter the list of **OLAP Connections** on all connections, only connections that point to an SAP BW system, only connections that point to a Cube or InfoProvider, or only connections that point to an SAP BEx query or SAP BEx query view. Select the correct OLAP connection and click **Connect**.

From this step onward, you can continue from Step 5 of Section 6.1.1, as all options to select an SAP BEx query or InfoProvider, and all further options, are similar (Figure 6.2).

SAP BW limitations

Two significant limitations of SAP BW are as follows:

- **Geo Maps**
  Currently, Geo Maps for SAP BW online data sources are not supported. A workaround would be to import or acquire the dataset from SAP BW and create a geographic hierarchy.

- **Dimensions**
  When using the live connection to an SAP BEx query or InfoProvider, it's not possible to define in which presentation manner they should be displayed: As **Text**, **Key**, or both. For more information regarding this limitation, please refer to SAP KBA **2549103**.

6.2 SAP HANA

SAP Lumira, discovery edition can connect to SAP HANA to view its data and create visualizations based on views. These views are data models, built on top of the physical tables where the data resides in SAP HANA. SAP Lumira, discovery edition supports connecting to analytical and calculation views.

Connecting to an SAP HANA view can be done in two ways:

- **Direct connection to SAP HANA**
  Here you have to provide all the connection details in SAP Lumira, discovery edition to connect to the SAP HANA system.

- **Connection via managed OLAP connection on the SAP BusinessObjects BI platform**

SAP Lumira, discovery edition uses the connections that are defined on the SAP BusinessObjects BI platform to connect to SAP HANA. Please note that a different type of OLAP connection (SAP HANA HTTP, see Chapter 21, Section 21.5.1) needs to be available on the SAP BusinessObjects BI platform compared with the scenario to import data from SAP HANA, as described in Chapter 5, Section 5.5.

As was also the case with the SAP BW live connection, the second scenario has a big advantage over the first one, in that with the managed OLAP connection the SAP Lumira documents are easily shared between users via the SAP BusinessObjects BI platform. The managed connection ensures that the same connectivity setup is used for all users and achieving single-sign on (SSO) becomes easy. For the dataset selection and result, both scenarios will lead to the same outcome.

Prerequisites

To be able to use the SAP HANA Live connection, either directly or via the SAP BusinessObjects BI platform, you need to ensure that:

- The SAP HANA XS port is up and running. This can be checked by entering the URL manually in a browser: *http(s)://<HANA_SYSTEM>:<WEB_DISPATCH_PORT>*. By default, the SAP HANA XS web server is configured to use the port numbers *80<SAP HANA instance number>* for HTTP and *43<SAP HANA instance number>* for HTTPS requests from clients.

- The SAP HANA Info Access service along with delivery unit *HCO_INA_SERVICE* is deployed on the SAP HANA platform. If it's deployed correctly, you can see the package: *sap\bc\ina\service* under *content* in the SAP HANA modeler. For more information, please refer to SAP KBA 2207175.

- The role *sap.bc.ina.service.v2.userRole::INA_USER* should be assigned to the SAP HANA user.

The supported SAP HANA versions are as follows:

- SAP HANA SPS 10, Revision 100 and above
- SAP HANA SPS 11, Revision 110 and above
- SAP HANA SPS 12, Revision 120 and above
- SAP HANA 2.0 SPS 01

Product Availability Matrix

The most up to date overview of supported source systems can be found in the Product Availability Matrix (PAM) for SAP Lumira. You can find this at *http://support.sap.com/pam*.

Exposing SAP BW Data via SAP HANA Views

In an SAP BW powered by SAP HANA environment, you can import SAP BW models as InfoCubes and DSOs, but also as SAP BEx queries, analytic views, and calculation views. For more information on this topic, see *http://bit.ly/2hrwgv6*.

6.2.1 Direct Connection to SAP HANA

To connect to an SAP HANA system using a direct connection, follow these steps:

1. Select **SAP HANA Live** from the **Data Source** menu on the home page of SAP Lumira, discovery edition. In case you want to add a data source to an SAP Lumira document, use the **New Dataset** option in the **Data** menu (see Chapter 3).

2. By default, **SAP HANA** is selected as the connectivity method. Enter the SAP HANA **Server** in the format of "<XS engine URL>:<port>", **User Name**, and **Password** (Figure 6.7).

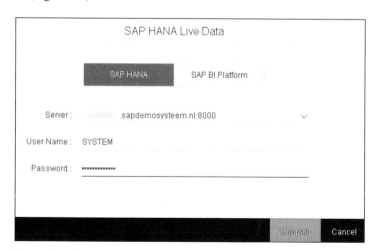

Figure 6.7 Direct Connection to SAP HANA

3. Click **Connect** to connect to the SAP HANA system.

4. Use the **Search** option to find a specific view (Figure 6.8). Only the views for your account are shown. Alternatively, you can switch to the **Folders** tab. With this view you can browse through the package structure in which the SAP HANA views are organized represented as folders and sub-folders.

Figure 6.8 Search and Select an SAP HANA View

5. Select the view that you want to use and click **OK**.

6. If you selected an SAP HANA view that contains mandatory variables or input parameters, the **Prompts** screen is shown (Figure 6.9). Enter the necessary values for each variable or input parameter and click **OK** to create an SAP Lumira document.

Input Parameters versus Variables

Input parameters are not used to filter data, but are used as input to perform certain calculations. An input parameter could for example be a target currency to perform a currency conversion. As an input parameter is used in such way, it can only have a single value as its input.

A variable on the other hand, is used to filter an attribute of the view, to limit the dataset. Here it is possible to use single or multiple values, intervals, or ranges of values.

Figure 6.9 SAP HANA Prompts

6.2.2 Connection via Managed OLAP Connection on SAP BusinessObjects BI Platform

The steps to connect to an SAP HANA view via a managed OLAP connection on the SAP BusinessObjects BI platform are almost completely similar to the SAP BW situation. After logging in to the SAP BusinessObjects BI platform, the steps to select a data source are the same as in the direct connection scenario.

> **OLAP Connection**
>
> Connecting to SAP HANA Live requires a different type of OLAP connection than when you import or acquire a dataset: the SAP HANA HTTP connection.
>
> Learn more on how to enable and create the SAP HANA HTTP connection on the SAP BusinessObjects BI platform in Chapter 21, Section 21.5.1 and Section 21.5.2.

To connect to an SAP HANA system via a managed OLAP connection on the SAP BusinessObjects BI platform, follow these steps:

1. Select **SAP HANA Live** from the **Data Source** menu on the home page of SAP Lumira, discovery edition. If you want to add a data source to an SAP Lumira document, use the **New Dataset** option in the **Data** menu (see Chapter 3).

2. Select the **SAP BI Platform** connectivity method (Figure 6.10).

3. Fill in the **System**, **User Name**, and **Password**.

4. Click **Next**.

5. An overview of available **OLAP Connections** is shown (Figure 6.11). Only the SAP HANA HTTP OLAP connections are included. With the **Show Connections** drop-down menu, you can select all connections (default), only connections that point

to a system, or only connections that point to a Cube or InfoProvider. Browse or **Search** for the OLAP connection that you want to use. Select it and click **Connect**.

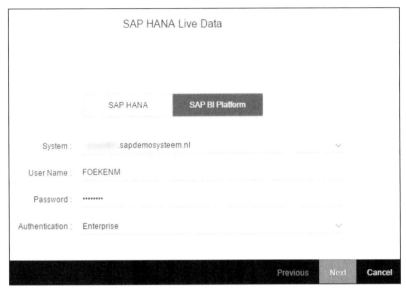

Figure 6.10 Connecting to the SAP BusinessObjects BI Platform

Figure 6.11 SAP HANA HTTP OLAP Connections on the SAP BusinessObjects BI Platform

6. From this step onward, you can continue from Step 4 of Section 6.2.1. All the options to select an SAP HANA view, and all further options, are similar.

6.3   Summary

In this chapter, we had a detailed look at how to use the live connectivity in SAP Lumira, discovery edition to connect to SAP BW and SAP HANA. The main difference between importing data versus connecting to the data source is that the data is not imported into your SAP Lumira document.

Furthermore, we provided an overview of the differences between using a direct connection and utilizing the various types of OLAP connections defined on the SAP BusinessObjects BI platform. The latter has many advantages over using a direct connection so we recommend you define and use the required OLAP connection(s) before creating Lumira documents. For more information, check out Chapter 21, Section 21.5.

The next chapter covers the options that SAP Lumira, discovery edition provides to perform data analysis actions.

6

Chapter 7
Data Analysis

The process of analyzing data consists of steps to inspect, cleanse, transform, and model data. The goal of this process is to discover useful information and support decision-making in your organization. This chapter describes how to use the data view of SAP Lumira, discovery edition to analyze and inspect your datasets via the grid and facet views.

7

An important step when turning data into information is analyzing or inspecting the elements, structure, and values of the dataset. In Chapter 5 and Chapter 6, we provided a detailed overview of how to acquire data from or connect to a wide range of supported data sources. In this chapter, we focus on the capabilities that SAP Lumira, discovery edition has to offer to analyze your dataset using the **DataView** mode before creating visualizations and stories.

To analyze the data, the **DataView** option offers two views:

- Grid view: The data is displayed in rows and columns, similar to a spreadsheet or table.
- Facet view: Shows distinct or unique values per column and the number of times these values occur.

The following sections explain in more detail how to use the data view by toggling between the grid and facet views.

> **Note**
>
> The data view, as described in this chapter, is only available for data sources that have been imported or acquired. For live data, only the design view is available and data analysis can be performed for instance by using a crosstab as chart.

> **Note**
>
> The source files used for the excercises in this chapter are available for download at *www.sap-press.com/4511.*

7.1   Data View

In Part I, we introduced the data view as part of the SAP Lumira, discovery edition user interface and briefly touched on some of the functionalities of the grid and facet view. Switching between the **DesignView** and the **DataView** tabs can be done by clicking on the button in the upper-right corner, as shown in Figure 7.1.

Figure 7.1 Switch to the Data View

Depending on previous actions performed, either the grid or the facet view is displayed. You can switch between the two views by clicking on the icons in the global toolbar, as shown in Figure 7.2. Here the grid view is selected with the facet view icon to the right. Please note that there is also the option to filter the dataset using the filter icon. You learn more on filtering in Chapter 16.

Figure 7.2 Toggle Between the Grid and Facet View

Besides toggling between the grid and facet view, the data view also offers a **Summary** tab in the left side pane. This tab displays the distinct values of a selected column in descending order based on the count of the number of occurrences. An example is displayed in Figure 7.3, based on the column **FIRST_NAME**.

By clicking on the sorting icons in the header, you can toggle between sorting based on the values or the number of occurrences in ascending or descending order.

In the following sections, we describe the main functionality of the grid and facet view to analyze and understand your dataset. Data manipulation actions that are available via the various context menus are not in scope and will be described in Chapter 8.

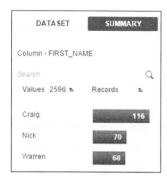

Figure 7.3 Summary Tab

7.2   Grid View

The grid view displays all acquired records and allows horizontal and vertical scrolling to view each column and row. Each dimension listed in the **Dataset** tab of the side pane is listed as a column. Measures are not available as columns in the grid view, as they only represent a certain aggregation type of a numeric dimension, for instance **Sum** or **Average**.

Now let's perform a couple of navigation actions to familiarize ourselves with the grid view:

1. Select the scrollbar at the bottom and scroll to the last column. Depending on the size of your dataset and type of data source, SAP Lumira, discovery edition will load and display the requested columns and rows.

2. Click on **City** in the left side pane's **Dataset** tab to directly jump to this column in the grid view, as shown in Figure 7.4.

    As you might have noticed, the dimensions listed in the **Dataset** tab of the side pane are sorted in ascending order, while the columns in the grid view are in the order defined in the data source. You can change the order in which the columns are displayed by selecting the header and dragging this in front or at the back of another column header.

3. Click on the header of the **HOBBIES** column and drag it in front of the **CITY** column. In Figure 7.5, you can see a thick blue line that indicates where the column is shifted. Release the mouse to apply the change.

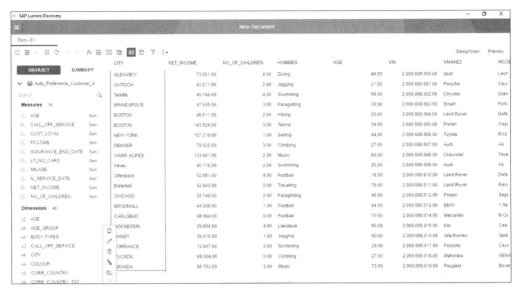

Figure 7.4 Select Dimension in Grid View

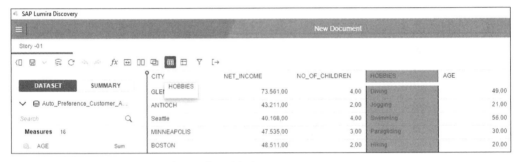

Figure 7.5 Rearrange Columns in Grid View

4. Besides rearranging the order of the columns in the grid view, you can also change the cell width. Hovering across the right edge of a column will display a thick blue line and icon, which can be dragged to either increase or decrease the width. Another option is to select a column header and click on the **Fit cell width to content** icon, as shown in Figure 7.6.

Please note that adjusting the cell width has to be done separately for each column. If you select multiple columns in the grid view, the only options (based on the data type) available in the context menu are to delete, replace values, or concatenate the selected columns.

Figure 7.6 Change Cell Width to Fit the Content

5. The grid view also offers basic sorting capabilities. You can change the order in which the values in the rows are displayed to either ascending or descending. Select the header of the **FIRST_NAME** column and click on the sorting icon. Select either **Ascending** or **Descending**, as shown in Figure 7.7, to change the order in which the rows are displayed.

Figure 7.7 Change the Sorting Order of a Column

Please note that sorting can only be applied on a single column at the same time. If you apply sorting on a second column, the sorting of the first column is automatically set to **None**.

7.3   Facet View

The facet view, as shown in Figure 7.8, displays the distinct values in each column and, by default, a count of the number of occurrences. Next to the column header, a number displays how many distinct values are present in the dataset. Any column that has more than 100 distinct values is marked as **100+**. The exact amount of distinct values is available via the **Summary** tab in the left side pane.

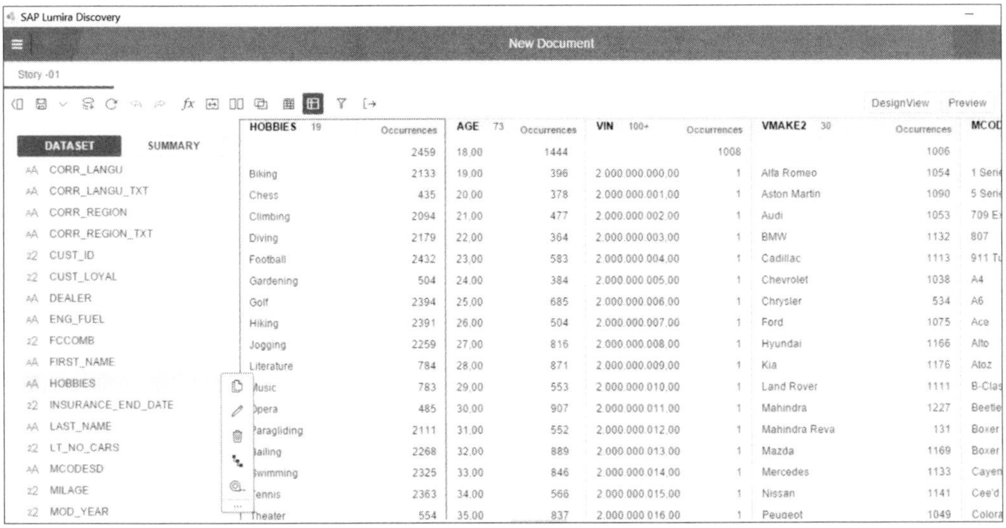

Figure 7.8 Facet View

The default view based on a count of the number of occurrences can be changed to any measure available in the dataset by following these steps:

1. Select **HOBBIES** in the **Dataset** left side panel.
2. Right-click in the header of the **HOBBIES** column and select **Show Measures** from the expanded context menu, as shown in Figure 7.9. A left-click on the column header only displays the first five icons.

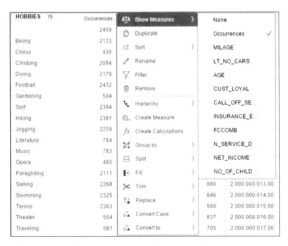

Figure 7.9 Change Measure in Facet View

A list of available measures is displayed in the context menu and can be selected to change the view of your data.

3. Select **AGE.** Make sure that the aggregation level of the measure **AGE** is set to **Average** in the **Dataset** tab.

4. The **HOBBIES** column now displays the average age of customers with a certain hobby. Similar to the grid view, sorting can be applied, but in this case both on the dimension value as well as on the measure.

5. Right-click again on the header of the **HOBBIES** column and expand the **Sort** context menu.

6. Select the last option, **Sort by Descending Measure**, as shown in Figure 7.10.

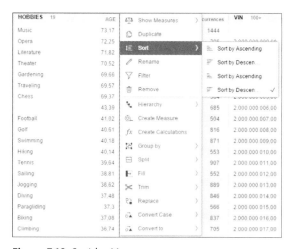

Figure 7.10 Sort by Measure

Now the column sorts the hobbies with the highest average age on top. As expected, hobbies like **Opera** are listed at the top while more active hobbies like **Climbing** and **Paragliding** are at the bottom with the lowest average age.

This example perfectly shows that even without creating a visualization, you can inspect and analyze your dataset using the facet view in SAP Lumira, discovery edition.

7.4   Summary

The data view of SAP Lumira, discovery edition enables end users to analyze their dataset before and during the process of creating visualizations or stories. As we have shown, the grid and facet view support this process with their capabilities to browse through the rows and columns and to display the distinct values and the number of occurrences in your dataset.

When analyzing the dataset using the grid and facet view, you often encounter anomalies or opportunities to enrich the data for visualization purposes. In the next chapter, we teach you all there is to learn about the available data manipulation actions available in SAP Lumira, discovery edition.

Chapter 8
Data Manipulation

After acquiring the data and performing a first analysis, it's time to prepare the dataset to use in visualizations and create stories. Being able to manipulate and enrich your datasets without any dependency on your IT department is the key to supporting the self-service needs of your business.

In this chapter, we discuss the tools that SAP Lumira, discovery edition offers to manipulate datasets. Data manipulation is one of the key requirements often mentioned by data analysts for self-service and data discovery scenarios. Being able to add calculated objects based on formulas or to enrich data with hierarchical information helps you shape the dataset for the intended purpose: delivering data using visualizations to clearly communicate your message.

As discussed in Chapter 5 and Chapter 6, datasets in SAP Lumira, discovery edition can be imported into an SAP Lumira document or the data remains in the source system and a live connection is used to fetch the required data given the created visualizations, filters, etc.

Deciding whether to import your dataset or use a live connection mainly depends on the need to be able to manipulate your dataset while analyzing and creating stories. While importing a dataset provides you with all the available data manipulation options described in the following sections, a live scenario will not offer any of them. The live scenario is limited to consuming the objects available in the dataset (including object and data types). No data manipulation actions are available.

Let's now dive into the different types of objects, hierarchies, calculations, and all the data manipulation actions that can be performed.

> **Note**
>
> The source files used for the exercises in this chapter are available for download via *www.sap-press.com/4511*.

8.1   Objects

Objects in SAP Lumira, discovery edition describe the data in your dataset and how this data can be used to create visualizations and stories. As mentioned in previous chapters, there are two types of objects:

- Dimensions
- Measures

In the side pane on the **Dataset** tab there is a clear distinction between the two types of objects (Figure 8.1). Let's take a closer look at dimensions first.

Figure 8.1 Measures and Dimensions

8.1.1   Dimensions

A dimension is an object that represents categorical data in your dataset. Examples are market, business, channel, customer, fiscal period, etc. Dimensions are represented as columns and they can have the following data types:

- **String**: Any object can be represented as text. It's the default data type if SAP Lumira, discovery edition can't detect the data type automatically.
- **Numeric**: A numeric object can contain any type of decimal number.
- **Integer**: Object that can only contain positive and negative whole numbers including zero.
- **Date/time**: Can be used in, for instance, time series charts and is the required data type to create date/time hierarchies (Section 8.2.2).

In SAP Lumira, discovery edition, each object available in the side panel has associated actions. The list of possible actions for a dimension are as follows:

- **Duplicate**
  Creates a copy of the object. Its associated column in the dataset is duplicated with **(2)** as suffix. You can use a duplicate object if you want to perform certain data actions but want to keep the original values for reference.

- **Create Date/Time Objects**
  Creates four additional dimensions on **Day**, **Month**, **Quarter**, and **Year** level based on the **Date/Time** data type dimension only.

- **Rename**
  Changes the name of the object.

- **Remove**
  Removes the object and the associated column in the dataset. If there are any derived or depending objects, a warning will be displayed that associated objects will be removed (Figure 8.2). This warning is limited to objects and will not indicate which filters, visualizations, or stories are impacted.

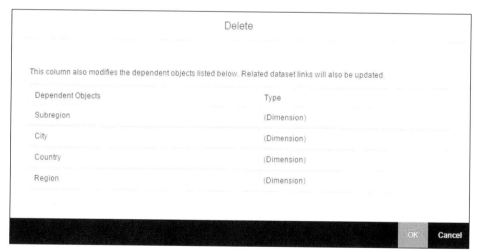

Figure 8.2 Dependencies Displayed When Removing an Object

The impact of the actions depends on the type of object:

- Dimensions and measures are deleted.
- Visualizations will have the object removed from the chart.
- Objects used as filters are removed.

- **Hierarchy**

  Based on the data type of the object, different available types of hierarchies will be displayed. Creating hierarchies is discussed in Section 8.2.

- **Create Measure**

  Objects of a numeric data type can be directly created as a measure with any type of aggregation. Other data type based objects are created with an aggregation **Count(All)**, which can only be changed to **Count(Distinct)**. More information on measures in can be found in Section 8.1.2.

- **Create Calculations**

  Shortcut to create calculated objects; Section 8.3 for more details.

- **Convert to**

  Depending on the data type of the object, you can convert it to another data type. A numeric object can be converted to a string while a string, or text object, can be converted to a **Number**, **Integer**, or **Date/Time** object (Figure 8.3).

Figure 8.3 Convert String Object to Different Data Type

- Converting to a **Number** or **Integer** is automatic. For conversions to **Date/Time**, a source format has to be selected, as shown in Figure 8.4.

Figure 8.4 Select Source Format for Date/Time Conversion

8.1.2   Measures

A measure is a numeric value that provides meaning to dimensions by calculating the result based on the selected aggregation type. An example would be sales revenue or costs. Only numeric or integer data types can be used as measures, because these values can be aggregated. SAP Lumira, discovery edition supports the following aggregation types:

- **Sum**: Adds all the values for a given measure.
- **Average**: Calculates the sum and then divides by the number of values.
- **Max**: Returns the maximum or highest value.
- **Min**: Returns the minimum or lowest value.
- **Count(Distinct)**: Counts each distinct item.
- **Count(All)**: Counts the total number of items in your dataset.

A measure can only have one aggregation type applied at the same time. If you want to visualize, for instance, the highest, lowest, and average sales per customer, you need to create three separate sales measure objects, one for each aggregation type.

For measures, the following list of object actions is available:

- **Change Aggregation**
  Enables you to change the aggregation of a measure, for example from **Sum** to **Average**.
- **Rename**
  Changes the name of the object.
- **Remove**
  Similar to removing a dimension when an impact assessment is performed. For more information, see Section 8.1.
- **Create Calculations**
  Shortcut to create calculated objects; see Section 8.3 for more details.
- **Display Formatting**
  Enables you to change the display format of a measure. As shown in Figure 8.5, you can select a value format: **Number** or **Percentage**. Furthermore, you can add a custom symbol like **$** as a **Prefix** or **Suffix**. Changing the scaling factor or decimal places is done through the number format option, accessible for each visualization on the canvas.

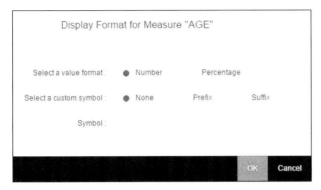

Figure 8.5 Display Format Options for Measure Objects

In the next section, we look at how different types of hierarchies are used to create relationships between dimension objects.

8.2   Hierarchies

If a dataset contains dimensions that logically form a hierarchy, you can define different types of hierarchies in SAP Lumira, discovery edition. Hierarchies can be used to view data at different levels of granularity and allow drilling up and down to gain insight into the relationship between dimensions and measures. An example would be a date/time hierarchy based on the dimensions **<Year>-<Month>-<Day>**.

In the next sections, we describe how to create the different types of hierarchies supported by SAP Lumira, discovery edition.

Live Data Hierarchies

SAP Lumira, discovery edition supports hierarchies defined in live data sources. If hierarchies are present, they will be obtained by default, which makes reporting much easier for users. However, none of the hierarchy types described in this section can be created when using a live data source.

8.2.1   Geographic Hierarchies

To plot data containing location information onto a geographic chart, we have to create a geographic hierarchy first. SAP Lumira, discovery edition supports two types of geographic hierarchies by:

- Names
- Latitude/longitude

SAP Lumira, discovery edition comes with an internal database of location information that contains countries, regions, sub-regions, and cities values plus their latitude and longitude coordinates. This can be used to create hierarchies by names. For the second type of geographic hierarchy, your dataset needs to contain latitude and longitude coordinates.

In the following sections, we explain how to create a geographic hierarchy to be able to enrich your SAP Lumira stories with geo maps.

Names

The first of the two options to create a geographic hierarchy is **By Names**. Please follow these steps:

1. To create a geographic hierarchy using names, right-click on a dimension or column that contains geographic information, in our example **CITY**, and select **Hierarchy · Geo · By Names** (Figure 8.6).

Figure 8.6 Create Geographic Hierarchy By Names

2. The **Geographic Hierarchy** dialog is displayed (Figure 8.7). Select which dimensions in your dataset you want to use to populate the geographic hierarchy. By default, the available dimensions that can be selected are limited to those detected by SAP Lumira, discovery edition as **Geo Dimensions**. You can change this by selecting **All Dimensions** next to **Show**.

3. In our example we have additional geographic information available for the **Country** and **Region**. If a geographic level is not available in your dataset, leave it to **None** (Figure 8.8). Click on **Confirm** to continue.

Figure 8.7 Geographic Hierarchy By Names Dialog

Figure 8.8 Select Available Geographic Dimensions from Dataset

4. The final step before creating the geographic hierarchy by names is to validate the analyzed values. As shown in Figure 8.9, an overview is presented of all values, which are **Solved** (locations mapped exactly, marked with green), **Unsolved** (locations with more than one possible match, marked with yellow), or **Not Found** (locations not found in the database, marked with red). To improve the reconciliation, there are three possibilities:

- Edit the original values in your dataset and try to match them with the values in the SAP Lumira, discovery edition database. This can be quite cumbersome because this database is not accessible. It can therefore be hard to create an exact match.

- Browse through the list of **Unsolved** items and select one of the possible matches. A probability is displayed that provides an indication if the displayed values indeed match the value in your dataset.

- Decide to not use additional geo dimensions from your dataset but leave them to **None** and use those from the SAP Lumira, discovery edition database. This might lead to a higher percentage of **Solved** values.

Please be aware that the SAP Lumira, discovery edition database containing geographic information is limited.

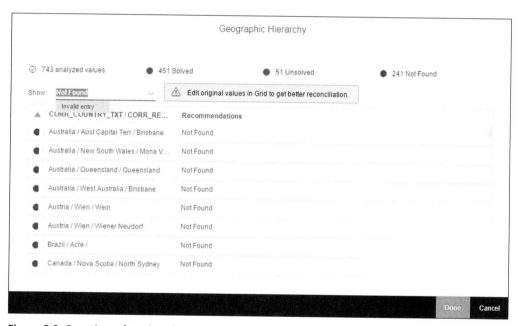

Figure 8.9 Overview of Analyzed Values

5. After selecting a match for **Unsolved** items, click **Done** to create the geographic hierarchy by names (Figure 8.10).

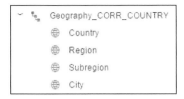

Figure 8.10 Geographic Hierarchy By Names

6. Switch to the data view to look at the additional objects created in your dataset (Figure 8.11).

Country	Region	Subregion	City
<unresolved>	<unresolved>	<unresolved>	<unresolved>
Germany	Saxony	Leipzig (Stadt)	Leipzig
India	Uttar Pradesh	Ghaziabad	Ghaziabad
Germany	Hesse	Cassel	Cassel
<unresolved>	<unresolved>	<unresolved>	<unresolved>
<unresolved>	<unresolved>	<unresolved>	<unresolved>
Germany	North-Rhine-Westphalia	Wuppertal	Wuppertal
<unresolved>	<unresolved>	<unresolved>	<unresolved>
India	West Bengal	Kolkata	Kolkata

Figure 8.11 Additional Geographic Hierarchy By Names Dimensions

Latitude/Longitude

A second option to create a geographic hierarchy is one based on latitude/longitude information. The main difference is that this allows a mapping of all possible locations, in addition to the available values in the geographic information database used by SAP Lumira, discovery edition. A prerequisite however is that you need to have latitude and longitude information present in your dataset.

In the following example, we create a geographic hierarchy by latitude/longitude based on a **county** dimension:

1. Right-click on a dimension or column that contains geographic information and select **Hierarchy · Geo · By Latitude / Longitude** (Figure 8.12).

2. The **Geographic Hierarchy** dialog is displayed (Figure 8.13). Here you need to specify which dimension contains the latitude and longitude information. Please note

that only numeric dimensions are available. If your latitude and longitude dimensions are not numeric, you need to convert them to the numeric data type first.

Figure 8.12 Create Geographic Hierarchy by Latitude/Longitude

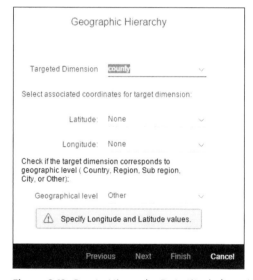

Figure 8.13 Create Hierarchy By Latitude/Longitude Dialog

3. If the **Targeted Dimension**, in our example **county**, corresponds to a geographic level (**Country**, **Region**, **Sub-Region**, or **City**), you can select this. If this is not the case, select **Other**. Click **Next** to continue.

4. Next, decide which **Parent Levels** you want to generate and how to name each generated level (Figure 8.14). Click **Finish** to create the geographic hierarchy by latitude/longitude.

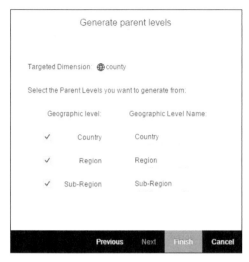

Figure 8.14 Generate Parent Levels Dialog

5. On the **Dataset** tab of the side pane, the geographic hierarchy by latitude/longitude including the generated parent levels are now available for use in geo charts (Figure 8.15).

Figure 8.15 Geographic Hierarchy by Latitude/Longitude

6. Switch to the data view to take a look at the parent level objects and values created in the dataset (Figure 8.16).

Country	Region	Sub-Region	county_LongLat
United States	Florida	Clay	CLAY COUNTY
United States	Florida	Clay	CLAY COUNTY
United States	Florida	Clay	CLAY COUNTY
United States	Florida	Clay	CLAY COUNTY
United States	Florida	Clay	CLAY COUNTY
United States	Florida	Clay	CLAY COUNTY

Figure 8.16 Additional Parent Level Data

In the next section, we focus on a different type of hierarchy: the date/time based hierarchy.

8.2.2   Date/Time Hierarchies

With date/time hierarchies you can view and analyze data at different date/time levels, by drilling up and down and rolling up the data.

To create a date/time based hierarchy, your dataset needs to contain at least one dimension that has a valid date or date/time format, for example: 26/07/2017 3:12:29 AM. If your dataset does not contain a single dimension that is formatted in a valid date or date/time format, you can use one or a combination of formulas, as described in Section 8.3.2 to create such a dimension first.

Please follow the next steps to define a date/time hierarchy based on the dimension **REGISTRATION_DATE**:

1. Right-click on a dimension of the data type date/time and select **Hierarchy • Date/ Time** (Figure 8.17).

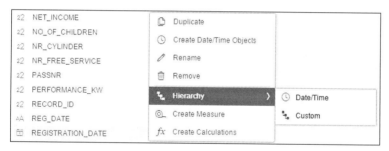

Figure 8.17 Create Date/Time Hierarchy

2. As a result, a date hierarchy is created (Figure 8.18), as our example is based on a dimension with only a date format. Please note that additional dimensions have been created which are now part of the dataset and can be used to roll up the data.

Figure 8.18 Date Hierarchy

3. Switch to the data view to look at the additional objects created in your dataset (Figure 8.19).

REGISTRATION_DATE	Year	Quarter	Month	Day
19-1-2012	2012	2012/Q1	2012/Q1/1	2012/Q1/1/19
19-6-2013	2013	2013/Q2	2013/Q2/6	2013/Q2/6/19
13-5-2013	2013	2013/Q2	2013/Q2/5	2013/Q2/5/13
6-10-2012	2012	2012/Q4	2012/Q4/10	2012/Q4/10/6
28-2-2010	2010	2010/Q1	2010/Q1/2	2010/Q1/2/28
4-1-2011	2011	2011/Q1	2011/Q1/1	2011/Q1/1/4
10-10-2011	2011	2011/Q4	2011/Q4/10	2011/Q4/10/10

Figure 8.19 Additional Date/Time Hierarchy Objects

8.2.3   Custom Hierarchies

The third and final type of hierarchy supported by SAP Lumira, discovery edition is a custom hierarchy. With this type of hierarchy, you can define your own levels based on the dimensions available in the dataset to drill down and filter.

In the following example, we explain how to create a custom hierarchy:

1. Right-click on one of the dimensions you want to include in the custom hierarchy and select **Hierarchy · Custom** (Figure 8.20).

Figure 8.20 Create a Custom Hierarchy

2. The **Create Hierarchy** dialog is displayed (Figure 8.21). Let's first define a name for the hierarchy.

3. Select the dimensions that need to be included in the custom hierarchy. Use the search bar to limit the number of dimensions displayed. Use the icons in the center and on the right side to add/remove dimensions and to change the order.

4. Click on **Create**.

5. After creating the custom hierarchy, you can rename the dimensions to give the different levels a more meaningful description (Figure 8.22).

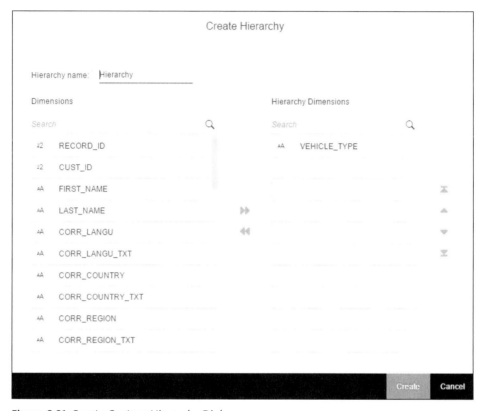

Figure 8.21 Create Custom Hierarchy Dialog

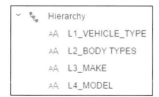

Figure 8.22 Custom Hierarchy

Now that you have learned all about creating different types of hierarchies, we will focus on discussing how to create calculated objects.

8.3   Calculated Objects

SAP Lumira, discovery edition has a formula language that can be used to create calculated dimensions and measures and create custom objects.

A calculated object can be created in multiple ways. One of the easiest ways is to use the **Create Calculations** icon in the main toolbar or to right-click on a dimension or measure in the side panel and select **Create Calculations** from the context menu.

In the sections ahead, we discuss the different types of calculated objects and the formulas available that allow you to create complex calculations, data conversions, etc.

8.3.1   Calculated Dimension

To create a calculated dimension, follow these steps:

1. Click on the **Create Calculations** icon *fx* in the main toolbar.

2. The **Calculations** dialog, as shown in Figure 8.23, is displayed. Select whether you want to create **Dimensions** or **Measures** using the radio buttons.

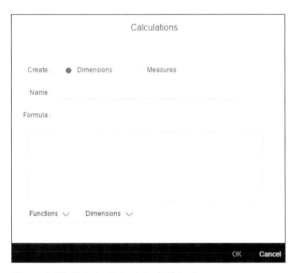

Figure 8.23 Create Calculated Object

3. Provide a **Name** for the calculated object.

4. The next step is to define which formula to use to create the calculated object. In this example, we want to create a calculated dimension that indicates for which customers their warranty period will expire in 30 days.

5. Click on **Functions** and select **AddDayToDate** from the **Date and Time** category of available functions. When you select a function, the syntax, a short description, and an example are shown on the right side. **Dimensions** displays the list of dimensions that can be used to construct the formula.

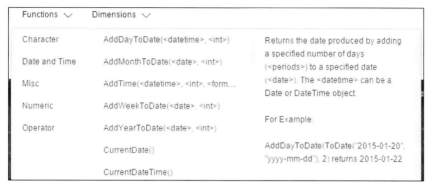

Figure 8.24 Select Functions

6. Because the dimension **WARRANTY_END_DATE** in this example is not in data/ time format, you'll use an additional formula (ToDate) to convert the data type and define the syntax without creating an additional dimension first.

7. Construct or enter the following syntax in the formula text area (Figure 8.25): AddDayToDate(ToDate({WARRANTY_END_DATE},"yyyy-mm-dd"),-30).

Figure 8.25 Formula to Create Calculated Dimension

8. Click **OK** to create the calculated dimension. As shown in Figure 8.26, the calculated dimension displays the date minus 30 days.

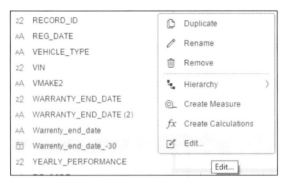

Warrenty_end_date	Warrenty_end_date_-30
2012-08-18	19-7-2012
2012-08-19	20-7-2012
2012-08-20	21-7-2012
2012-08-21	22-7-2012
2012-08-22	23-7-2012
2012-08-23	24-7-2012
2012-08-24	25-7-2012
2012-08-25	26-7-2012
2012-08-26	27-7-2012
2012-08-27	28-7-2012
2012-08-28	29-7-2012

Figure 8.26 Result of Calculated Dimension

If you need to edit the calculated dimension, right-click on the dimension and select **Edit** (Figure 8.27). A dialog will be displayed that allows changing the formula defined.

22 RECORD_ID	🗋 Duplicate
AA REG_DATE	✏ Rename
AA VEHICLE_TYPE	
22 VIN	🗑 Remove
AA VMAKE2	🐾 Hierarchy ⟩
22 WARRANTY_END_DATE	⊙_ Create Measure
AA WARRANTY_END_DATE (2)	
AA Warrenty_end_date	*fx* Create Calculations
🛱 Warrenty_end_date_-30	☑ Edit...
22 YEARLY_PERFORMANCE	

Edit...

Figure 8.27 Edit Calculated Object

Calculated Measure

A calculated measure is constructed similar to a calculated dimension. The only difference is that the result returned is numeric. An aggregation type can be applied after creating a calculated measure.

8.3.2   Formula Syntax and Functions

To construct a formula that can be successfully parsed, you need to follow a couple of basic rules:

- Objects can be referenced but must be enclosed with { }, for example {Customer}.
- Values can be expressed directly where strings should be enclosed with " and ", for example "this syntax is ok".
- Numeric values should be expressed as numbers, for example 75.6.
- Standard operations and logical expressions can be used, like if, then, else, +, *, /, etc.

If the syntax is not correct, SAP Lumira, discovery edition will display an error message and you will not be able to create, or save changes to, a calculated object. Figure 8.28 displays an example of an error message with some description regarding which part of the syntax is responsible for the error.

> ⓘ Function ToDate uses an invalid date format 'yyyy-mm-' for parameter format. Try rewriting the formula.

Figure 8.28 Example of Syntax Error

Table 8.1 provides an overview of all functions available to manipulate character strings.

Function	Definition
Concatenate(str1, str2)	Concatenates two strings into a single string. Example: Concatenate("New", "York") returns NewYork.
ExceptFirstWord(str, sep)	Returns a copy of a string, with the first word removed. Example: ExceptFirstWord("Hello world", " ") returns Hello.
ExceptLastWord(str, sep)	Returns a copy of a string, with the last word removed. Example: ExceptLastWord("Hello world", " ") returns world.

Table 8.1 Overview of Character Functions

Function	Definition
FirstWord(str, sep)	Returns the first word of a string. Example: FirstWord(Lumira Discovery, " ") returns Lumira.
LastWord(str, sep)	Returns the last word of a string. Example: LastWord(Lumira Discovery, " ") returns Discovery.
Length(str)	Returns the length of a string. Example: Length("How long") returns 8.
LowerCase(str)	Returns a copy of a string, with all characters converted to lowercase. Example: LowerCase("LOWER CASE") returns lower case.
Lpad(str, length, pad)	Returns a copy of a string, padded with leading characters to the specified total length. Example: Lpad("Incomplete string", 20, "#") returns ###Incomplete string.
Replace(str, target, replacement)	Returns a string, with all occurrences of a specified string replaced with another specified string. Example: Replace("Waldorf", "Wal", "Wall") returns Walldorf.
Rpad(str, length, pad)	Returns a copy of a string, padded with trailing characters to the specified total length. Example: Rpad("Incomplete string", 20, "#") returns Incomplete string###.
SubString(str, start, length)	Returns a substring (of a specific length) of a string. Example: SubString("Lumira", 3, 2) returns mi.
SubString(str, start)	Returns a substring of a string. Example: SubString("Lumira", 2) returns mira.

Table 8.1 Overview of Character Functions (Cont.)

Function	Definition
Trim(str, toTrim)	Returns a copy of the string, with the leading and trailing repetitions of a character removed. This function is case-sensitive. Example: Trim("Hello", "H") returns ello.
TrimLeft(str, toTrim)	Returns a copy of the string, with the leading repetitions of a character removed. This function is case-sensitive. Example: TrimLeft("Netherlands", "r") returns lands.
TrimRight(str, toTrim)	Returns a copy of a string, with trailing repetitions of a character removed. This function is case-sensitive. Example: TrimRight("Martijn", "n") returns Martij.
UpperCase(str)	Returns a copy of a string, with all characters converted to uppercase. Example: UpperCase("Haler") returns "HALER".

Table 8.1 Overview of Character Functions (Cont.)

Table 8.2 provides an overview of all functions available that return date and time data.

Function	Definition
AddDayToDate(date,periods)	Returns date by adding a specified number of days (periods) to a specified date (date). Example: AddDayToDate(ToDateTime("2017-11-26 13:29:48", "yyyy-mm-dd hh:mi:ss"), 2) returns 2017-11-28 1:29:48 PM.
AddMonthToDate(#date#, periods)	Returns date by adding a specified number of months to a specified date. Example: AddMonthToDate(#2017-01-01#,1) returns 2017-02-01.

Table 8.2 Overview of Data and Time Functions

Function	Definition
AddTime(datetime, numberOfUnits,format)	Returns time by adding a specified amount of time (number of units) to a specified time (datetime), in the specified format (format). Example: AddTime(ToDateTime("2017-01-20 23:59:45", "yyyy-mm-dd hh:mi:ss"),1, "hh") returns 2017-01-21 00:59:45 AM.
AddWeekToDate(#date#, periods)	Returns date by adding a specified number of weeks to a specified date. Example: AddWeekToDate(#2017-01-01#,1) returns 2017-01-08.
AddYearToDate(#date#, periods)	Returns date by adding a specified number of years to a specified date. Example: AddYearToDate(#2017-01-01#,-1) returns 2016-01-01.
CurrentDate()	Returns the current date as a Date object. Example: CurrentDate() returns the current date: 2017-11-28.
CurrentDateTime()	Returns the current DateTime (combined date and time). Example: CurrentDateTime() returns the current DateTime: 2017-11-28 3:34:23 PM.
CurrentTime()	Returns the current time as a Time object. Example: CurrentTime() returns the current time: 3:34:23 PM.
DateDiffInDays(#start#, #end#)	Returns the number of days between two dates. Example: DateDiffInDays(#2017-03-23#, #2017-01-30#) returns -52.

Table 8.2 Overview of Data and Time Functions (Cont.)

Function	Definition
DateDiffInMonths(#start#, #end#)	Returns the number of months between two specified dates. Example: DateDiffInMonths(#2017-02-01#, #2016-01-01#) returns -13.
Day(#date#)	Returns the day of the month as a number from 1 to 31. Example: Day(#2017-03-25#) returns 25.
DayOfWeek(#date#)	Returns the day of the week as a number from 1 (Sunday) to 7 (Saturday). Example: DayOfWeek(#2017-06-18#) returns 7.
DayOfYear(#date#)	Returns the day of the year as a number. Example: DayOfYear(#2017-07-26#) returns 207.
Hour(time)	For a specified time (time), returns the hour. Example: Hour(ToTime("21:19:45","hh:mi:ss")) returns 21.
LastDayOfMonth(#date#)	Returns the date produced by computing the last day of the month of a specified date. Example: LastDayOfMonth(#2017-06-14#) returns 2017-06-30.
LastDayOfWeek(#date#)	Returns the date produced by computing the last day of the week of a specified date. Example: LastDayOfWeek(#2017-04-18#) returns 2017-04-23.
MakeDate(year,month,day)	Returns the date that is built from a specified year, month, and day. Example: MakeDate(2017,7,7) returns 2017-07-07.

Table 8.2 Overview of Data and Time Functions (Cont.)

Function	Definition
MakeDateTime(date,time)	Returns the DateTime (combined date and time) that corresponds to the specified date and time. Example: MakeDateTime(MakeDate(2017,6,11), MakeTime(10,25,58)) returns 2017-06-11 10:25:58 AM.
MakeTime(hour,minute, second)	Returns the time that corresponds to the specified hours, minutes, and seconds. Example: MakeTime(9,13,24) returns 9:13:24 AM.
Minute(time)	For a specified time (time), returns the minute. Example: Minute(ToTime("9:13:24 ", "hh:mi:ss")) returns 13.
Month(#date#)	Returns month of the year as a number from 1 to 12. Example: Month(#2017-02-24#) returns 2.
Quarter(#date#)	Returns the number that represents the quarter of a specified date. Example: Quarter(#2017-08-17#) returns 3.
Second(time)	For a specified time (time), returns the seconds. Example: Second(ToTime("16:54:18", "hh:mi:ss")) returns 18.
TimeDiff(start,end,format)	Returns the amount of time between a specified start time (start) and a specified end time (end), in the specified format (format). Example: TimeDiff(MakeDateTime(Make-Date(2017,1,12), MakeTime(11,12,34)), MakeDateTime(MakeDate(2017,2,15), MakeTime(5,39,11)),"ss") returns 2917597.

Table 8.2 Overview of Data and Time Functions (Cont.)

Function	Definition
ToDate(string, format)	Converts input string to a date in a specified format, when the dates in a column of an original data source are in string format. Example: ToDate(Obj, 'yyyy/dd/MM') converts a string in the format yyyy/dd/MM to a date.
ToDateTime(datetime, format)	Converts specified input string (datetime) in the specified format (format) to a DateTime (combined date and time). Example: ToDateTime("2016-05-17 10:29:25", "yyyy-mm-dd hh:mi:ss") returns 2016-05-17 10:29:25 AM.
ToTime(time, format)	Converts a specified input string (time) in the specified format (format) to a Time object. Example: ToTime("23:12:27", "hh:mi:ss") returns 11:12:27 PM.
Week(#date#)	Returns the number that represents the week of a specified date. Example: Week(#2017-09-23#) returns 38.
Year(#date#)	Returns the year of a specified date. Example: Year(#2015-03-23#) returns 2015.

Table 8.2 Overview of Data and Time Functions (Cont.)

Table 8.3 provides an overview of all expression functions available that can be used to create custom calculations on aggregated values.

Function	Definition
<calculation> For <context>	Returns context for a calculation. Example: RunningSum({Costs}) For [{Country}, {Product}] returns the running sum of Costs and resets it at Country and Product level.

Table 8.3 Overview of Expression Functions

Function	Definition
`<calculation> ForAllExcept <context>`	Returns everything else in the dimensions as the context for a calculation. Example: `Previous({Sales}) ForAllExcept [{Customer}, {Product}]` returns previous value of `Sales`, resetting at all dimensions other than `Customer` and `Product`.
`CumulativeDistribution(obj, bool)`	Returns cumulative distribution of a measure object (obj). Parameter (bool) is used to set relative rank order: (true) is ascending order and (false) is descending order. Example: `CumulativeDistribution({Sales}, false)` returns the relative rank of the current sales value.
`DenseRank(obj, bool)`	Returns density rank of a measure. The second parameter is a Boolean value used to set the dense rank order: true ranks the number from high to low and false ranks the number from low to high. Example: `DenseRank({Sales}, true)` returns `Sales` in a ranked manner.
`First(obj)`	Returns first value of a measure. Example: `First(Sales)` returns the first value of `Sales` in the result set.
`Index()`	Returns row number of the current row in the result set.
`Key(obj)`	Returns key value of a dimension member. Example: `Key(Month)` returns the key value of the `Month` level in a time hierarchy.
`Last(obj)`	Returns last value of a measure. Example: `Last(Sales)` returns the last value of `Sales` in the result set.
`Median(obj)`	Returns median of a measure.

Table 8.3 Overview of Expression Functions (Cont.)

Function	Definition
MovingAverage(obj, int, int, bool)	The moving average returns the sum of the previous n values and the current value divided by n+1.
	Example: MovingAverage([Cost],1,0,true) For [Customer]). The moving average returns the sum of the previous Cost value and the current value divided by 2. The For operator is used to reset the moving average at the Customer level.
MovingSum(obj, int, int, bool)	Returns moving sum of a measure.
Next(obj, int)	Returns next value of a measure.
NthValue(obj, int)	Returns nth value of a measure.
	Example: NthValue({Sales}, 2) returns the Sales value at the second row of the result set (counting from 1); returns null if there is no such row.
PercentRank(obj, bool)	Returns percent rank of a measure.
	bool; true is ascending order, false is descending order.
Previous(obj, int)	Returns previous value of a measure.
Rank(obj, bool)	Returns rank value of a measure.
	bool; true ranks from high to low, and false ranks from low to high.
RunningAverage([Sales], true) for [Country])	Returns running average of a measure. The parameter true excludes empty sales values.
	Example: RunningAverage([Sales], true) for [Customer]) returns running average of Sales and resets it at the Customer level.
RunningCount([Sales], true)	Returns running count of a measure.
	Example: RunningCount([Sales] for [Country]) returns running count of sales and resets it at the country level.

Table 8.3 Overview of Expression Functions (Cont.)

Function	Definition
RunningMax([Sales])	Returns the running maximum of a measure. Example: RunningMax([Sales] for [Country]) returns running maximum of Sales and resets it at the Country level.
RunningMin([Sales])	Returns the running minimum of a measure. Example: RunningMin([Sales] for [Country]) returns running minimum of Sales and resets it at the Country level.
RunningSum([Sales])	Returns the running sum of a measure. Example: RunningSum([Sales] for [Country]) returns running sum of Sales and resets it at the Country level.
Value(obj)	Returns value of a dimension member.
Variance(obj)	Returns variance value of a member.

Table 8.3 Overview of Expression Functions (Cont.)

Table 8.4 provides an overview of the available miscellaneous functions.

Function	Definition
Contain(whereStr, whatStr)	Returns occurrences of a string within another string. The search is not case-sensitive. Example: Contain("Lumira, discovery edition", "CoV") returns true.
GroupValues(column, ListOfValues, newValue)	Groups a list of values. Example: GroupValues(CountryColumn, ["Netherlands", "Germany", "Belgium"], "My Countries") returns "My Countries" when the CountryColumn column contains "Netherlands", "Germany", or "Belgium".

Table 8.4 Overview of Miscellaneous Functions

Function	Definition
`if<cond> then <alt1> else <alt2>`	Chooses between two alternatives, based on a Boolean condition. The second alternative is optional and evaluates to null when missing. Example: `if {AGE}=40 then 1 else 0` returns `1` for each row where `{AGE}=40`.
`IsNotNull(obj)`	Returns a Boolean value that indicates whether the object contains a null value. If a field contains a null value, the function returns `false`. Otherwise it returns `true`.
`IsNull(obj)`	Returns a Boolean value that indicates whether the object contains a null value. If a field contains a null value, the function returns `true`. Otherwise it returns `false`.
`ToNumber(param)`	Converts any type of parameter to a numeric value. Numbers are truncated to zero decimal places.
`ToText(num, digits)`	Converts a specified number to a string. The number is truncated to the specified number of decimal places. Example: `ToText(10.4519, 1)` returns `10.4`.
`ToText(param)`	Converts a parameter to a string.

Table 8.4 Overview of Miscellaneous Functions (Cont.)

Table 8.5 provides an overview of the available numeric functions.

Function	Definition
`Abs(num)`	Returns the absolute value of a number. Example: `Abs(-64)` returns `64`.
`Ceil(num)`	Returns the smallest integer that is greater than or equal to a specified number. Example: `Ceil(89.4)` returns `90`.

Table 8.5 Overview of Numeric Functions

Function	Definition
Floor(num)	Returns the largest integer that is not greater than a specified number. Example: Floor(89.4) returns 89.
Log(num)	Returns the natural logarithm of a specified number. Example: Log(100) returns 4.605.
Log10(num)	Returns the base 10 logarithm of a specified number. Example: Log10(100) returns 2.
Mod(num, divisor)	Returns the remainder of the division of a number by another number. Example: Mod(22,3) returns 1.
Power(num, exponent)	Raises a number to a power. Example: Power(3,3) returns 27.
Round(num, digits)	Returns a numeric value, rounded to a specified number of decimal places. Example: Round(12.63, 1) returns 12.6.
Sign(num)	Returns -1 if a specified number is negative, 0 if the specified number is zero, or +1 if the specified number is positive. Example: Sign(-1) returns -1.
Truncate(num, digits)	Returns a numeric value, truncated at a specified number of decimal places. Example: Truncate(33.457, 1) returns 33.400.

Table 8.5 Overview of Numeric Functions (Cont.)

Table 8.6 provides an overview of the available operator functions. Operator functions include logical and other functions that return true or false.

Function	Definition
And operator `<left> and <right>`	Returns the logical conjunction of its Boolean inputs. This function returns `false`: true and false.
Or operator `<left> or <right>`	Returns the logical disjunction of its Boolean inputs. This function returns `true`: true or false.
Like pattern `<matchExpr> like <pattern>`	Determines whether a character string matches a specified pattern. The search is not case-sensitive.
In List `<testExpr> in <candidate-List>`	Determines whether a first input matches a value in a second input list. Example: 13 in [2, 5, 19] returns `false`.
Not operator `not<bool>`	Negates a Boolean input. Example: `not true` returns `false`.

Table 8.6 Overview of Operator Functions

In the next section, we focus on the additional data actions that are available in the grid view, which is part of the **DataView** mode. The object actions described in this section are available from both the data view and the design view.

8.4   Data Actions

In addition to the object actions described in Section 8.1, SAP Lumira, discovery edition offers a number of data actions that can be used to manipulate the values in the dataset. This section is limited to the additional functions that are not available from the side panel.

> **Data Actions for Live Data Sources**
>
> The data actions described in this section can only be accessed through the grid view in the **DataView** mode. This mode is not available when using live data sources and hence these actions can't be performed. If any of the actions below are necessary in your use case, please switch from a live to an import scenario.

Let's switch to the grid in the **DataView** mode and take a look at the additional data actions that are applicable for any data type. Right-click on the column header to display the context menu:

- **Sort**
  Allows sorting the values in a particular column in ascending or descending order.

- **Filter**
  Displays the filter dialog that can be used to define a filter. Any filters applied to the dataset in the data view are applied to all visualizations based on this dataset. More detail on filtering can be found in Chapter 16.

- **Fit to content**
  Easy way to adjust the width of each column to the length of the value.

- **Group by**
  Allows the creation of groups that contain one or multiple values either through **Selection** or using the **Range** option. Using the **Group By** action creates a new dimension where each value assigned to a group is displayed with the group name.

In the example in Figure 8.29, based on **Selection**, a new dimension called **Manufacturer_Continent** will be created, where for each continent one or multiple manufacturer values are added. Any remaining dimension values not assigned to a group are displayed as **Others**. However, the description for this group can be changed at the bottom to any string.

A second option to create one or multiple groups is to use the **Group By Range** option. The dialog, **Create Groups By Range**, displays the minimum and maximum value present in the dataset. Similar to creating groups by selection, you have to enter a name for the new dimension and determine the number of intervals and the range.

In the example in Figure 8.30, we create eight **AGE** groups based on the dimension **Ag** and named it "AGE Intervals". SAP Lumira, discovery edition proposes the interval based on the available values.

Figure 8.29 Group By Selection

Figure 8.30 Create Groups By Range

The following data actions are only applicable for objects of the data type **string** (or **text**):

- **Split**

  Enables you to split the values in a column based on a **<Space>** or any other character (Figure 8.31). As a result of clicking **Apply**, two additional columns are created that contain the split values.

Figure 8.31 Split Based on <Space> or Other Characters

- **Fill**

  Allows you to add characters at the **Beginning** or **End** of a string up to the given length (Figure 8.32).

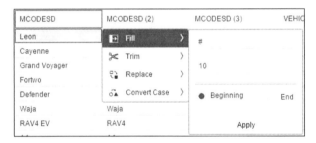

Figure 8.32 Fill Data Action

- **Trim**

  Using **trim** allows you to remove **<Space>** or any **Other Character** at the **Beginning** or **End** of the value in a column (Figure 8.33).

Figure 8.33 Trim Values at the Beginning or End Based on a Character

- **Replace**

  The **Replace** options replaces a given string with the second value entered (Figure 8.34).

Figure 8.34 Replace Value

- **Convert Case**

  This option allows you to convert values to upper- or lowercase.

The last four data actions can also be applied when selecting one or multiple values instead of the column header (Figure 8.35).

Figure 8.35 Available Data Action When Selecting One or Multiple Values

In the next sections, you learn how SAP Lumira, discovery edition enables working with multiple datasets in a single SAP Lumira document through the concepts of merging and appending.

8.5   Merging Datasets

SAP Lumira, discovery edition allows you to work with multiple datasets in a single SAP Lumira document. However, to combine data from different datasets into a single visualization, these datasets have to be merged (or linked, see Chapter 18) into a single dataset using the selected join operator. In order to merge the datasets, the following prerequisites have to be taken into account:

- The merging dataset must have a key dimension. Each dimension that qualifies is indicated by the word **Key**.
- Only dimensions that have a similar data type can be merged.
- The SAP Lumira document requires a minimum of two datasets. If that is not the case, an information dialog is displayed with the following text: **This operation requires two datasets**.

> **Live Data Limitation**
>
> Merging datasets is not supported for live datasets. If you need to combine dimensions from two live datasets into a single visualization, SAP Lumira offers the concept of linking, as described in Chapter 18.

Let's look how we can merge two datasets by following the next steps:

1. Click on the menu bar and select **Data · Combine · Merge** or use the following shortcut key: Ctrl + Shift + M (Figure 8.36). Another option is to click on the **Merge Datasets** icon ⊞ available in the toolbar.

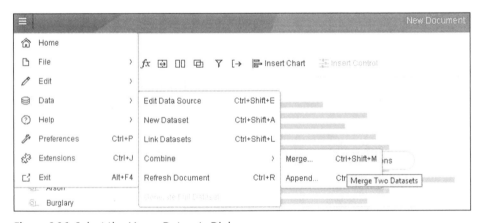

Figure 8.36 Select the Merge Datasets Dialog

2. The **Merge Datasets** dialog (Figure 8.37) is displayed. By using the dropdown boxes in the left and right pane, you can select which two datasets, available in the SAP Lumira document, need to be merged.

Please keep in mind while selecting the datasets that, based on the selected join operator, the selected dimension(s) in the second (right pane) dataset are matched to key dimensions in the original (left pane) dataset.

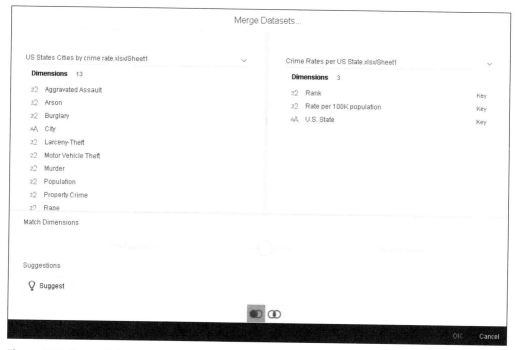

Figure 8.37 Merge Datasets

Before selecting any dimensions, let's briefly discuss the two types of join operators available when merging datasets:

– **Left Outer Join** ◉: All rows from the dataset selected in the left pane are preserved when performing the merge operation. If no matching value is found in the dataset selected in the right pane, NULL values are added for those merged dimensions.

– **Inner Join** ◎ : Only the rows that have a matching key dimension value in both datasets are preserved. Rows from both datasets that don't have a matching key dimension value are lost.

3. Based on your requirements for merging the two datasets selected, please select the join operator at the bottom of the **Merge Datasets** dialog.

4. The next step is to select the matching dimensions in the left and right pane. The selected dimensions will be listed in the **Match Dimensions** area. If the two dimensions selected are compatible, the **OK** button will be enabled (Figure 8.38). You can simply remove or adjust the dimensions selected by hovering across one of them in the upper right-corner. An **X** is displayed that deletes the dimension from the **Match Dimensions** area.

Suggest Matching Dimensions

If you have no understanding of the datasets yet, SAP Lumira, discovery edition can provide you with a suggestion as to which dimensions in both datasets could be a match. To use this option, please click on **Suggest**.

Figure 8.38 Selected Dimensions

An information bar displayed at the bottom indicates which percentage of matching columns are compatible. In our example, the percentage is 97% caused by the fact that two values in the original dataset for the dimension **State** are not present in the second dataset. Based on the **Left Outer Join** operator selected, these rows are kept in the original dataset and the merged dimensions are displayed as **NULL**.

If the selected dimensions do not constitute a unique key, you'll receive the following error message: **The selected lookup columns do not constitute a unique key**. This means you have to select a different set of dimensions or adjust your original data source so it contains at least one dimension with a unique value for each row of data.

5. Click **OK** to perform the merge operation. The result of the merge operation is that the dimensions in the second dataset (right pane) are now available as part of the first dataset (left pane) and can be combined in a single visualization.

It's possible to perform a merge operation based on multiple selected dimensions from both datasets. This scenario is called a *composite merge*.

Restoring the original dataset can be done using the undo option, or just remove the merged dataset and acquire the original dataset again.

8.6   Appending Data

In addition to merging datasets, SAP Lumira, discovery edition also provides capabilities to append datasets. Appending data is not based on a join between two datasets, but on a union that combines two datasets by adding data to the bottom of the original dataset. This scenario can be very useful when you have periodic datasets that you want to combine.

To be able to append datasets, the following prerequisites need to be met:

- The SAP Lumira document contains at least two datasets.
- Both datasets have columns that contain compatible data types.
- The SAP Lumira document requires a minimum of two datasets. If that is not the case an information dialog is displayed with the following text: **This operation requires two datasets**.

The following steps explain how to append datasets:

1. Click on the menu bar and select **Data** · **Combine** · **APPEND** or use the following shortcut key: ⌈Ctrl⌉+⌈Shift⌉+⌈P⌉ (Figure 8.39). Another option is to click on the **Append Datasets** icon ▯▯ available in the toolbar.

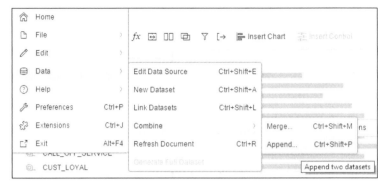

Figure 8.39 Append Two Datasets

2. The **Append Data** dialog (Figure 8.40) is displayed. On the left side you select the dataset to which you want to append the data in the dataset on the right side. For instance, you want to add **2017** data (right side) to an original dataset (left side) with **2016** data.

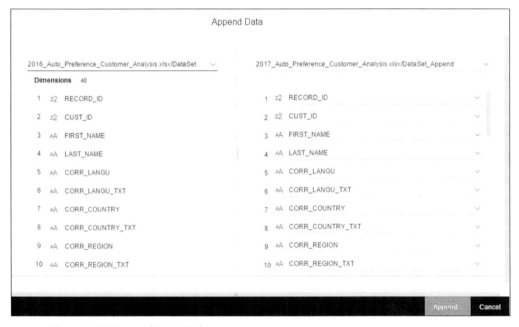

Figure 8.40 Append Data Dialog

Columns are mapped (based on the column name) in order from 1 to *n*, and by selecting a column name you can change the column for each position. If the dataset that contains the rows that you want to append to the original dataset has a different order, you can still map each column correctly. Furthermore, if the column name is different, you can still append the data as long as the data type is consistent. If this is not the case, an error message will appear, indicating that the **Union Cannot Happen** (Figure 8.41).

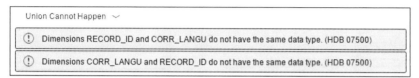

Figure 8.41 Union Cannot Happen

3. Click on **Append**. All rows from the lookup dataset will be added to the original dataset, based on the mapping. The combined dataset retains the column names from the original dataset.

If you want to restore the original dataset, you can undo the append operation using the undo option, or remove the combined dataset and acquire the original dataset again.

8.7   Configuring Auto-Enrichment

SAP Lumira, discovery edition is able to auto-enrich your imported dataset and create objects with a certain data type based on rules. To ensure that objects, based on the column header, are created with unwanted data types, you can maintain these rules manually.

For each installed version of SAP Lumira, discovery edition the enrichment file is created and can be found in your Windows personal folder (Figure 8.42); for example: *C:/ users/<user>/.sapvi2.*

Whenever you create a rule or make a change to the file, these are not migrated or copied when a new version of SAP Lumira, discovery edition is installed.

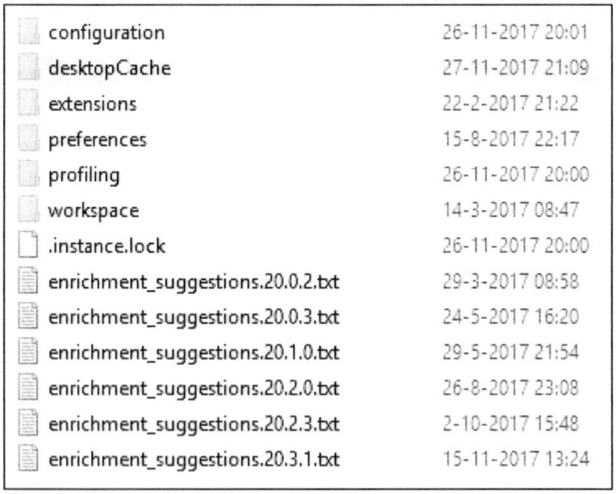

Figure 8.42 Available Enrichment Files

The rules defined in the enrichment file basically define what should *not* happen. An example of one of the suggestion rules is displayed in Listing 8.1. This means that any column with key in the header should not be created as a Measure and Time data type.

```
{
    "objectName":" (?i).*key.* ",
    "dataTypes":["integer", "biginteger", "double"],
    "enrichment":"MEASURE",
    "rule":"hide"
},
{
    "objectName":" (?i).*key.* ",
    "dataTypes":["integer", "biginteger", "double"],
    "enrichment":"TIME",
    "rule":"hide"
},
```

Listing 8.1 Suggestion Rules

The enrichment file is written in JavaScript Object Notation (JSON), which is comparable to, for example, XML. By using an online syntax checker or JSON editor, you can easily ensure that the definition is valid by parsing the code.

The JSON attributes are defined in Table 8.7.

JSON Attribute	Description
objectName	The name of an expression that can be matched to the column header of the object.
dataType	The data type or types that are associated with the column. Possible types include the following: ■ Integer ■ Biginteger ■ String ■ Date ■ Boolean You can specify none or all types. If none is specified, all types are considered.
enrichment	This specifies the type of enrichment. You can specify the following: ■ Measure ■ Time ■ Geo Selecting one of these means that you are excluding the object from enrichment.
Rule	The only supported value is Hide, meaning that the enrichment will not be applied.

Table 8.7 Auto-Configuration Rules

Auto-configuration adjustments may not be something that you will need to use very often. However, if there are some common datasets that you are using and you do not want to manually remove the default enrichments, then it can be of value.

8.8   Summary

With data manipulation actions, it's possible to clean your dataset, create objects, define hierarchies, etc. These actions, however, are only available when importing data into the SAP Lumira document.

Now that you have fully prepared your dataset(s), we show you how you can create different types of visualizations in the next chapters.

PART III

Data Visualization and Stories

Chapter 9

Chart Creation

After bringing in and manipulating the data, it is time to start visualizing. In this chapter, we look at how to set up charts in SAP Lumira, discovery edition.

It is finally time to start making some visualization out of all that (raw) data that we brought into SAP Lumira, discovery edition. In this chapter, we discuss the various ways to create charts with SAP Lumira, discovery edition.

First, we look at the options that the SAP Lumira, discovery edition canvas brings you to quickly set up a chart. Next, we dive into the Chart Builder to explore the more detailed approach for creating and managing charts. We also touch base on the formatting options for visualizations. Finally, we enhance the charts with reference lines and conditional formatting.

9.1   Chart Canvas

The easiest and quickest way to create a new chart in SAP Lumira, discovery edition is by directly using the canvas. When you create a new story, by default one empty visualization is added to the upper-left corner of the canvas (Figure 9.1). You can add visualizations by either clicking the **Insert Chart** button in the menu bar or right-clicking on an empty area of the canvas and selecting **Insert Chart**.

Before you insert a new visualization, you have to choose the type of visualization (Figure 9.2). Don't worry if you are not exactly sure which one to pick; you can change this afterward. In Chapter 10 through Chapter 15, we discuss all these different chart types in detail.

Figure 9.1 Default Canvas

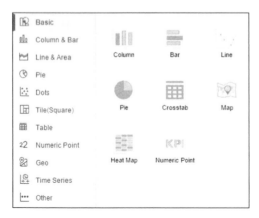

Figure 9.2 Visualization Picker

To set up the chart, start dragging and dropping the measures and dimensions from the **Dataset** menu in the side pane onto the visualization. You can drop the measures and dimensions on different portions of the visualization, depending on the visualization type. A checkmark will show up when you are allowed to drop an item on a certain area of the chart (Figure 9.3).

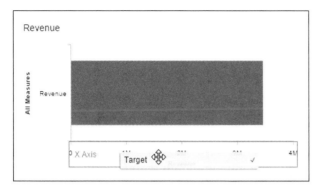

Figure 9.3 Drag and Drop a Measure Directly on a Visualization in the Canvas

An **X** will appear when it not possible to drop an item in a particular area (Figure 9.4).

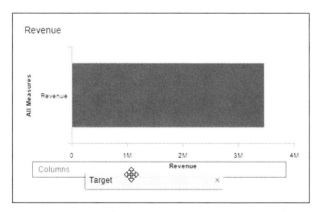

Figure 9.4 Drag and Drop a Measure on an Incompatible Position

For example, in case of a bar chart, you can drag a measure onto the chart area or the x-axis (the value axis) to display its total value as a bar. Dimensions can be dropped on the y-axis of the chart area to show the measure(s) by dimension member. Also, it is possible to drop a dimension on the **Rows** or **Columns** areas, which you can find at the far left, or lower area of the visualization. This will activate the **Trellis** option.

As you might have experienced already, building charts directly on the canvas can be quick, but there are also some limitations. After dropping a measure or dimension on the visualization, it is not possible to reposition this item anymore. The only option that you have is to use the **Undo** button to revert the action(s). Also, not all chart setup features can be applied, for example using the **Color** option.

The next section shows how you can access these more advanced features with the Chart Builder.

9.2   Chart Builder

With the Chart Builder, you can further customize a chart or visualization. In this section we first go through the features of the Chart Builder, secondly we look at the chart properties.

9.2.1   Using the Chart Builder

To activate the Chart Builder (Figure 9.5), you need to maximize the visualization on the canvas. You can quickly do this by clicking the visualization and choosing the first option (**Maximize**).

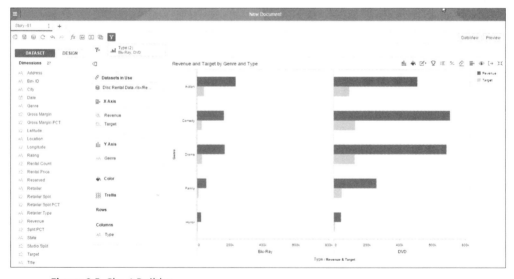

Figure 9.5 Chart Builder

As shown in Figure 9.5, the visualization now takes up about 70% of the screen, and an additional pane is introduced between the side pane and the visualization. This is called the feeding panel. Here all the different parts of the visualization are displayed, including the measures and dimensions that were already assigned. The properties displayed in the Feeding panel depend on the type of visualization. The example in Figure 9.5 shows the properties of a bar chart. Next to the **Datasets in Use**, you can use the **X-Axis**, **Y-Axis**, **Color**, and **Trellis** options. The details for each visualization type are discussed in the Chapters 10 through 15.

You can add or remove dimensions and measures using drag and drop between the **Dataset** tab in the side pane and the feeding panel. Also here the checkmarks and Xs show if a dimension or measure is allowed to be used in a certain part of the visualization. A different way to add dimensions or measures is to use the + icon in the upper-right corner of each section in the feeding panel. Here only applicable objects are shown (Figure 9.6).

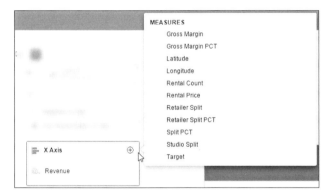

Figure 9.6 Adding a Measure in the Feeding Panel with the + Menu

A measure that is added to the feeding panel has two additional options (Figure 9.7). You can activate these options via the context menu of the measure (right-click):

- **Change Chart Type for Series**
  With this option, you can determine what type of visualization is used for the measure. This can be a line, bar, or stacked area chart. This way you can create combination charts.

- **Assign to Secondary Axis**
  This option introduces a secondary axis with its own scale and labels. This can be useful when you, for example, want to show nominal values and a percentage in the same chart.

Figure 9.7 Measure Options in the Feeding Panel

9.2.2   Chart Properties

The chart properties can be toggled from the context menu that you see after right-clicking on the chart (Figure 9.8). Depending on the visualization type, a different menu will be displayed. Be aware that these properties can also be adjusted from the preview mode. The following options are available:

- **Normal Stacking or 100% Stacking**
  This option is only available in stacked or area charts. With **Normal Stacking**, the absolute values of the measures are displayed. With **100% Stacking**, the values are presented as a percentage from the whole.

- **Horizontal or Vertical**

- **Show Title**
  Shows or hides the title of the chart. By default, the title is always shown. To change the text of the title, double-click the title and edit the text.

- **Show Legend**
  Shows or hides the legend at the side of the chart that shows a different color for each measure. By default, the legend is always shown.

- **Show Data Labels**
  Displays the value of each data point in the chart. By default, the data labels are hidden.

- **Use Measures as a Dimension**
  With this option, you can display and compare two or more measures in a series of charts, where each measure will become a dimension member. When adding this new dimension in the trellis, you can for example quickly set up different charts for each measure, rather than having all measures in a single chart (Figure 9.8).

- **Set Axis Scale...**

  With this option, you can switch to a fixed scale on a chart, by entering a bottom and top value (Figure 9.9). By default, the range of the axis scale is set as **Automatic**.

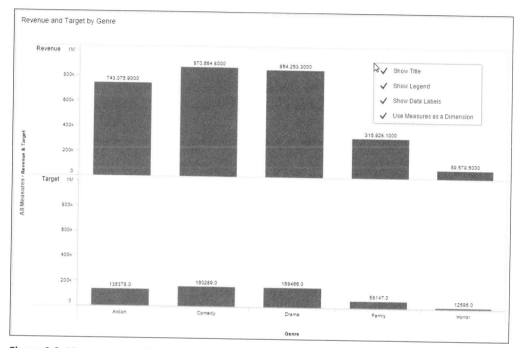

Figure 9.8 Measures as a Dimension

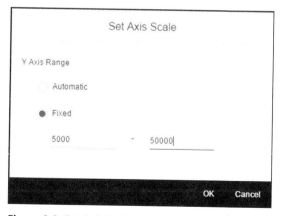

Figure 9.9 Set Axis Scale

- **Show Grid Lines**
  This option simply shows or hides the gridlines on a chart. By default, the gridlines are not shown.

- **Enable Ad-hoc Data Comparison**
  With **Ad-hoc Data Comparison**, you can easily compare the values of different members within a chart. As shown in Figure 9.10, the difference in both percentage and nominal value is shown between the selected bars. Hold the Ctrl key to make multiple selections.

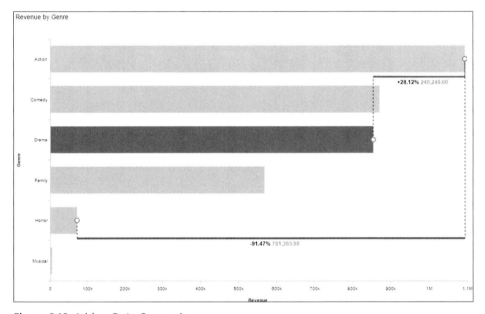

Figure 9.10 Ad-hoc Data Comparison

If you don't hold the Ctrl key and select three or more members in the chart, a popup window is shown (Figure 9.11). This gives a short summary of the selected values, and gives the sum, average, max, min, and median values.

The popup has a second page, which can be entered by clicking the arrow on the right side of the popup window. Now a tag cloud of the selected members is shown (Figure 9.12).

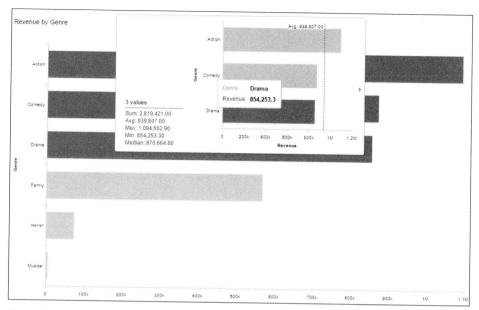

Figure 9.11 Summary Popup

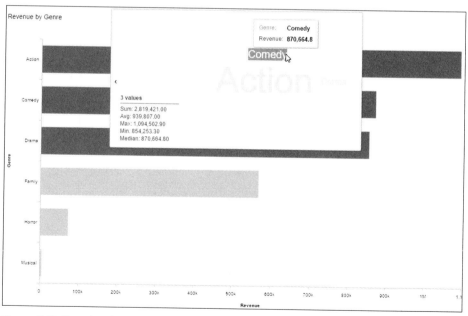

Figure 9.12 Tag Cloud

- **Add Trendline**
  Based on the values in the chart, SAP Lumira, discovery edition can calculate a
  trendline using linear regression (Figure 9.13). This option activates the trendline.

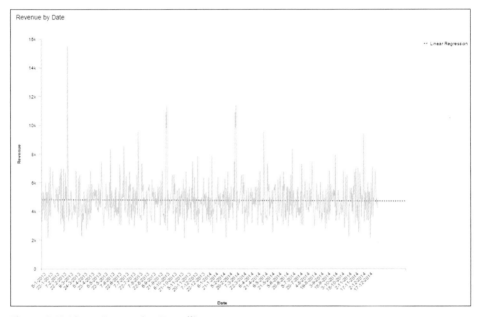

Figure 9.13 Linear Regression Trendline

- **Edit Trendline Setting**
  After activating the trendline, it can be extended to additional periods (Figure
  9.14). Figure 9.13 shows the result of this.

Figure 9.14 Trendline Setting

- **Remove Trendline**
  This final option removes the trendline from the chart.

9.3   Visualization Formatting

We have several options to change the visuals of a chart. We can change the color palette and edit each part of the chart in detail in the **Visualization Properties** menu.

9.3.1   Colors Palette

SAP Lumira, discovery edition uses a number of standard color palettes to apply a color range to the visualizations in a story (Figure 9.15). You can easily select a different palette from this menu.

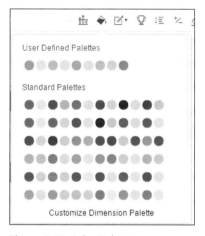

Figure 9.15 Color Palette

In addition, it is possible to define and save your custom color palettes (see Figure 9.16) using the **Customize Dimension Palette** option. Here you can define a number of colors using the color picker or by entering the RGB or HEX color codes.

Depending on the type of visualization, specific color palettes for measures can be used, for example in case of heat maps, tree maps, Geo Maps, or tag clouds. In these situations, the color gives an indication of the relative measure value, rather than differentiating the members of a dimension.

> **Default Color Palettes**
>
> By default, all charts in your story use the color palettes that are selected in the **Charts** section of the **Preference** menu (see Chapter 3, Section 3.6).

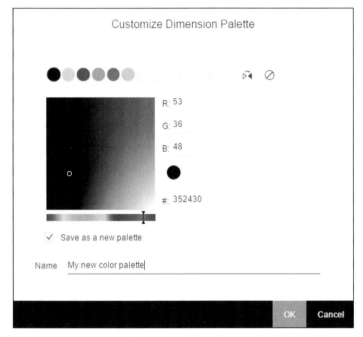

Customize Dimension Palette

R: 53

G: 36

B: 48

#: 352430

✓ Save as a new palette

Name   My new color palette|

OK   Cancel

Figure 9.16 Customize/Create Color Palette

9.3.2   Visualization Properties

The side pane provides, next to the **Dataset** tab, a **Design** tab. After selecting a visualization, we can edit its properties in the **Visualization Properties** menu—the fourth icon in the **Design** tab (Figure 9.17). This menu contains a number of generic properties, which are included in all charts, and a bunch of specific ones. In this section, we look at the generic properties; the specific properties are discussed in Chapters 10 through 15 for each chart type.

In addition to using the dropdown menu to select a certain property, you can also just click in the visualization to activate the properties menu for the selected area. In Figure 9.18, the chart title is selected in the chart (see the dotted rectangular around the chart title), and the respective properties are shown in the side pane.

Figure 9.17 Visualization Properties

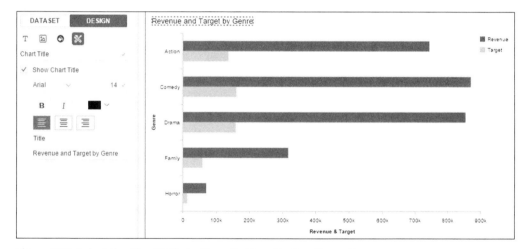

Figure 9.18 Select the Chart Title to Show Its Visualization Properties

The following generic properties are available:

- **Data Label**
  Provides the option to show a data label for each data point. You can also choose to

replace the data label with a pictogram (for example, an airplane or a person) and set its color, size, and direction.

- **Horizontal Axis**
  Gives options to show or hide the horizontal axis labels, axis line, and tick marks. Here you can also change the formatting of the labels and line and set a fixed or automatic axis scale.

- **Horizontal Axis Title**
  Displays or hides the title of the horizontal axis and format it.

- **Vertical Axis**
  Gives options to show or hide the vertical axis labels, axis line, and tick marks. Here you can also change the formatting of the labels and line and set a fixed or automatic axis scale.

- **Vertical Axis Title**
  Displays or hides the title of the vertical axis and format it.

- **Chart Area**
  Provides options to set the background color of the chart, and show or hide a border around the chart, including settings to change the formatting of the border. Also, with the **Enable Interactive Mode**, you can enable the interactivity settings for mobile and desktop devices, which allows the user to adjust the look and feel of the chart.

- **Chart Title**
  Displays or hides the title of the chart and format it. Here you can also overwrite the default title text.

- **Plot Area**
  Provides options to use a background color for the area where the actual chart is plotted, show or hide the border and gridlines, and format them. You can also activate or deactivate the **Fit Data Point into the Plot Area** option here. By default, this is activated, and all the data points are displayed within the room that the chart has. If you have a lot of data points, this may become unreadable. If you uncheck this option, a scrollbar will appear within the chart, so that there is more room for all the data points. The disadvantage is of course that you need to scroll to see all the values.

- **Legend**
  Display or hide a legend next to the chart, position it, and set the formatting.

9.4   Reference Line

You can add one or more *reference lines* to a chart to display important values that need to stand out. For example, if you want to show a target value, an industry benchmark, or an important date, you could use a reference line for that. There are two types of reference lines:

- **Fixed**

  Reference lines with a fixed value have a pre-set reference value. This value won't change whenever the data in the chart changes.

- **Dynamic**

  Reference lines with a dynamic value will change whenever the data in the chart is changed, for example when applying a filter.

To create a reference line, click the first icon in the visualization toolbar above the chart in the Chart Builder. When you are in canvas mode, just right-click the chart and select **Reference Lines**. In the **Edit Reference Line** menu, you can set the type of reference line to **Fixed** or **Dynamic**.

For a fixed reference line, you need to determine the axis you want to display the reference line one (if applicable) and set the fixed value. You can edit the label and check whether the label should be shown or not (Figure 9.19).

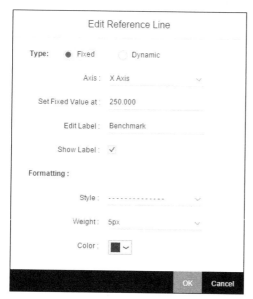

Figure 9.19 Edit Fixed Reference Line

For a dynamic reference line, you must select the measure and the aggregation type (Figure 9.20). Both types have the option to do some formatting adjustments, by change the style of the line (dotted or not), its weight, and color.

Figure 9.20 Edit Dynamic Reference Line

Figure 9.21 shows an example of these two reference lines on a bar chart.

After adding a reference line to a chart, the **Manage Reference Lines** menu will appear when you go to the **Reference Lines** option for a second time (Figure 9.22). This menu allows you to edit, add, or remove the reference lines. Also, you can turn off or on a reference line by using the checkbox.

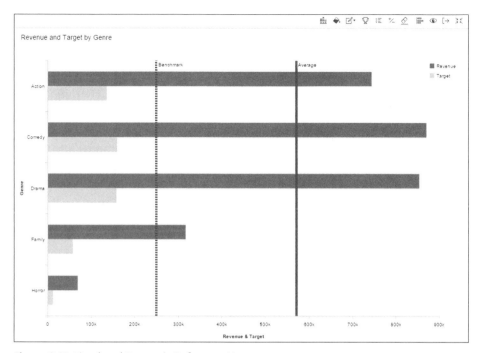

Figure 9.21 Fixed and Dynamic Reference Lines

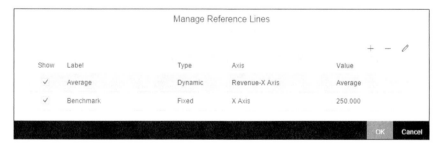

Figure 9.22 Manage Reference Lines

9.5 Conditional Formatting

With *conditional formatting*, you can set rules that determine the visual display of data points on a chart. For example, if a value is below a certain number, the data points that apply to this rule should be colored red.

To set up a conditional formatting rule, click the third icon in the visualization toolbar when you are in the Chart Builder. If you are on the canvas, just right-click the chart and choose **Conditional Formatting**.

The **Conditional Formatting Settings** menu appears (Figure 9.23). Here you can create, delete, duplicate, and edit the rules. Using the checkmarks, you can determine which rules should be applied. You can reuse rules throughout your story and apply the same rule on multiple visualizations. Also in this menu, you can change the prioritization of the rules. This is useful in case you have multiple conditional formatting rules that apply on the same measure or dimension. This could lead to conflicts, where data points in the visualization meet multiple rules. In that case, the higher prioritized rule is applied.

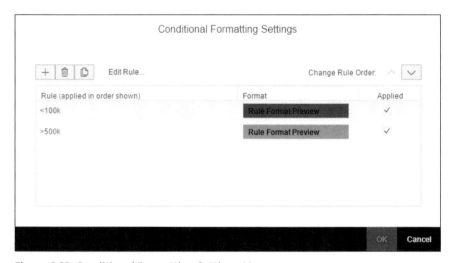

Figure 9.23 Conditional Formatting Settings Menu

Use the + icon to create a new rule. On the **Edit Formatting Rule** page that appears, you start by entering a name for the rule (Figure 9.24).

On the second line you need to determine the rule itself. First select whether the rule should be based on a measure or a dimension. Next, you can select the specific measure or dimension from the second dropdown list. The third option is the operator (greater than, between, is null, etc.). Depending on the operator you choose, you can fill in one or more values or select members from a list.

The third line offers options to set up the formatting of the rule. You can select a fill color and change the text formatting.

Figure 9.24 Edit Formatting Rule Menu

Conditional Formatting on Text

Only crosstabs support conditional formatting for the text (weight, font, and color). For charts, the coloring of the bars, columns, lines, and pie slices is possible.

Figure 9.25 shows a bar chart with two formatting rules applied. As you can see, the formatting rules are also included in the legend.

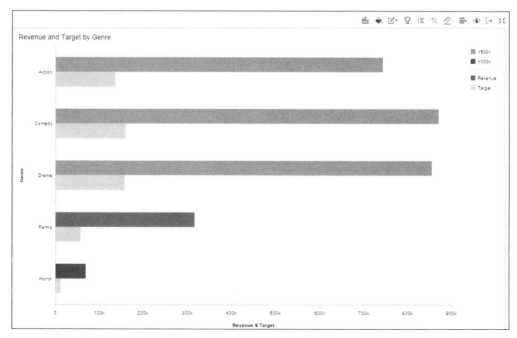

Figure 9.25 Chart After Applying Conditional Formatting Rules

9.6   Summary

In this chapter, we walked through the several options to create and set up charts in SAP Lumira, discovery edition. We looked at the fastest way of chart creation on the canvas and dove into the more detailed approach of the Chart Builder. Next, we discussed the generic visualization options to format a chart. Finally, we created reference lines and conditional formatting rules and applied them on top of our charts.

In the next chapter, we take a more in-depth look at the crosstab.

Chapter 10
Crosstabs

SAP Lumira, discovery edition offers different ways to visualize and interact with data. One of the most popular forms is the crosstab.

In a crosstab table, numbers are presented along rows and columns. This is very useful when you want to display and analyze exact information. You can show a lot of detailed data in an efficient way. It also allows you to include data from multiple measures that have different scales or units of measurement.

However, crosstabs aren't very useful for identifying trends and other relations between data points. You can highlight outliers by changing the layout of numbers that are outside of the main trend, but you can't show how much or how good or bad something is.

In this chapter, we first create a new crosstab and explore the available formatting and display options. Next, we look at the analysis options. As there are specific features available when using the crosstab in a live data scenario, we take a look at that as well.

10.1 Creating a Crosstab

Like most tasks within SAP Lumira, discovery edition, you can create a crosstab completely by using drag and drop. In the following sections, let's look at how you can create a crosstab, and what kind of customizing options are available.

10.1.1 Adding a New Crosstab

To create a new crosstab, follow these steps:

1. Insert a new chart on the canvas and select the **Crosstab** option.

2. As you saw in Chapter 9, you can start adding dimensions and measures on the crosstab component on the canvas. In this case, we want to use some detailed features. Maximize the crosstab by clicking the **Maximize** button.

3. Drag the **Revenue** measure into the **Measures** box.

4. You'll see that, by default, another **Measures** object appears in the **Columns** box. This object can be moved to the **Rows** box if you want to see the measures in the rows. For now, just add the **Genre** dimension to the **Rows** and **Year** to the **Columns** (Figure 10.1).

Figure 10.1 Creating a Crosstab

10.1.2   Formatting

You can adjust the look of a crosstab. This includes not only the way the elements of the crosstab are visually displayed, for example using coloring, but also how the values of the dimensions and measures are presented, for example without decimals.

You can enlarge the width of a column by dragging the column border between two columns. To rename the title of the crosstab, just double-click it or right-click it and choose **Rename Title**.

By right-clicking on any element of the crosstab, the associated context menu will pop up. Here you can find the **Formatting** options for that part of the crosstab. This includes the **Font Type**, **Font Size**, **Alignment**, font weight (**Bold**), and style (*Italic*), as shown in Figure 10.2.

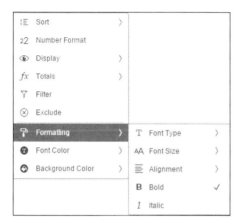

Figure 10.2 Formatting Options

Furthermore, there are options to change the **Font Color** (Figure 10.3) and the **Background Color**. There are four areas that can be formatted individually: **Headers**, **Row** objects, **Column** objects, and the **Result** area. Note that this kind of formatting is in no way related to the values themselves. For that functionality we can use conditional formatting, discussed in Chapter 9.

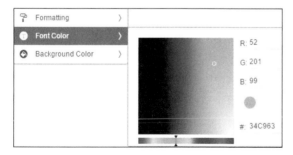

Figure 10.3 Font Color Option

The context menu also contains a **Display** option. Here you can change whether only the **Text** value of a dimension member, or also the **Key** value should be shown (Figure 10.4). You can also show both and choose the required order.

Figure 10.4 Display Options

The **Number Format** option (Figure 10.5) determines how a measure value should be displayed in the result area. Here you can set the **Scaling Factor**, the number of **Decimal Places**, and how the **Units and Scaling Factors** should be represented in the crosstab. For this last option, you can choose between **Display Both in Header**, **Display Units in Data Cells**, or **Do not Display**.

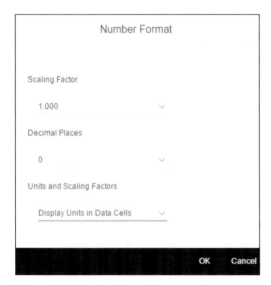

Figure 10.5 Number Format

Figure 10.6 shows these three options side by side.

Revenue by Year and Genre

	Revenue		
Year	2013	2014	Overall Result
Genre	* 1.000 EUR	* 1.000 EUR	* 1.000 EUR
Action	415	679	1.095
Comedy	556	315	871
Drama	312	543	854
Family	375	193	568
Horror	70	3	73
Musical	5		5
Overall Result	1.733	1.733	3.466

Revenue by Year and Genre

	Revenue		
Genre | Year	2013	2014	Overall Result
Action	EUR 415	EUR 679	EUR 1.095
Comedy	EUR 556	EUR 315	EUR 871
Drama	EUR 312	EUR 543	EUR 854
Family	EUR 375	EUR 193	EUR 568
Horror	EUR 70	EUR 3	EUR 73
Musical	EUR 5		EUR 5
Overall Result	EUR 1.733	EUR 1.733	EUR 3.466

Revenue by Year and Genre

	Revenue		
Genre | Year	2013	2014	Overall Result
Action	415	679	1.095
Comedy	556	315	871
Drama	312	543	854
Family	375	193	568
Horror	70	3	73
Musical	5		5
Overall Result	1.733	1.733	3.466

Figure 10.6 Units and Scaling Factor Display Options

10.2 Analysis Options

The crosstab is a very popular way to analyze data. It gives you the ability to easily dive into your dataset to understand the details of it. You could start with two values that for some unknown reason are different, and by using filters and adding dimensions to the crosstab, more details about the origin of these values will become clear.

Therefore, almost all data visualization tools include some kind of option to visualize data in a tabular form. This is also the case for the tools in the SAP BusinessObjects BI portfolio. The most advanced tabular analysis can be done in SAP BusinessObjects Analysis for Microsoft Office, which is a plugin on Microsoft Excel that runs SAP BEx queries and SAP HANA views (see Chapter 1). However, feature-wise, the crosstab in SAP Lumira, discovery edition comes very close to this tool, in both offline and live scenarios. In addition, when you run an SAP Lumira, discovery edition story on the BI Launchpad in your browser, you don't even need Microsoft Excel and the SAP Analysis for Microsoft Office plugin to be installed on your computer!

Let's look now at the analysis options of the crosstab in SAP Lumira, discovery edition.

> **Conditional Formatting and Ranking**
>
> There are two analysis options which were discussed in other chapters already. For details on **Conditional Formatting**, please see Chapter 9. For **Ranking**, please see Chapter 16.

10.2.1   Sorting

Dimensions and measures can be sorted in ascending or descending order. You can find this option in the context menu after right-clicking on a dimension or measure in the crosstab (Figure 10.7).

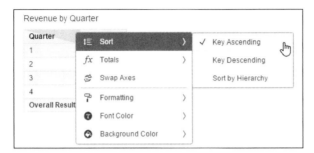

Figure 10.7 Sorting in the Context Menu

You can also use the sort icon in the visualization toolbar to sort by measures (Figure 10.8).

Figure 10.8 Sorting in the Visualization Toolbar (Third Icon)

10.2.2   Totals

With the **Totals** option, we can **Show** or **Hide** the totals for each individual dimension. The **Hide Totals If Only One Member** option makes sure no (unnecessary) repetitions of total values are displayed in the crosstab. Figure 10.9 clearly demonstrates this feature for the **Genre** dimension. A result row is shown only for the 2014 results, as only in those cases is more than one value for genre present.

An interesting feature is **Select Multiple Totals**. Here you can select additional calculations, and you can adjust the order in which they should be displayed: **Result**, **Sum**, **Count**, **Average**, **Minimum**, and **Maximum** (Figure 10.10). Result is always selected by default. Figure 10.9 shows three of these additional totals. In case the aggregation type of a measure is **Sum**, then the **Sum** total will show the same result as the **Result** total.

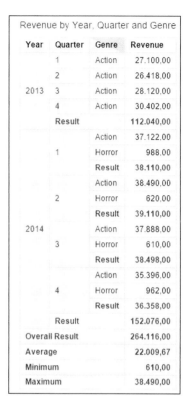

			Revenue by Year, Quarter and Genre
Year	**Quarter**	**Genre**	**Revenue**
	1	Action	27.100,00
	2	Action	26.418,00
2013	3	Action	28.120,00
	4	Action	30.402,00
		Result	**112.040,00**
	1	Action	37.122,00
		Horror	988,00
		Result	**38.110,00**
	2	Action	38.490,00
		Horror	620,00
		Result	**39.110,00**
2014	3	Action	37.888,00
		Horror	610,00
		Result	**38.498,00**
	4	Action	35.396,00
		Horror	962,00
		Result	**36.358,00**
	Result		**152.076,00**
Overall Result			**264.116,00**
Average			22.009,67
Minimum			610,00
Maximum			38.490,00

Figure 10.9 Totals

Figure 10.10 Multiple Totals

10.2.3   Filtering

There are several methods to filter a crosstab. If you are in the **Maximize** mode of the crosstab, you can quickly filter a dimension member by right-clicking it and selecting the option **Filter** (Figure 10.11). This will immediately filter the crosstab, without giving you a popup screen to change your selection. By using the ⌞Ctrl⌟ key, you can make selections of multiple members, even in multiple dimensions at the same time.

Next to the **Filter** option, there is the **Exclude** option. This does the exact opposite of the filter, and only shows the members that you didn't select.

It is also possible to filter using a measure value. When you do this, all the unique dimension members that make up this measure value are filtered at once.

Figure 10.11 Filter and Exclude Dimension Members

Whatever selection you made, the filters are always displayed in the filter bar above the canvas (Figure 10.12). Here you can also create filters on dimensions that are not used in the crosstab visualization. This option also allows the usage of operators.

Figure 10.12 Filter Bar

When you are not in **Maximize** mode, you don't have the option to quickly filter on a selected dimension member. But, you can use the **Filter** option in the context menu to select a dimension and create a filter, or do the same from the filter bar.

Finally, there is the option to create a **Filter by Measure** (Figure 10.13). This way, the crosstab is filtered on the measure value, either for all the dimensions or a specific dimension.

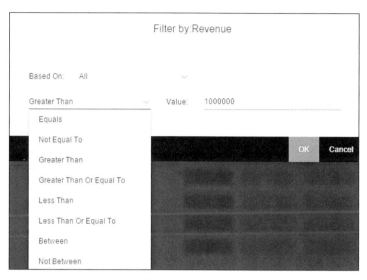

Figure 10.13 Create a Filter by Measure

For more information and details on filtering of visualizations, please see Chapter 16.

10.2.4   Drilling

If a dimension contains a hierarchy, it is possible to drill through this hierarchy. The drill options appear in the context menu of the dimension (Figure 10.14).

Figure 10.14 Drill Options

This is an easy way to move through the levels of the hierarchy, without having to add (or remove) the individual dimensions between the dataset and the crosstab (Figure 10.15). For additional details on this functionality, please see Chapter 16.

Revenue by Year and Genre			Revenue by Year, Quarter and Genre				Revenue by Year, Quarter, Month and Genre				
Year	Genre	Revenue	Year	Quarter	Genre	Revenue	Year	Quarter	Month	Genre	Revenue
2013	Action	28.120,00	2014	3	Action	37.888,00			7	Action	14.428,00
2014	Action	37.888,00			Horror	610,00				Horror	136,00
	Horror	610,00	Overall Result			38.498,00			8	Action	11.708,00
Overall Result		66.618,00								Horror	298,00
							2014	3	9	Action	11.752,00
										Horror	176,00
									Result		38.498,00
							Overall Result				38.498,00

Figure 10.15 Drilling Through a Date/Time Hierarchy

10.2.5 Swap Axes

The **Swap Axes** option switches the objects that are displayed in the rows with those in the columns, and vice versa (Figure 10.16). You can find this option by right-clicking on a dimension header in the rows.

Revenue by Year, Quarter and Genre				Revenue by Year, Quarter and Genre				
Year	Quarter	Genre	Revenue	Year	2013			
2013	1	Action	27.100,00	Quarter	1	2	3	4
	2	Action	26.418,00	Genre	Action	Action	Action	Action
	3	Action	28.120,00	Revenue	27.100,00	26.418,00	28.120,00	30.402,00
	4	Action	30.402,00					

Figure 10.16 Swap Axes

10.3 SAP BW and SAP HANA Live Data

When you use a live SAP BW data source instead of an offline source, some additional analysis options are available in the crosstab. If you are familiar with data analysis using SAP BEx queries in tools like SAP BusinessObjects Analysis for Microsoft Office, SAP BEx Analyzer, or even the crosstab in SAP Lumira, designer edition, you'll see that a lot of those SAP BEx-specific features are now available in this SAP Lumira, discovery edition online scenario as well.

In this section, we discuss these SAP BEx-specific features one by one. As you will see, some of the features are also available when using a live SAP HANA data source.

10.3.1   Hierarchy

When using an SAP BW data source, and one or more hierarchies are available for a dimension, the **Select Hierarchy** is visible in the context menu (Figure 10.17). After clicking this option, a list of available hierarchies is given. When you don't want to use a hierarchy, there is always the option to select **No Hierarchy**. This is always the first option in the list.

After you selected a hierarchy, you'll notice that the dimension is now displayed in a hierarchical form (Figure 10.18). Also, the context menu has expanded with some more hierarchy related options. **Expand All** shows the full hierarchical structure, while **Collapse All** rolls up the structure again. With **Expand to Level,** you can quickly expand the structure to a specific level. That way, you don't need to expand or collapse each level manually.

Figure 10.17 SAP BW Live Scenario, Dimension Context Menu

Product Costs by Product

Product	Product Costs EUR
⊟ All Products	6,258,252,000
⊟ Notebooks	3,144,886,250
⊟ Mobile Workstation	1,207,808,250
⊟ 15 Inch	608,918,750
Notebook Standard 15	608,918,750
⊞ 17 Inch	598,889,500
⊟ Basic Notebooks	1,937,078,000
⊞ 15 Inch	990,030,250
⊞ 17 Inch	947,047,750
⊞ Monitors	1,898,393,750
⊞ Mobile Devices	1,214,972,000

Figure 10.18 SAP BW Hierarchy in Crosstab

10.3.2 Attributes

SAP BW dimensions (within SAP BW these objects are called *characteristics*) may contain attributes. These attributes give some more information about the dimension member. For example, the dimension **Person** (Rob) can contain the attributes **Gender** (Male), **Date of Birth** (14 October 1969), and **Nationality** (Dutch). With this option, you can display these attributes next to the dimension members. Attributes are directly linked to their dimensions, and are therefore not represented as separate objects in the row or column boxes. Also, attributes can only be displayed. It is not possible to use them for filtering. The attribute is comparable to the detail object in an SAP BusinessObjects Universe.

10.3.3 Suppress Zeros in Rows/Columns

With the **Suppress Zeros in Rows** (or **Columns**) option, you can determine whether rows that contain only zeros as value must be shown or hidden. This feature is available for both live SAP BW and SAP HANA data sources.

10.3.4 Compact Display in Rows/Columns

Instead of displaying the dimension values next to each other, in separate rows or columns, with the **Compact Display in Rows** (or **Columns**) option, the dimensions are nested and displayed as if they were a hierarchical structure. The first dimension is always the top node in this structure, which you can expand to see the other dimensions. Figure 10.19 shows as crosstab with three dimensions in the rows. After activating **Compact Display in Rows**, they are displayed in a structure. This option is only available for live SAP BW data sources.

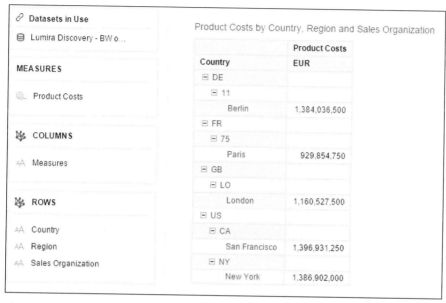

Figure 10.19 Compact Display

10.3.5   Add Dynamic Calculation

Each measure can be extended with a number of dynamic calculations (Figure 10.20). The **Add Dynamic Calculation** option provides a list of auto-generated calculations, such as **Rank Number** and **Percentage Contribution**. After selecting a dynamic calculation, a new column or row is created in the crosstab, and the new measure is also available in the **Measures** box. You can use **Edit Name** or **Remove** from the context menu of the dynamic calculation to change the name or delete the measure.

Table 10.1 describes all dynamic calculation options. All these options are available for live SAP BW data sources. For live SAP HANA data sources, only **Rank Number** and **Olympic Rank Number** are available.

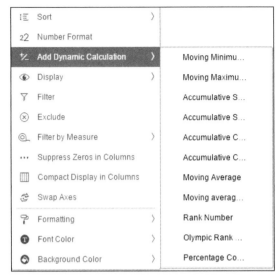

Figure 10.20 BW Live Scenario, Measure Context Menu

Dynamic Calculation	Description
Moving Minimum Value	Shows the lowest value up to this point in the crosstab.
Moving Maximum Value	Shows the highest value up to this point.
Accumulative Sum	Sums all values up to this point.
Accumulative Sum of Rounded Values	Sums all rounded values up to this point.
Accumulative Count of All Values	Counts all values in a cumulative way.
Accumulative Count of All Values that are Not Zero, Null or Error	Counts all values in a cumulative way, excluding the zeros. In such a case, the last number is repeated.
Moving Average	Calculates the average of all the values up to this point.
Moving average for values that are not zero, null or empty	Calculates the average of all the values up to this point, excluding the zeros. In such a case, the last number is repeated.

Table 10.1 Dynamic Calculations

Dynamic Calculation	Description
Rank Number	Ranks the unique values. In case a value occurs multiple times, the same rank is given.
Olympic Rank Number	Ranks the unique values, where in case of multiple occurrences of the same value, the next value does not get the next number in rank, but the rank that corresponds to number of previous values.
	For example, when rank 7 occurs twice, the following value gets rank 9.
Percentage Contribution	Calculates the percentage of the value compared to the total result.

Table 10.1 Dynamic Calculations (Cont.)

10.4 Summary

In this chapter, we looked at one of the most popular visualization methods: the crosstab. We showed you how to create a crosstab in SAP Lumira, discovery edition and made you familiar with the analysis options it offers. Furthermore, we discussed the specific features of the crosstab when using a live data connection to SAP BW and SAP HANA sources.

In the next several chapters, we go through the available charts in SAP Lumira, discovery edition, starting with the comparison charts.

Chapter 11

Comparison Charts

Comparison charts are used to discover and accentuate differences between dimension members.

The first category of charts that we are going to discuss are the comparison charts. These charts visualize the differences between values for dimension members and multiple measures.

In this chapter, we introduce the bar chart, column chart, 100% Marimekko chart, radar chart, the tag cloud, heat map, and the numeric point. We discuss the purpose and possible application of all these chart types and show their specific settings and formatting options.

11.1 Bar Chart

The bar chart compares the values of several entities with each other, across dimension members that are plotted below each other. The length of the bar allows you to compare the values. Figure 11.1 shows an example, where it is clear that the genre **Comedy** generated the most revenue and **Horror** the least. In this example, the bar chart is also sorted, so the largest value appears on top and the smallest at the bottom. This makes the chart very easy to read.

Together with the line chart and the crosstab, the bar chart is probably the most used visualization method. An advantage of the bar chart over the column chart (Section 11.2) is that the labels are horizontal, which makes them easier to read.

As shown in Figure 11.2, the bar chart uses the x-axis for the measures and the y-axis for the dimensions. Furthermore, you can add dimensions that need to be displayed in separate colors for each member. In Figure 11.2, dimension **Rating** is added as a **Color**. In addition, **Trellis** can be used in both the rows and columns. In the example, we added dimension **Type** as the **Column Trellis**, which splits the bar chart in two charts side by side.

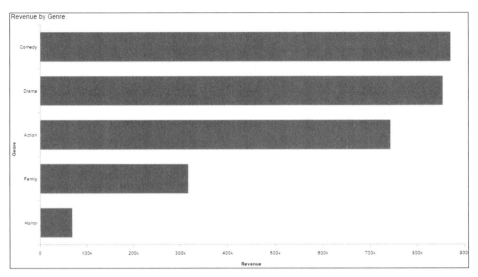

Figure 11.1 Bar Chart

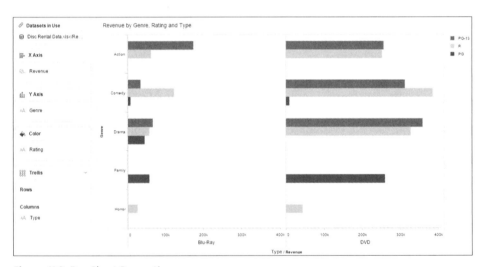

Figure 11.2 Bar Chart Properties

The bar chart has a few specific formatting options available in the formatting menu **Bar** (Figure 11.3). You can change the shape of the bars with the **Bar Shapes** option. By default, this is the rectangular bar, but you could also change this into pointers or arrow shaped bars. We wouldn't recommend using this, as these adjustments make it harder to read the chart and compare values.

With **Pictograms**, you can even replace the whole bar with an icon of, for example, a plane, person, or chicken. Again, this is not recommended.

Finally, you can change the **Color** of a bar or pictogram and quickly switch the chart type into a **Line** chart or an **Area** chart.

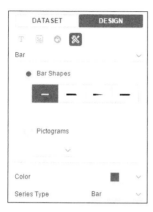

Figure 11.3 Bar Chart Formatting Options

In the **Formatting** menu for the **Data Labels**, you can show or hide the data labels, but in addition you can **Show Pictograms**. By double-clicking a data label of a single member, you can edit the pictogram (and by the way also the data label) for this particular member. In Figure 11.4 each member has its own pictogram.

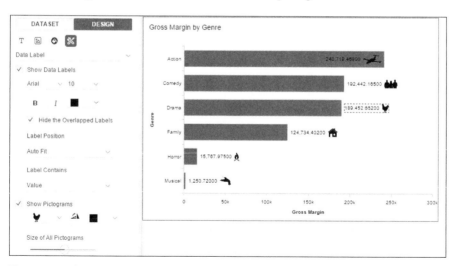

Figure 11.4 Pictograms in a Bar Chart

11.2 Column Chart

The column chart does the exact same thing as the bar chart, only instead of showing horizontal bars it shows them vertically, from left to right. The height of the bar represents the value.

The properties of the column chart are the same as for the bar chart, only the measures are now shown in the y-axis, and the dimensions in the x-axis, as shown in Figure 11.5.

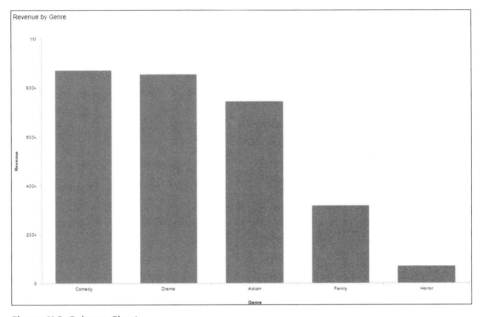

Figure 11.5 Column Chart

The formatting options are almost the same as those for the bar chart. The only difference is that the option to switch to a different chart type is not available here.

11.3 Marimekko Chart

The Marimekko chart is a special version of the column chart where the value of a measure is represented by not only the height of the bar, but also the width (Figure 11.6). Also noticeable is that there is no longer any space between the bars.

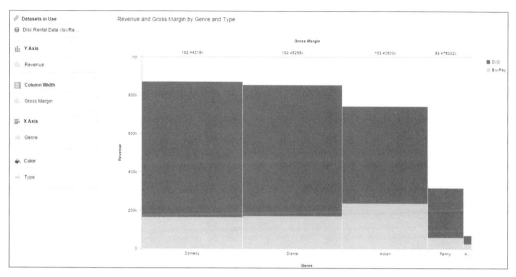

Figure 11.6 Marimekko Chart

The Marimekko chart has an additional property for the **Column Width**. It is only possible to use one measure for the y-axis and one for the **Column Width**. When you add a dimension in the **Color**, the bars are split up according to this dimension. In Figure 11.6, **Dimension Type** is used as a color, which splits all the bars into two stacks.

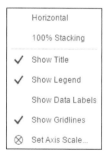

Figure 11.7 Marimekko Chart Context Menu

With the context menu option **Horizontal**, you can switch the direction of the chart (Figure 11.7). Here, you can also transform the chart into a **100% Stacking** chart. The y-axis now shows a range from 0 to 100%, and each value is represented as a part of the total value (Figure 11.8).

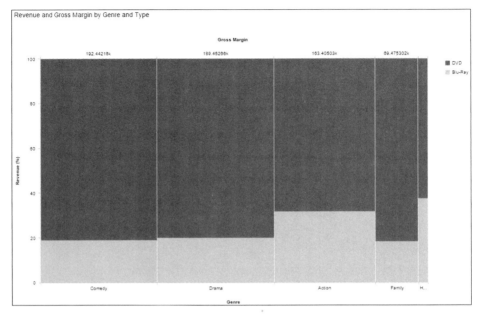

Figure 11.8 100% Stacking Marimekko Chart

There are no specific formatting options for the Marimekko chart, except for the **Color** column.

11.4   Radar Chart

The radar chart is basically a line chart, where the x-axis is a circle instead of a horizontal line (Figure 11.9). The result is a chart where a data point's distance from the center shows the value of the key figure. A radar chart can be useful for comparing the shape of properties for several entities or when you want to show data that is naturally ordered in a circular way, such as hours on a clock.

In the radar chart properties, you can set the dimension(s) that should represent the **Radar Branches**, and the measures that must be plotted on the branches. You can also use **Color** and **Trellis**.

With the **Line** formatting menu, you can change the **Line Width** and enable or disable a fill of the line area, using **Show Fill Color for Polygon** (Figure 11.10). It also allows you to change the level of **Transparency**.

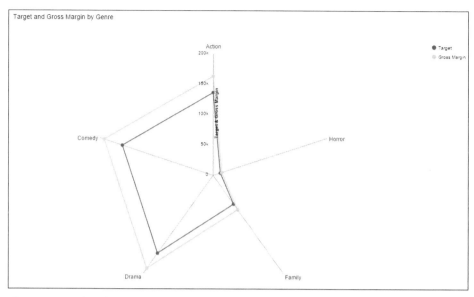

Figure 11.9 Radar Chart

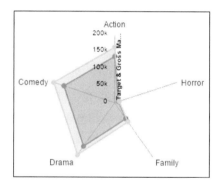

Figure 11.10 Radar Chart with Fill Color

11.5   Tag Cloud

The tag cloud is a visualization that we see often on websites or in infographics. It displays a mash-up of the selected dimension values, where the size of the words and the color intensity give an indication of the relative values of the two selected measures (Figure 11.11).

Tag clouds may be a cool way to display your data, but you should question if they are effective. Yes, you'll probably be able to immediately see which dimension members have the highest values or are the most important, but it is almost impossible to do exact comparisons and determine how much larger value A is compared to value B.

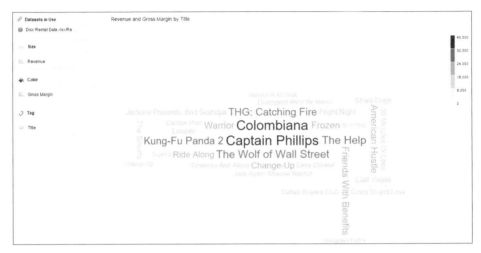

Figure 11.11 Tag Cloud

The tag cloud has only three properties: **Size**, **Color**, and **Tag**. **Size** and **Color** are made up by two measures; the **Tag** is the dimension that should be displayed.

There are no specific formatting options available for the tag cloud. To change the color, pick a different color palette from the **Choose Colors** option in the visualization toolbar.

11.6   Heat Map

The heat map uses the color palette colors to visualize the relative values of the dimension members (Figure 11.12). This quickly shows the outliers. Each tile has the same size (the tree map also uses the size of the tile to indicate the relative value of a secondary measure).

For the heat map, you have to use a measure as a **Color**, and you can use one or more dimensions to make up the tiles using the x-axis. In addition, you can use the y-axis to further split up the dataset.

There are no specific formatting options available for the heat map.

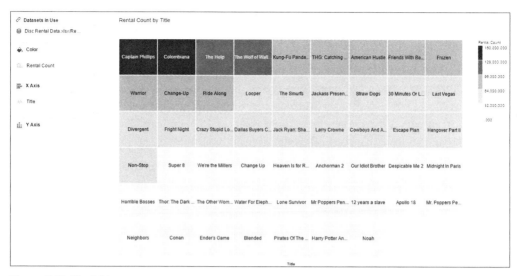

Figure 11.12 Heat Map

11.7   Numeric Point

The numeric point is not really a chart, and it is probably the simplest visualization option in SAP Lumira, discovery edition. It just shows a single value. You can use the numeric point to highlight a specific KPI or value in the report, as shown in Figure 11.13.

Figure 11.13 Numeric Point

As the visualization shows only a single value, the only option you have in the properties is to add a measure.

Compared to the properties, you have more possibilities in the formatting options of the numeric point. As shown in Figure 11.14, you have quite a few options to edit the formatting of the **Value**. You can change the font, its size, weight, and color, and set the alignment.

Next it is possible to display the value as a number or as a percentage. The number option gives some additional settings. You can choose to **Show 1000 Separator** (unticking the box will hide it), and choose to display the value using a **Metric Symbol**. This is an interesting option, as it allows you to shorten the values, which makes large numbers way easier to read. A value of, for example, $3,465,958.60 would be displayed as $3.47M. Using the **Auto** option, SAP Lumira, discovery edition determines by itself which metric symbol should be used, but you can also use a fixed option here and choose from **K** (thousands), **M** (millions), **B** (billions), and **T** (trillions).

Finally, you can set the number of **Decimal Places**, add a **Prefix**, and add a **Suffix**.

Figure 11.14 Numeric Point Formatting Options

11.8   Summary

In this chapter, we looked at the first batch of charts: the comparison charts. We introduced six different chart types, including their properties and specific formatting options.

In the next chapter, we dive into the percentage charts.

Chapter 12
Percentage Charts

Percentage charts show the relative values of parts compared to a whole.

We continue our journey through the SAP Lumira, discovery edition chart types and arrive at the percentage charts. These charts are used to visualize the relative values of parts of a dataset, rather than showing the nominal values.

In this chapter, we look at the pie chart, the donut chart, the stacked bar and stacked column charts, and finally the funnel chart. As in Chapter 11 on the comparison charts, we discuss the specific settings and formatting options for each chart type.

12.1 Pie Chart

The pie chart shows values as slices of a circle (Figure 12.1). A pie chart's strength is that it shows the part-to-whole relation in an easy-to-understand way. However, as the number of slices grows, it's more difficult to see which entity holds what part, so comparing values gets more difficult. It is possible to show data labels on the slices, but that undermines the whole point of data visualization again. Trends and exact values don't work with this chart.

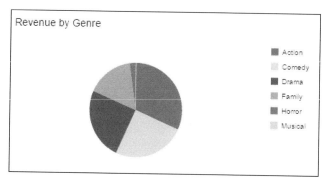

Figure 12.1 Pie Chart

We generally recommend bar or column charts over pie charts, but they may be effective when you need to compare only two or three values.

The pie chart uses a measure to determine the relative **Size** of the slices, and each dimension member is displayed in a different **Color**. Note that you could use multiple measures and dimensions here. The combination of the measures and/or dimensions will then be represented in the pies.

In addition to this, **Trellis** can be used in both the rows and columns. In the example, we added dimension **Rating** as the **Row Trellis**, and **Type** as the **Column Trellis** (Figure 12.2).

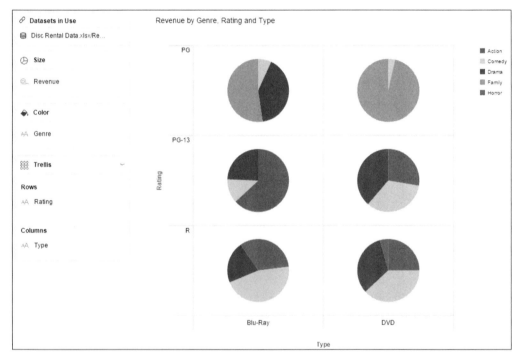

Figure 12.2 Pie Chart Properties

The pie chart has a few formatting options (Figure 12.3). From the **Slice** menu, you can change the color of each individual slice. In the **Data Label** menu, you can enable or disable the data labels and change the font, its size, weight, and color. You can also determine what to do with overlapping labels (hide or show), and change the **Label Position** (**Inside** or **Outside** the pie chart). With the final option, you can change what the **Label Contains**.

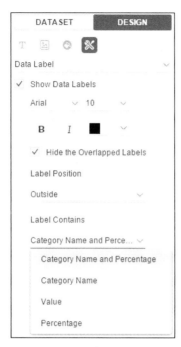

Figure 12.3 Pie Chart Formatting Options

12.2   Donut Chart

The donut chart is a variation on the pie chart, which has a hole in the middle of the pie (Figure 12.4). The same comments apply here: it might look like an attractive visualization, but as the number of entities grows, it becomes harder, or even nearly impossible, to make sound comparisons.

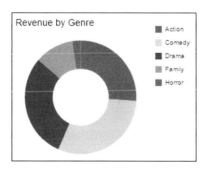

Figure 12.4 Donut Chart

The properties to set up a donut chart are almost the same as those for the pie chart. The donut chart has two additional features compared to the pie chart. You can **Highlight the Slice** that you select by clicking on it. In addition, you can show the dimension name and percentage and select a single color to represent all the other dimension members. Also, in the **Plot Area** property, you can change the size of the inner circle of the donut (Figure 12.5).

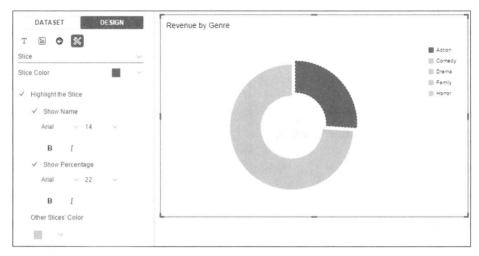

Figure 12.5 Donut Chart Formatting Options

12.3   Stacked Bar Chart

In a stacked bar chart, the bar itself is divided into colors based on the part-to-whole relationship of the underlying entities (Figure 12.6). The chart shows the part-to-whole relationship in the bar, and the bars themselves can be compared to each other. If you have only one bar, a standard bar chart with a bar for each entity is more useful. A stacked bar chart can be used when you have multiple whole values (e.g., sales per month) and the whole is divided by region.

Keep in mind, however, that comparing the colored parts across bars is difficult because the starting points are dependent on values of the entities, so you don't have a base value to compare. This type of chart is most useful when you want to compare a value across entities and also want to see something of the part-to-whole relationship with that entity. This chart doesn't show trends, outliers, or exact values well.

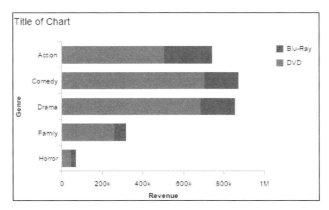

Figure 12.6 Stacked Bar Chart

The stacked bar chart uses the **X-axis** for the measures and the **Y-axis** for the dimensions (Figure 12.7). The dimensions that are in the **Color** area make up the values within the bars (in Figure 12.7, the **Type** dimension is selected for this). Furthermore, the **Trellis** options are available.

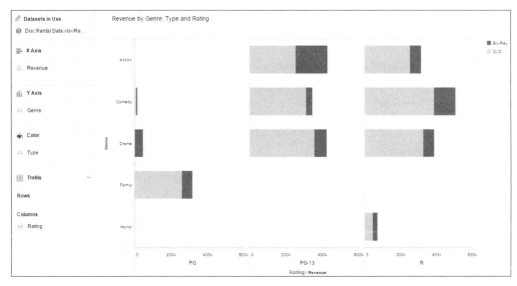

Figure 12.7 Stacked Bar Chart Properties

With the context-menu option **100% Stacking** (right-click in the chart area), you can turn your stacked bar chart into a 100% stacked bar chart. This chart type consists of horizontal bars that show the part-to-whole data (Figure 12.8).

285

This visualization allows you to show part-to-whole relations across a dimension. The disadvantage is that you can't compare the dimension itself because everything is added to 100%. An alternative that paints a part-to-whole relation more clearly is the bar or column chart, as it's easier to make comparisons with them.

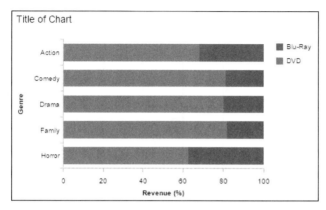

Figure 12.8 100% Stacked Bar Chart Properties

There are no specific formatting options for the stacked bar chart.

12.4   Stacked Column Chart

The stacked column chart has the same advantages and disadvantages as the stacked bar chart, but the labels are in vertical alignment (Figure 12.9).

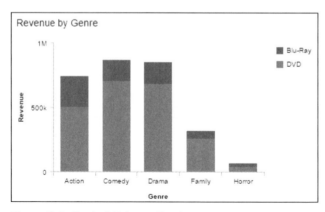

Figure 12.9 Stacked Column Chart

The properties of the stacked column chart are the same as for the stacked bar chart. It is also possible to switch to a 100% stacked column chart.

There are no specific formatting options for the stacked bar chart.

12.5 Funnel Chart

A funnel chart can be used to present different stages in a process, where the values are shown as a percentage of the total. This is literally displayed as a funnel, where the smaller values are at the end of the funnel (Figure 12.10).

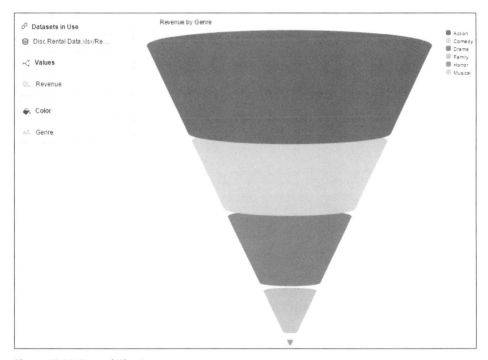

Figure 12.10 Funnel Chart

This chart type is often used to visualize the different stages in a sales process, where a sales manager starts with a large number of possible leads and ends up with a (smaller) number of actual sales at the end of the funnel.

The setup for the funnel chart is very simple. You can only use a single measure and a single dimension in this visualization (Figure 12.10).

There are no specific formatting options for the funnel chart.

12.6   Summary

In this chapter, we went through the second category of chart, the percentage charts. We discussed five different chart types with their specific properties and formatting settings.

In the next chapter, we continue with the correlation charts.

Chapter 13
Correlation Charts

Correlation charts are used to find relationships between values.

The next type of charts that we discuss are the correlation charts. We talk of correlation when there is a relationship between two or more variables. For example, data could show a relation between temperature and the number of ice creams sold (the higher the temperature, the higher the number of sales).

In this chapter, we introduce the scatter plot, bubble chart, network chart, and the tree.

13.1   Scatter Plot

A scatter plot shows the relationship between two measures. It's great at showing trends of a relationship as well as highlighting outliers—often you add trend lines to the scatter cloud to identify a trend that you can use for future predictions.

Figure 13.1 shows the relation between revenue and rental count. As expected, we see that the higher the rental count, the higher the revenue is for the titles.

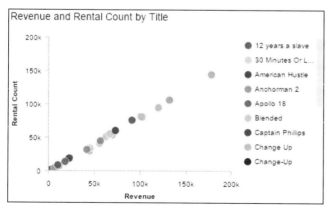

Figure 13.1 Scatter Plot

A scatter plot needs two measures: one on the **X Axis**, the other one on the **Y Axis**. In the **Color** box, we must add the dimension or dimensions that we want to plot in the chart. Each individual member gets its own color.

With the **Shape** option, we can differentiate the data points with different shapes, so that we can distinguish the different groups of data. Another interesting feature is the **Animation** option. This turns the chart into a movie by showing the states of the dataset one by one. In Figure 13.2 we added dimension **Month** as the **Animation**, and after pressing the **Play** button underneath the chart, the scatter plot will display the data points month by month. This is a nice way to show or discover a certain movement in the dataset over time. However, the **Trellis** option probably is a better alternative, as it gives you the option to show all the different states (in our example, the months) side by side in a single overview.

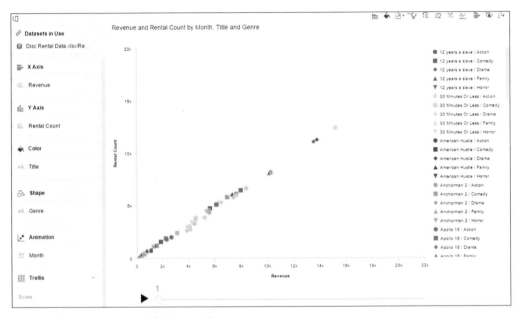

Figure 13.2 Scatter Plot Properties

Visualization Limit
The scatter plot can visualize a maximum of 10,000 data points.

The data points, or scatters, have their own formatting menu (Figure 13.3). Here we can change the **Color** and **Scatter Style** of all the scatters, or select an individual data point and change only that one. Also, the size of the scatter can be adjusted here.

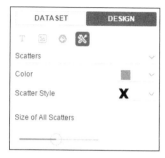

Figure 13.3 Scatter Plot Formatting Options

13.2   Scatter Plot for Time Series

The scatter plot for time series is a special version of the scatter plot, where instead of a second measure, a **Time Dimension** is used. As shown in Figure 13.4, this chart plots the results over time. As you can see, the chart shows a very readable time structure on the x-axis.

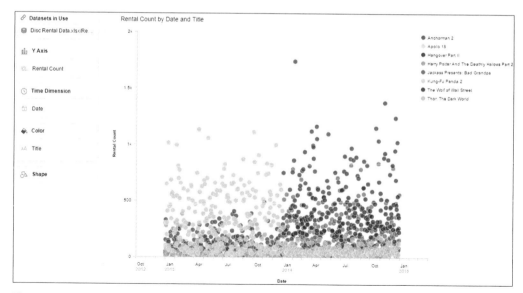

Figure 13.4 Scatter Plot for Time Series

The scatter plot for time series has the same properties and formatting options as the scatter plot, only the animation and trellis options are missing, and the measure on the x-axis is replaced by the time dimension. This time dimension can be a standard date/time object, but also an object of a date/time hierarchy (year, quarter, month, or date) that has been derived from a date/time object.

13.3   Bubble Chart

A bubble chart is very similar to a scatter plot, only it can also show data in three measures (Figure 13.5). You use three values: one shown on the x-axis, one shown on the y-axis, and one shown via the size of the bubble. In the example in Figure 13.5, you see that even though both the **Rotten Tomatoes** movie score and the **Audience Score** are very high for some of the **Titles**, their **Domestic Gross** (the size of the bubble) is relatively small—even smaller than titles that have gotten lower scores.

This type of chart is designed for comparison. The position of each bubble allows you to compare the values to each other. The sizes of the bubbles can also be used for comparison, but this is a less exact way of comparing because you can only tell if a bubble is large or not. You can't show exact numbers or trends with this chart. If you select a single data point, the popup shows all the details (Figure 13.6).

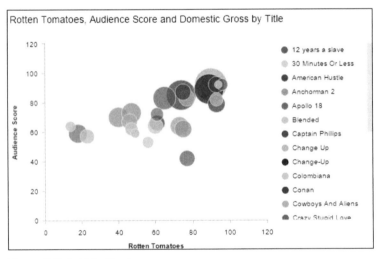

Figure 13.5 Bubble Chart

The bubble chart has the same properties as the scatter plot, with the addition of the measure that determines the **Size** of the bubbles (Figure 13.6).

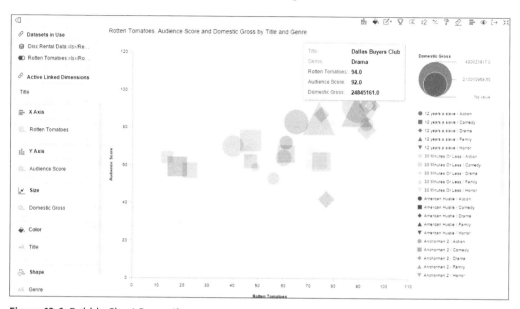

Figure 13.6 Bubble Chart Properties

The data points, or **Bubbles**, have their own formatting menu (see Figure 13.7), just like the scatters of the scatter plot. Here you can change the **Color** and **Bubble Style**. Of course, there is no option to change the size of the bubbles, as this is determined by the size measure.

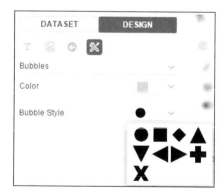

Figure 13.7 Bubble Chart Formatting Options

13.4   Bubble Chart for Time Series

Just as for the scatter plot there is a time series variant of the bubble chart (Figure 13.8). Compared to the bubble chart, instead of a third dimension, a **Time Dimension** is used on the x-axis, which shows up as a clear time structure. Furthermore, the bubble chart for time series has the same properties and formatting options as the bubble chart, except for the animation and trellis options.

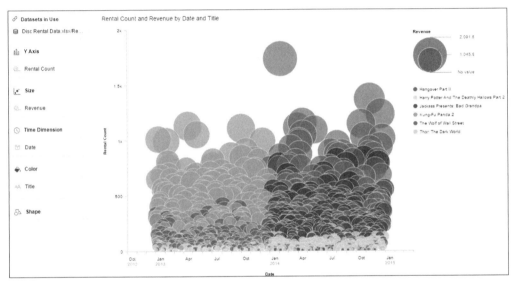

Figure 13.8 Bubble Chart for Time Series

13.5   Network Chart

The network chart shows relationships among the members of two dimensions (Figure 13.9). They do not use or require a measure. This chart type could help you quickly see if there are certain data groupings within your dataset.

The network chart can only show the relationships between two dimensions. The only property option is therefore to add these two dimensions to the chart.

There are no specific formatting options available for the network chart.

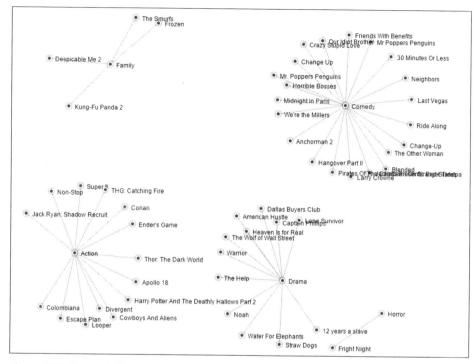

Figure 13.9 Network Chart

13.6   Tree

The tree is a simple visualization of the relation between two dimensions (Figure 13.10). The application of the tree is quite limited; it is only possible to add two dimensions, where only one value of the first dimension is used as the root node of the hierarchy. You could use the tree to highlight a list of related dimension members.

As shown in Figure 13.10, besides a **Dimension** area, there are no other properties available for the tree. By default, the first value of the first dimension is used as the root value (in the example, this is **Genre Action**). To show a different member, just put a filter on the dimension.

Except for the **Chart Title**, there are no formatting options for the tree.

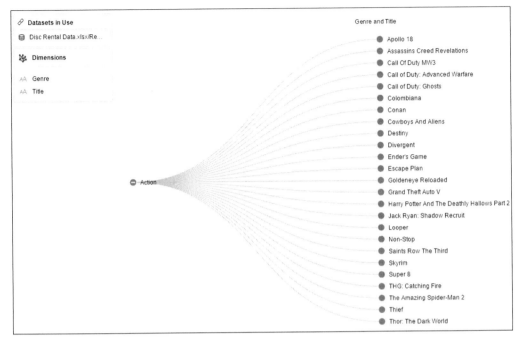

Figure 13.10 Tree

13.7   Summary

In this chapter, we discussed the correlation charts that we can use in SAP Lumira, discovery edition. This included the scatter plot, the bubble chart, the network chart, and the tree.

In the next chapter, we look at the final chart category: trend charts.

Chapter 14

Trend Charts

Trend charts show in what form or pattern data changes.

In this chapter, the final group of charts are discussed: trend charts. Trend charts show the change of values. Mostly, this is time related. Are sales increasing or decreasing? Is this pattern the same for all products? Is there a certain pattern or seasonality in the data? Trend charts can help find the answers to these questions.

The setup of this chapter is the same as the previous ones on the other chart types. We discuss the line chart (including the line chart for time series), the stacked area chart, the waterfall chart, the box plot, the parallel coordinates chart, and finally the combination chart.

Section 14.7 includes a comparison of all the chart types in SAP Lumira, discovery edition.

14.1 Line Chart

One of the most popular charts in data visualization is the line chart. In a line chart one or more lines flow from left to right (Figure 14.1). It usually involves time, plotted along the x-axis. Because of its format, a line chart is very useful to show trends in data. If you want to emphasize a comparison between values, then you should think about a column or bar chart instead of a line chart.

The line chart visualizes one or more measures on the y-axis against one or more dimensions on the x-axis. This chart however also has the option to switch between the default **Horizontal** mode and a **Vertical** mode (Figure 14.2). In the vertical mode, the line(s) go from top to bottom. If you have a specific need to display dimension labels on the vertical axis, this chart may be useful, but, in general, we don't recommend it. It's easier to read trends going from left to right, so the traditional line chart is usually best (and again, if you want to compare values, we recommend the bar chart).

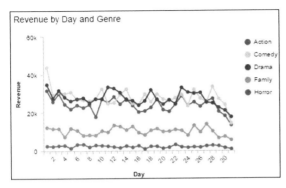

Figure 14.1 Line Chart

When adding a dimension to **Color**, a line will appear for each member. The option for **Trellis** is also available.

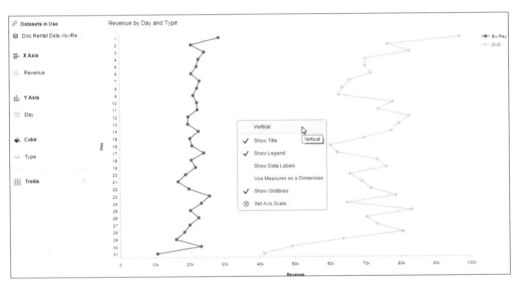

Figure 14.2 Line Chart Properties

In the **Formatting** options for the line chart, you'll find the option to change the **Line** and the **Marker** on the line. You can change the symbol that is used as a marker and adjust its rotation, color, and size.

For the line, you can change the color, width, and style (unbroken, striped, or dotted line) (Figure 14.3). You can use **Enable Smoothed Line** to make the lines look less edgy. This may look nice, but it removes a bit of the value of the data visualization, as it is not 100% representing the actual data. With the **Show All Lines** option, you can make the lines appear or disappear. In the latter case, only the markers are visible.

Note that adjustments on markers and lines can be done for all the lines at once, or for individually selected lines.

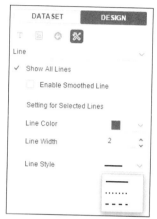

Figure 14.3 Line Chart Formatting Options

SAP Lumira, discovery edition also contains a special line chart type in case you are using a time dimension, like a date. This is the line chart for time series. The x-axis becomes the time dimension axis, and it is able to translate the date into a year, month, and day (Figure 14.4).

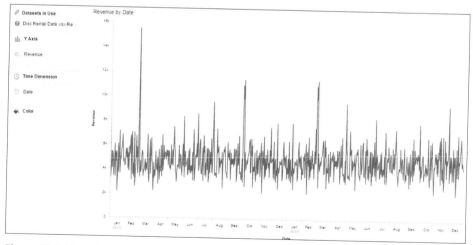

Figure 14.4 Line Chart for Time Series

14.2   Stacked Area Chart

A (stacked) area chart emphasizes trends of data and allows you to compare the trends of several entities (Figure 14.5). In fact, this is a line chart where the space between the lines is filled to emphasize the differences between the series, as part of a whole.

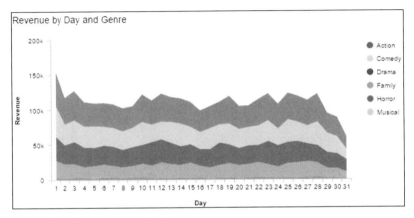

Figure 14.5 Stacked Area Chart

The properties for the stacked area chart are the same as for the line chart (Figure 14.6).

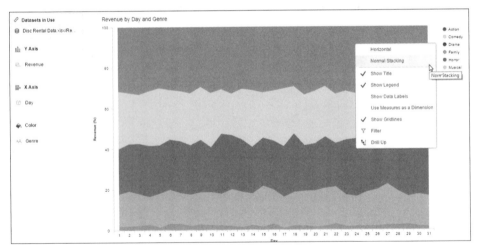

Figure 14.6 100% Stacked Area Chart Properties

Also, this chart has the ability to switch between a **Horizontal** and **Vertical** view. In addition, you can use **100% Stacking** to turn the chart into a 100% stacked area chart (Figure 14.6). In that case, the measure axis changes from nominal values to percentages, ranging from 0 to 100%.

The stacked area chart only has an **Area** option, where the color of the selected area can be adjusted.

14.3   Waterfall Chart

A waterfall chart emphasizes the cumulative addition to the end result with positive and negative values (Figure 14.7). A stacked bar chart would have difficulties presenting the negative values, so that is where the waterfall chart comes in handy. If you want to emphasize the comparison between values, a standard bar chart is a better choice.

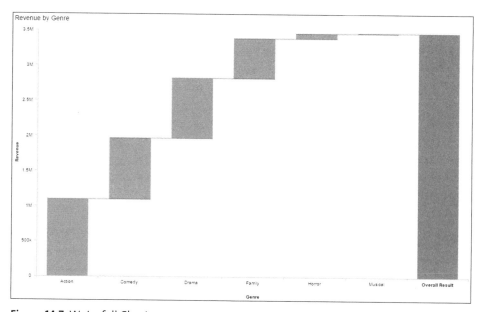

Figure 14.7 Waterfall Chart

In the properties for the waterfall chart, you can select the measure(s) for the **Y Axis** and dimension(s) for the **X Axis**. In addition, via the **Show/Hide Properties** menu

(Figure 14.8), you can show the **Totals** in the chart as an additional bar. Also, this chart can switch between **Vertical** and **Horizontal** mode.

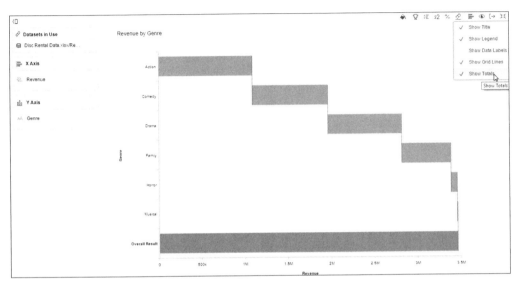

Figure 14.8 Waterfall Chart Properties

In the **Formatting Options** menu for the **Bar**, you can adjust the three colors that are used in the waterfall chart: **Increasing**, **Decreasing**, and **Total** values (Figure 14.9).

Figure 14.9 Waterfall Chart Formatting Options

14.4   Box Plot

A box plot aggregates the data for a dimension in order to determine the different quartiles of the data. This gives an overview of the spread and the skewness in data.

As shown in Figure 14.10, the line in the middle of the box is the median, and the bottom and top boxes are the first and third quartiles. The two whiskers are the minimum and maximum of the data (this chart type is also called a box-and-whisker plot). Outliers are plotted as individual points.

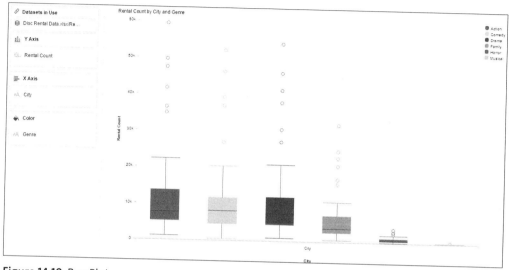

Figure 14.10 Box Plot

For the box plot, you have to select a measure and a dimension for which the spread of this measure has to be visualized. In addition, you can add a color to compare these spreads between the members of a dimension. In Figure 14.10, a box plot is shown for the **Rental Count** by **City** for each **Genre**. You see that there are some extreme outliers in the first four genres. Apparently there a few cities that have very high number of rentals compared to the others. Comparing the genres side-by-side, you can see that the spread is the highest in the action genre.

There are no specific formatting options available for the box plot.

14.5 Parallel Coordinates Chart

In a parallel coordinates chart, you can plot your data as a series of lines that links the measure values of each dimension member (Figure 14.11). The measures are displayed as vertical lines.

As shown in Figure 14.11, you can add multiple measures to this chart, but only one dimension can be visualized.

The parallel coordinates chart has no specific formatting options.

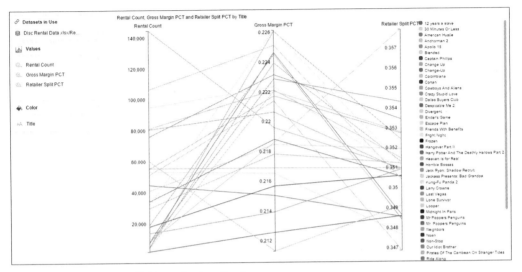

Figure 14.11 Parallel Coordinates Chart

14.6   Combination Chart

In Chapter 9, we discussed how to switch the chart type for a measure via the **Change Chart Type for Series** option. This can be done via the context menu of a measure that has been added to the chart. When we have multiple measures in the same chart, we can create a combination chart by using different chart types. For example, we can show the daily revenue as a line, while the gross margin percentage is visualized with bars. As you can see in Figure 14.12, the percentage is also assigned to the secondary axis.

After switching the chart type of a measure, an additional option becomes available in the formatting menu for the line: **Series Type**. With this feature, you can quickly change the line chart into a bar chart or area chart, like we already did with the option as shown in Figure 14.12. But, even better, in case you are using a dimension for color, you can now select a single series (i.e., a line) and change that specific dimension member into a different chart type (Figure 14.13).

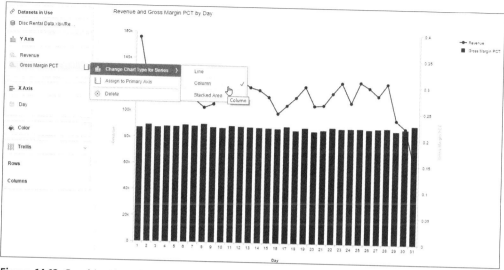

Figure 14.12 Combination Chart with Two Measures

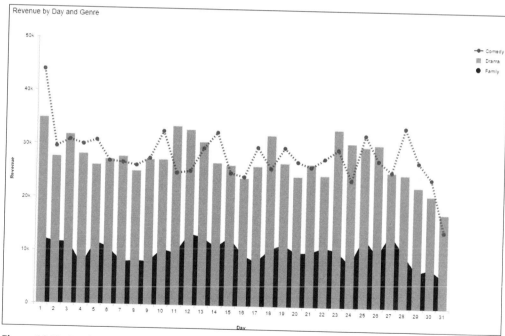

Figure 14.13 Combination Chart with Multiple Chart Types in a Single Series

14.7   Summary

In this chapter, we discussed the final group of charts in SAP Lumira, discovery edition: trend charts. We covered the line chart, the stacked area chart, the waterfall chart, the box plot, the parallel coordinates chart, and the combination chart.

After all these chapters in which we discussed the different chart types, it is time to summarize. Table 14.1 shows an overview of all chart types that are present in SAP Lumira, discovery edition, with their major strengths (+) and weaknesses (–).

	Trend	Comparison	Part-to-Whole	Outliers	Relationship	Exact
Numeric Point	––	–	––	––	––	++
Line Chart	++	+–	–	+–	––	––
Area Chart	+	+–	–	+–	––	––
100% Area Chart	+	+–	+	+–	––	––
Bar/Column Chart	+	++	+	+	––	–
Bar/Column Combination	++	+	+	+	––	–
100% Stacked Bar/Column Chart	–	+–	+–	–	–	––
Marimekko Chart	––	+–	+–	–	–	––
100% Stacked Marimekko Chart	––	+–	+–	–	–	––
Waterfall Chart	––	+	++	+	––	––

Table 14.1 Chart Comparison

	Trend	Compari-son	Part-to-Whole	Outliers	Relation-ship	Exact
Crosstab	——	—	—	+	—	++
Scatter Chart	+	+	——	++	++	——
Bubble Chart	——	+	——	++	+	——
Pie/Donut Chart	——	+—	+—	+—	——	——
Heat Map	——	+—	+	+	—	——
Tree Map	——	+—	+	+	+—	——
Tag Cloud	——	+—	—	+	——	——
Box Plot	——	+	++	++	—	—
Network Chart	——	——	——	——	++	——
Radar Chart	+—	+—	+	+	——	——
Funnel Chart	——	+—	+—	+—	+	——
Parallel Coor-dinates Chart	——	——	——	——	+	——
Tree	——	——	——	——	+—	——

Table 14.1 Chart Comparison (Cont.)

In the next chapter, we look at a completely different method of data visualization: the map.

14

Chapter 15
Geographic Visualizations

Geo maps visualize data on a map, which enables a location-based analysis of your dataset.

When your dataset contains a dimension that is location related, such as a country, city, or longitude/latitude coordinates, it is possible to visualize this geographical data on a map. SAP Lumira, discovery edition offers mapping solutions that allow you to quickly plot, find, and analyze data. You can even add multiple layers of data and use your own custom maps.

In this chapter, we first look at the difference between the online and offline map solution in SAP Lumira, discovery edition. Next, we walk through the properties of the geo map and the different layer types. Finally, we look at the available formatting options.

15

15.1 Online versus Offline Maps

By default, a new map is always an **ESRI Online Map**. This option requires an active network connection. If this isn't available, an error will be given and you have the option to switch to the offline map (Figure 15.1). You should check your Internet connection and proxy settings if this error appears.

Figure 15.1 ESRI Error

Besides the default Esri online map and the built-in offline map, you also have the option to use a customized online map. In this section, we discuss all these options.

15.1.1 Esri Online Map

The Esri online map uses the Esri base map and therefore requires an active network connection. Esri is a supplier of advanced mapping solutions. The Esri base maps that come with SAP Lumira, discovery edition are available for free and no Esri account is required. SAP Lumira, discovery edition takes care of this. Figure 15.2 shows one of the four default Esri base maps. In this example, we see two layers on top of the streets-based map: a **Choropleth** layer, which colors the regions based on revenue, and a layer with **Markers** for each store. Other options are the **Bubble** and **Pie** layers. For the base maps, we can choose from a **Satellite**, **Streets**, **Topo**, or **Grey** view.

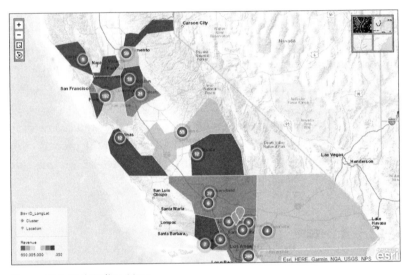

Figure 15.2 Esri Online Map

Base Maps

A base map is the fundamental layer of a geographical visualization. It typically contains geographic features, like country or region borders, streets, rivers, and city names. It depends on the purpose of the map what kind of base map is sufficient. In some cases, it might be necessary to show the earth's elevation, while in other cases only the country borders are enough.

You can use SAP Lumira, discovery edition to add information to such a base map by adding additional layers on top of it, for example the weather forecast.

A collection of Esri base maps can be found here: *http://www.esri.com/data/base-maps*.

If you want to use your own custom Esri maps, you can connect to the Esri ArcGIS online service with your credentials or connect to your Esri on-premise environment. These settings can be adjusted in the SAP Lumira, discovery edition properties (see Chapter 3).

ESRI ArcGIS

For more information about the Esri ArcGIS product, check the following site: *http:// www.esri.com/software/arcgis/arcgisonline.*

15.1.2   Offline Map

With the **Offline Map** option, the base map is loaded locally and no network connectivity is required. Compared to the online Esri map, the looks of the local map are not as smooth and detailed, but we can still use it to plot layers for countries, regions, sub-regions, and cities. As Figure 15.3 shows, we can plot the same layers on top of an offline map as on an online map.

Figure 15.3 Offline Map

15.1.3 Customized Online Map

With the **Customized Online Map** option, you can use your own base map, or one of the freely available base maps that can be found on the Internet. As shown in Figure 15.4, you need to enter the **Base Map URL** and an optional **Base Map Copyright** label, which will be displayed in the bottom-right corner of the geo map.

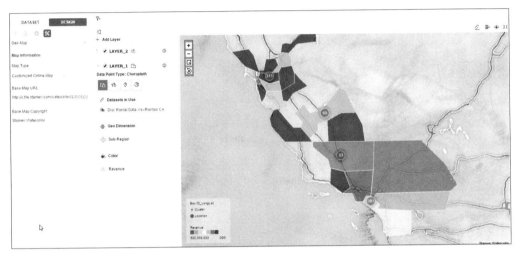

Figure 15.4 Customized Online Map

Custom Base Maps

A collection of Esri base maps can be found here: *http://www.esri.com/data/basemaps*.

A list of OpenStreet base maps can be found here: *http://wiki.openstreetmap.org/wiki/Tile_servers*.

15.2 Setting Up a Geo Map

The main prerequisite to using a geo map is that your dataset contains a geographical dimension. See Chapter 8 for details on the creation of a geographical hierarchy.

There are four different layer types available in the geo map: **Choropleth**, **Bubble**, **Marker** and **Pie**. In the following section, we discuss each of them.

We can add multiple layers on top of each other. With **+ Add Layer**, we can add additional layers (Figure 15.5). Via the gear symbol, we have the option to change the order of the layers, clear all their properties, change the color palette, or delete the layer. With the checkbox in front of the layer name, we can deactivate (and activate) each layer, without having to delete it. The name of a layer can be changed by double-clicking it.

With the **Import ESRI Custom Service** option, you can use your own customized maps from your Esri ArcGIS account or your Esri on-premise server.

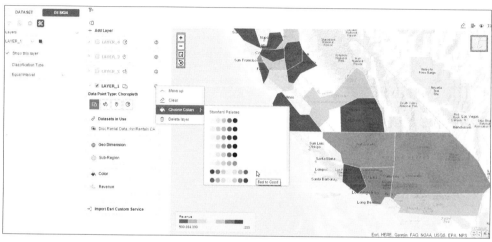

Figure 15.5 Choropleth Properties

15.2.1   Choropleth

In a choropleth map, each geographic region is colored based on its measure value (Figure 15.5). In the **Layers** formatting option, you can change the **Classification Type** from **Equal** interval into **Quantile**. With an **Equal** interval, the colors are divided equally over the value scale, while with **Quantile**, each color represents the same number of member values.

15.2.2   Bubble

Bubbles are shown for each region, where the **Size** is determined by a measure and the **Color** by a dimension (Figure 15.6). In addition, you can create an **Animation** of this map to see how the bubble develops over time, or between the different members of a dimension. The **Cluster adjacent locations** option in the **Layers** formatting option groups bubbles together for regions that are very close to each other. When you zoom in on the map, the bubbles will leave the clusters again, as there is more room to display them individually. In addition, the **Color Palette** colors can be over-ruled here.

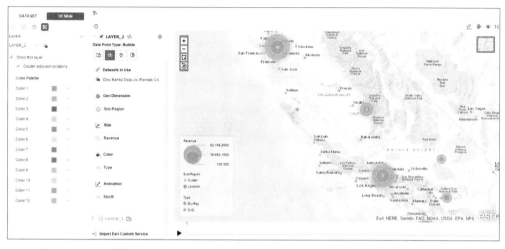

Figure 15.6 Bubble Properties

15.2.3   Marker

A marker is shown for each geographic region (Figure 15.7). With **Cluster adjacent locations** in the **Layers** formatting option, these points are grouped together when they are very close to each other. You can also adjust the color of the markers.

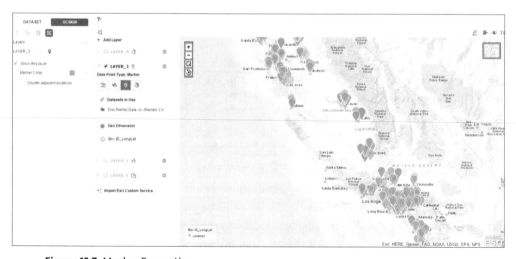

Figure 15.7 Marker Properties

15.2.4   Pie

For each region a pie chart is shown, where the size of the pie is determined by the measure value, and the division of the pie by the selected dimension (Figure 15.8). The pies can be turned into donuts by selecting **Show as Doughnut Chart** in the **Layers** formatting options. Here also the **Color Palette** can be adjusted.

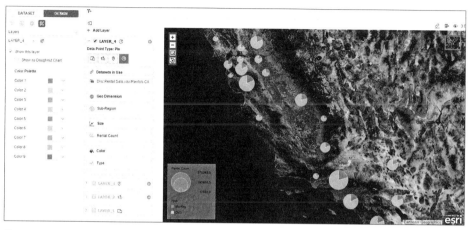

Figure 15.8 Pie Properties

For the offline map, you can make some more adjustments to the formatting (Figure 15.9). You can change the color for the **Land**, **Water**, and **Borders**, and decide whether you want to see the ocean names and in which format.

Figure 15.9 Offline Map Formatting Settings

15.3   Summary

In this chapter, we explored the capabilities of SAP Lumira, discovery edition in geographical visualizations. We saw that we can use the advanced online Esri maps, but also can fall back on the integrated, offline maps that SAP Lumira, discovery edition contains, or even use a custom base map. We discussed the several properties and layer visualization options of the geo map component.

In the next chapter, we describe the filter capabilities of SAP Lumira, discovery edition.

Chapter 16
Filters

Creating filters on datasets reduces the amount of data displayed in visualizations and stories. Using filters is extremely powerful to turn data into information and knowledge and enables you to make better data-driven and fact-based decisions in your business processes.

Now that you are familiar with the different chart types, let's take a closer look at the capabilities that SAP Lumira, discovery edition has to offer to filter data in datasets, visualizations, pages, and stories.

Filtering data helps communicate information to users in a more efficient way. For example, if you are only interested in seeing year-to-date (YTD) sales results for Europe or a particular product, hiding data from other regions and products by applying a filter helps better understand and interpret the information. It reduces the density of data in visualizations. Applying filters will only hide data; removing the filters will show the data again.

You create a filter by choosing values or ranges of values from one or multiple dimensions or measures (only on visualizations) to include or exclude using operators. When designing and interacting with stories, data filters can be applied to different levels: datasets (limited to data acquisition), individual visualizations, on the entire page, or to the whole story. This chapter describes how to apply data filters on these different levels and which types of filtering are available in SAP Lumira, discovery edition.

> **Note**
>
> The source files used for the exercises in this chapter are available for downloading via *www.sap-press.com/4511*.

16

16.1   Filtering Data in Datasets

The first level of filtering can be applied to datasets using the data view. All visualizations based on data from this dataset will be affected by this type of filter. As mentioned earlier, the data view is only available for datasets that have been acquired or imported, so filtering on complete datasets is not available when using live connections.

Now let's look at how you can apply filtering on a dataset by following the next steps:

1. Switch to the data view and click on the filter icon in the menu toolbar to show the filter bar if it's not visible.

2. Click on **Add Filters**. Optionally, you can right-click on the header of a column in the grid or facet view and select the filter option from there.

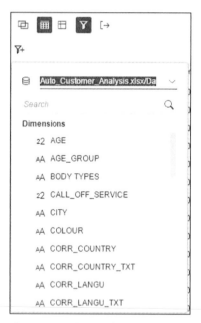

Figure 16.1 Filter Dialog in DataView Mode

3. A filter dialog will be displayed (Figure 16.1). Here you can select a dimension by scrolling down the list of available objects or by using the search bar.

4. Select **VMAKE2** as the dimension and add **Porsche** as a filter (Figure 16.2), as you are only interested in data about cars of this manufacturer.

Figure 16.2 Select Value to Apply Filter on Dataset

5. As a result, all the rows of data are filtered based on the value **Porsche** for the dimension **VMAKE2**. This is visually indicated in the filter bar, as shown in Figure 16.3.

Figure 16.3 Filter on Dataset

Please note that filters applied to a dataset are not displayed in the filter bar when switching to the design view.

If you want to delete a filter applied to the dataset, please hover over the filter and click on the **X** to remove the filter.

16.2   Filtering Data in Visualizations

The second level on which a filter can be applied is on a single visualization or chart. All other visualizations on your page or story will not be affected by this type of filter.

In the following sections, we describe how to add a filter to a visualization and interact with existing filters. Furthermore, we explain how to apply a filter based on selecting data points instead of dimensions and how to filter by applying a rank, displaying only the highest and lowest values within the dataset.

16.2.1   Adding Filters

Applying a filter to a visualization can be done in multiple ways. Let's take a closer look at the available options to apply a filter on a single visualization with the following example:

1. Click on **Insert Chart** and add a new bar chart to the canvas.
2. Add **BODY TYPES** and **PERFORMANCE_KW** to the visualization, as shown in Figure 16.4. Make sure you change the aggregation type of **PERFORMANCE_KW** to **Average**.

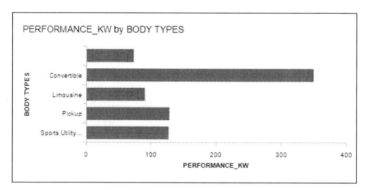

Figure 16.4 Example of a Bar Chart

3. Let's assume we are interested in displaying the average **PERFORMANCE_KW**, which stands for horsepower, but only for vehicles with a hybrid power unit. Select the visualization and click on the filter icon that appears at the right side of the visualization window, or drag and drop a dimension onto the filter bar. This will display the dialog box shown in Figure 16.5, which allows selecting the dimension on which to apply a filter. The dropdown menu at the top allows switching between linked datasets within the SAP Lumira document to select a dimension.

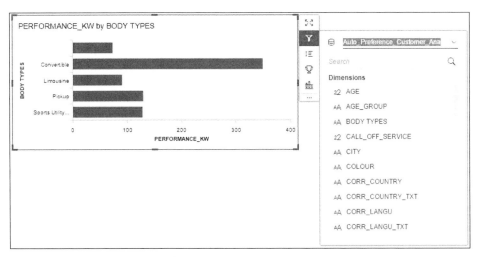

Figure 16.5 Select a Dimension for Filtering

4. Enter "ENG_FUEL" in the search bar to limit the list of dimensions or scroll through the list and select the dimension. SAP Lumira, discovery edition now displays the dialog box shown in Figure 16.6 to assist you to create a filter based on the selected dimension.

Figure 16.6 Filter Dialog Box

5. Next, select the operator in the top-left corner. The operator determines which action will be performed on the dataset. Table 16.1 displays a list of all available operators per dimension data type together with a short description.

Operator	Description	Available for Text	Available for Numeric and Date
Between or Not Between	Enter a beginning value and end value to specify the included or excluded range.	No	Yes
Equals, Not Equals	Select one or multiple values to include or exclude.	Yes	Yes
Greater than, Greater than equal, Less than, or Less than equal	Type a single value on which the operator is applied.	No	Yes
Contains, or Not Contains	Type a string that is contained in all values that need to be included or excluded.	Yes	No

Table 16.1 Overview of Filter Operators

Not all operators are available for each data type. The dialog box will only list the operators applicable to the data type of the selected dimension.

Clicking on the + icon in the top-right corner of the dialog box allows building complex filters. With this option multiple filters can be combined, for instance **Less Than** 20 and **Greater** than 80. For now, keep **Equals** as the (default) operator.

If the data type of the dimension is **Date**, the **Filter By** dialog box will display an additional date picker icon. With this you can easily select a calendar day and define for instance a range using the operator **Between**, as shown in Figure 16.7.

The search bar allows you to limit the number of dimension values displayed based on the entered search string. This feature is useful when the dimension has a large number of unique values. By default, if there are more than 100 members in the dataset for the selected dimension, the filter dialog box displays the following warning: **Too many filter values are available. Search for the required value.**

Figure 16.7 Date Picker Option

> **Change Maximum Members**
> The default value for the maximum number of members to be displayed is set to 100. You can adjust the number by changing the value in the *SAPLumiraDiscovery.ini* file: -Dhilo.filter.maxMembers=100. This file is located in your install directory, for example: *C:\Program Files\SAP BusinessObjects Lumira\Lumira Discovery\Desktop*.

6. Select **Hybrid** from the list and click **OK**. An alternative is to enter the value of a member directly into the text box next to the selected operator.

The data displayed in the bar chart, as shown in Figure 16.8, is quite different than Figure 16.5. Not only are the values of **PERFORMANCE_KW** significantly lower, but also the **BODY TYPES** called **Pickup** and **Convertible** are not present in our dataset with a hybrid engine.

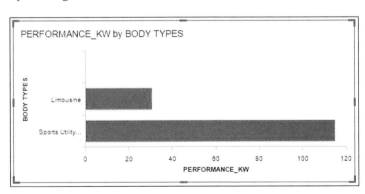

Figure 16.8 Filter on Hybrid ENG_TYPE

16.2.2   Filtering on Measures

SAP Lumira, discovery edition offers a second workflow to apply a filter to a visualization and it introduces a new functionality: filter on measures. Please follow these
steps to familiarize yourself with this workflow:

1. Select a visualization and click on the **Maximize** icon.

2. If it's not visible, show the filter bar by toggling the **Show/Hide Filter Bar** icon, as
   shown in Figure 16.9.

Figure 16.9 Show/Hide Filter Bar

3. Click on the **Add Filters** icon or drag and drop the measure onto the filter bar. As
   shown in Figure 16.10, besides dimensions, it's now possible to select measure
   objects as well as apply filtering.

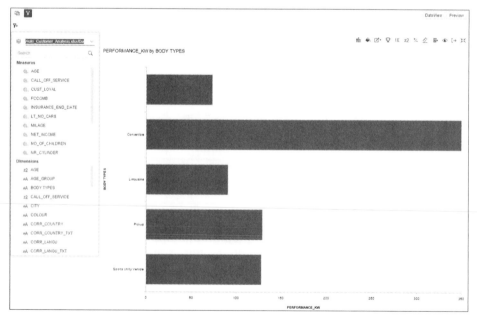

Figure 16.10 Filtering a Visualization Based on a Measure Object

4. Select **Milage** as we are interested in applying a filter based on a range between 20,000 and 50,000 miles. The **Filter by** dialog is displayed (Figure 16.11). Enter the requested information and click on **OK** to apply the filter.

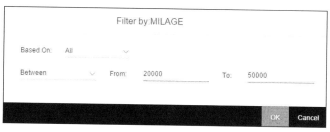

Figure 16.11 The Filter By Dialog

5. Click on **Minimize** to return to the canvas.

As we explain in more detail in Section 16.3, the filter bar can only be used to add visualization filters on dimensions and measures in **Maximize** mode. If you use the filter bar to apply filters when the canvas is visible, this filter can only be applied to the page or story level and only based on dimension objects.

In the next section, we explain how to view which filters have been applied to visualizations and how filters can be edited and removed.

16.2.3   Interacting with Filters

Interacting with filters applied to visualizations is done via the filter bar. As shown in Figure 16.12, the filter bar displays the filters currently applied to the dataset, selected visualization, page, or story with a token, listed in Table 16.2.

Token	Description
🗄	Filter applied to a dataset. This filter is only visible from the **DataView** mode.
📊	Filter applied to a single visualization. This filter is only visible when a visualization is selected on the canvas.
🗒	Filter applied to the current page. Each visualization on the page is filtered.
🗖	Filter applied to a story. Each visualization in the story is filtered.
🏆	Filter as a result of applying a rank on a single visualization.

Table 16.2 Token Icons for Filtering

325

Please note that behind the dimension name, the number of selected members is displayed between brackets. In this example only one member was selected which value listed as part of the filter. If multiple members are selected only the first values are displayed based on the available string length. Furthermore, the operator symbol is displayed in front of the selected values.

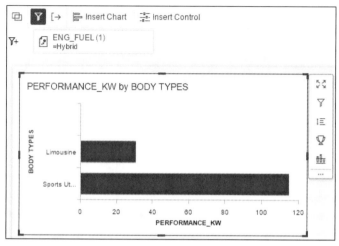

Figure 16.12 Display Applied Filters

Editing a filter can be done by clicking on the filter token displayed in the filter bar. The dialog box as shown in Figure 16.6 will be displayed where the necessary changes can be made.

To delete a filter, hover across the filter in the filter bar. As shown in Figure 16.13, an **X** appears in the top-right corner of the filter. Click on the **X** to delete the filter.

Figure 16.13 Delete a Filter

16.2.4   Selecting Data Points

A second option to filter data is by selecting data points directly from the visualization, instead of by selecting a dimension first. Follow these steps to learn how to apply a filter based on selecting data points:

1. **Maximize** a visualization or switch to the Preview mode. It's not possible to select data points in design view.

2. Hover across a visualization and use a lasso to select the data points, as shown in Figure 16.14. It's also possible to select multiple individual values or to select data points directly from the **Legend** or the **Axes** labels.

   Notice that the data points that are not included in the selection are colored gray after you select one or multiple data points.

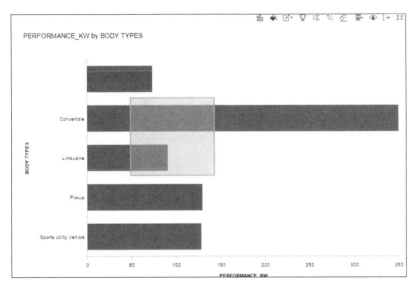

Figure 16.14 Selecting Multiple Data Points

   An information box summarizes the number of data points selected. When selecting or hovering across individual data points, the corresponding dimension and measure values are displayed.

3. Right-click on one of the selected data points to display the context menu, as shown in Figure 16.15. Click either on **Filter** or **Exclude**.

Figure 16.15 Data Points Context Menu

A filter is created that filters on the data points selected or excludes the data points from the visualization.

In the next section, we take a look at using hierarchies to filter visualizations.

16.2.5   Filtering Using Hierarchies

A third option to filter data in visualizations is by using hierarchies. As described in Chapter 8, SAP Lumira, discovery edition offers capabilities to create date/time, geo, and custom hierarchies. If the visualization contains a dimension that is part of a hierarchy, you can drill up or down dimensions to explore the data at different levels. When you're drilling, a filter token appears in the filter bar, or the filter may be added to an existing token.

The available drill options are listed in Table 16.3.

Item	Description
Drill Down	With **Drill Down**, a filter will be applied to the selected members and the dimension will be replaced with the dimension one level down in the hierarchy.
Drill By	The **Drill By** option is similar to drilling down apart from replacing the dimension. Instead, the dimension representing one level down in the hierarchy will be added to the visualization.
Drill Up	**Drill Up** will replace the current dimension displayed in the visualization with the dimension one level up in the hierarchy. If a filter was applied earlier by drilling down, this will be removed.
Drill Path...	A dimension can be part of multiple hierarchies. With the **Drill Path** option, you can switch between multiple hierarchies.

Table 16.3 Interact with Hierarchies

Drill Path Limitation
Currently **Drill Path** hierarchies are only supported with offline or SAP HANA online data sources with level based hierarchies.

Please follow these steps to learn how to use hierarchies to filter data:

1. Add a line chart to the canvas.

2. Drag and drop **Mileage**, **Year**, and **VEHICLE_TYPE** into the visualization. Ensure that the visualization looks similar to Figure 16.16.

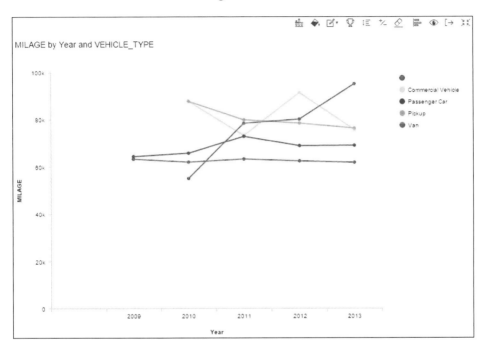

Figure 16.16 Line Chart with Date/Time Hierarchy

3. Right-click on the x-axis label value Year **2011** and select **Drill Down**. The **Year** dimension will be replaced with **Quarter**, which is one level down in the hierarchy, and a filter will be applied to **Year**. The visualization should be similar to Figure 16.17. Notice the filter on **Year** equals 2011 in the top-left corner. Furthermore, the title of the visualization changes from **Mileage by Year** to **Mileage by Quarter**.

4. Right-click on **Quarter 2** and select the option **Drill By**. A filter is applied to **Quarter** and the dimension **Month** is added to the visualization. This option, compared to **Drill Down**, makes it easier and more intuitive to interpret the current navigation state, because the values of previous navigation/filter actions remain visible, as shown in Figure 16.18.

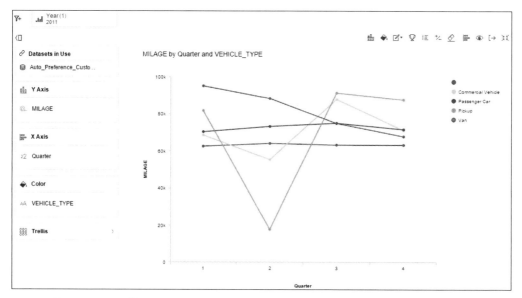

Figure 16.17 Drill Down to Quarter

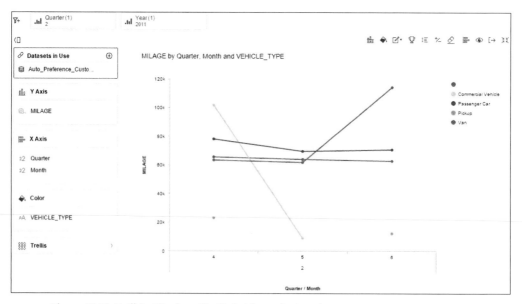

Figure 16.18 Drill By Displays Multiple Hierarchy Levels

X-Axis Visibility of Dimensions

When using the **Drill By** option, please ensure that enough space below the x-axis is available to display the label values of each dimension. If one or multiple dimensions are displayed in gray, as shown in Figure 16.19, adjust the position of the x-axis to increase the space to display all dimension values.

Figure 16.19 Increase Space to Display X-Axis Dimension Values

5. Select one of the **Month** values on the x-axis and select **Drill Up**. The visualization will return to the state, as displayed in Figure 16.17.

6. If the visualization contains a dimension that's part of multiple hierarchies, selecting the **Drill path** option allows switching between different hierarchies defined.

7. Please be aware that performing drill activities changes the state of your visualization and applies a filter. Removing the filter directly from the filter bar will not always reverse the visualization to its original state.

16.2.6   Ranking

Another method of filtering data in visualizations is by using the rank option. Ranking allows you to display the top or bottom values of the dataset based on the highest or lowest values. To apply a rank, select a visualization on the canvas and click the **Rank** icon ♔. Alternatively, you can expand the visualization and select **Rank** in the toolbar in the top-right corner.

Figure 16.20 displays the **Ranking** dialog box, which allows you to select the **Measure**, **Value**, and **Dimension** that drive the calculation. The difference with the other filter options is that you are able to select a measure to apply a filter instead of a dimension.

Figure 16.20 Ranking Options

In Figure 16.21 and Figure 16.22, we created a top three ranking filter on the measures **NET_INCOME** and **MILEAGE** applied to the dimension **HOBBIES** to visualize which hobbies have the highest net income and mileage associated with them.

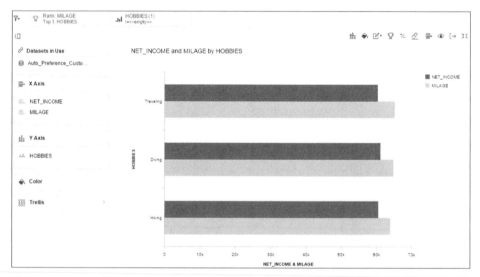

Figure 16.21 Top Three Hobbies Based on the Highest Average Mileage

Based on the two visualizations, you can conclude that outdoor hobbies like travel-ing, diving, and hiking have the highest average mileage. On the contrary the top three hobbies with the highest net income are associated with theater, football, and biking. This example shows it's very easy to use ranking to visualize the highest and lowest values in your dataset.

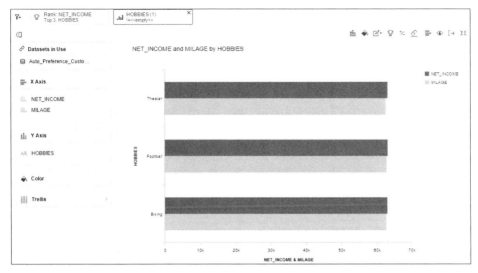

Figure 16.22 Top Three Hobbies Based on the Highest Average Net Income

When a ranking is applied to a visualization, the **Filter Bar** displays the **Rank** token, as shown in Figure 16.23. Editing the filter or deleting the filter is done similarly to all other filters. Either select the filter to reopen the **Ranking** dialog box or hover over to display the **X** to delete the ranking applied.

Figure 16.23 Rank Filter

There are a couple of limitations when applying ranking to filter data in a visualization:

- Measures and dimensions that are not part of the visualization can't be selected in the **Ranking** dialog box.
- When using linked datasets, only measures and dimensions that originate from a single dataset can be selected. It's not possible to apply a ranking based on measure A from dataset 1 and dimension B from dataset 2.
- Only one ranking can be applied at the same time to a single visualization.
- Ranking can't be applied to a page or story.

16.2.7   Linked Analysis

The final way to filter data in visualizations is via linked analysis. With linked analysis it's possible to define how visualizations or charts interact, based on a dimension in the source chart. Linked analysis can be used for charts based on the same dataset or based on different datasets that contain linked dimensions (see Chapter 18 for more information on linking datasets). The target chart does not have to contain the dimension selected in the source chart for filtering.

Now let's look at how to set up linked analysis by following next steps:

1. Right-click on the source visualization to display the context menu and select **Linked Analysis** (Figure 16.24).

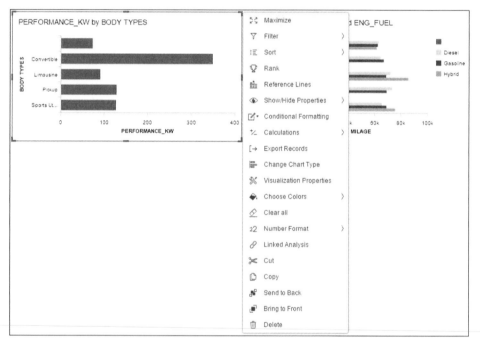

Figure 16.24 Select Linked Analysis

2. The dialog, as shown in Figure 16.25, is displayed.
3. Here you can select a dimension and select for which visualizations on which page you want to apply the linked analysis. In our example we select the dimension **BODY_TYPES** and check the **MILAGE by ENG_FUEL and BODY_TYPES** chart, which is part of **Page -01**.

Figure 16.25 Linked Analysis Dialog

4. Click **OK**.

5. Switch to preview mode to see the linked analysis in action. If you select one or multiple values for the dimension **BODY_TYPES** in the source chart, the target chart will be filtered based on the selected values (Figure 16.26).

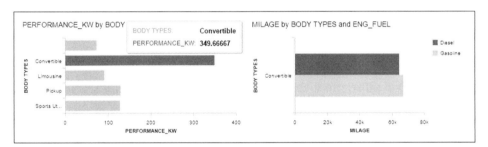

Figure 16.26 Target Chart Is Filtered Based on Selected Value

If you want to edit or delete the linked analysis, switch back to the design view and perform the following steps:

1. Select the source visualization and right-click to show the context menu. The **Linked Analysis** option now shows two additional actions, as displayed in Figure 16.27.

Figure 16.27 Select to Edit or Delete a Linked Analysis

2. Click on **Delete Link** to remove the linked analysis. A confirmation dialog is displayed with the following message: **Do you want to delete all links?** Click **Ok** or **Cancel** to proceed.

3. If you select **Edit Link**, the **Linked Analysis** dialog is shown again. From the edit link mode, however, it's only possible to change the target visualizations and not the dimension itself. Changing the dimension of the source chart would require a deletion first.

Please keep in mind the following when using linked analysis:

- Only a single dimension can be selected for each source chart.
- When the dimension is removed from the source chart, the linked analysis is also removed without any warning message.

In the next section, we look at how to apply filters and the level of pages and stories instead of individual visualizations.

16.3   Filtering Data in Stories

Besides applying filters to datasets and individual visualizations, filters can be applied to a page or story. In the following sections, we focus on the differences between applying filters to a single visualization versus an entire story. As mentioned, selecting data points, using hierarchies, or filtering data by using ranking is not applicable to pages or stories.

16.3.1   Applying Filters

Please follow the next steps to apply a filter on a page or story:

Note

For this example, a map has been added to the canvas displaying the average mileage per country.

1. In **DesignView** mode, click on the **Add Filters** icon or drag and drop a dimension onto the filter bar.

2. Select **HOBBIES** from the list of available dimensions. The filter dialog box, as shown in Figure 16.28, is displayed with one additional option compared to applying a filter on a single visualization. The **Filter Scope** option allows you to define whether the filter has to be applied to the current page or all pages within your story.

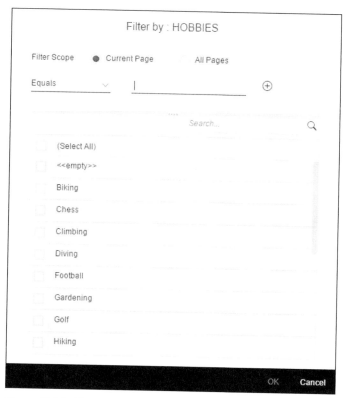

Figure 16.28 Filter on Current Page

3. Keep the default option to apply the filter to the **Current Page** and select **Biking** and **Football**. Click on **OK** to apply the filter.

In Figure 16.29, a story filter is applied to **COLOR**, the filter on **HOBBIES** is applied to the page, and **ENG_FUEL** is applied to the selected visualization only.

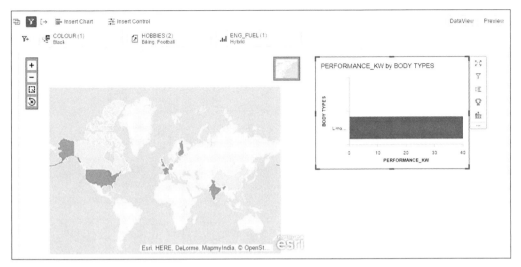

Figure 16.29 Filters Applied to the Story, Page, and Visualization Level

16.3.2   Interacting with Filters

Similar to visualization filters, you can edit page and story filters by clicking on the token in the filter bar. Hovering across the filter will display the **X** icon to remove a filter.

Please note that editing or deleting a filter applied to the page or story can only be done from the canvas. If a visualization is maximized, the page and story filters will be grayed out.

16.4   Using Controls

Instead of using the filter bar to interact with filters applied to a visualization, page, or story, as described in the previous sections, SAP Lumira, discovery edition also allows users to create controls to act as filters that are placed directly onto the canvas. Controls add interactivity to your story and can overlay a visualization. You're not bound to the filter bar to interact with your story. A box indicates the placement of the control on the canvas and allows resizing and moving the control across the story.

In the following sections, we show you how to add controls to your stories, how to edit the controls, and how to delete them.

16.4.1   Add Controls to the Canvas

A control can be added simply by clicking on **Insert Control** from the toolbar menu and selecting a dimension or by dragging and dropping an existing filter token from the filter bar onto the canvas. Please follow these steps to add a control:

1. Drag and drop an existing filter token, in this example **Country**, from the filter bar and release it on the canvas, as shown in Figure 16.30. Please note that only page or story filters can be placed onto the canvas. Filters on visualizations can't be selected. In this example, our filter is defined as a country that contains *United*, which means that all members that have the string *United* are included.

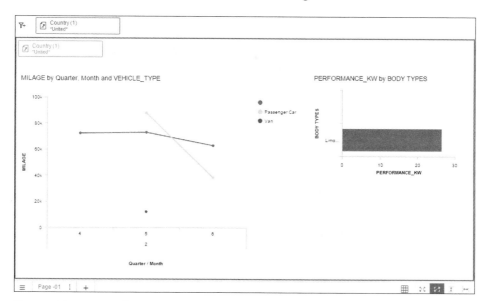

Figure 16.30 Drag and Drop a Filter to Create Control

2. Once you release the control on the canvas, the **Control Type** dialog box, as shown Figure 16.31, is displayed. Here you select which type of control to add. Depending on the data type of the selected dimension filter and the selected operator, certain control types will be available. A full overview is provided in Table 16.4.

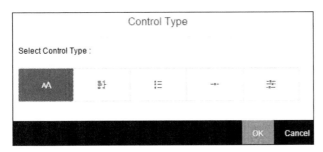

Figure 16.31 Control Type Dialog Box

Option	Description
Text Box ᴬᴬ	Displays a text box where you can type in values.
Choice ≔	The choice control is useful to view, search through, and sort the list of members to apply a filter.
Dropdown ≝↑	Similar to the choice control. Main difference is that the drop-down control is more appropriate if space on the canvas is limited.
Date 📅	Date control can be used to view and organize visualizations for a specified time period. Depending on the operator, you can select single or multiple dates.
Slider ⊸	The slider is only available for numeric values and allows filtering on specific ranges. You can choose between a single or double slider.
Complex Filter ≣	Control displays the value of the filter for one or more conditions. If you have created a complex filter, which contains more than one operator, this control type is the only available one to select.

Table 16.4 Control Types Options

3. Select **Text Box** as your **Control Type** and click **OK**.

4. Change the visualization from **Line** to **Crosstab** using the chart picker and add **Country** to the rows.

5. To interact with the control added to our story, we have to switch to preview mode. As shown in Figure 16.32, the filter on **Country** in the filter bar is grayed out. You are

only able to interact with the filter by typing in values corresponding with members in the dataset.

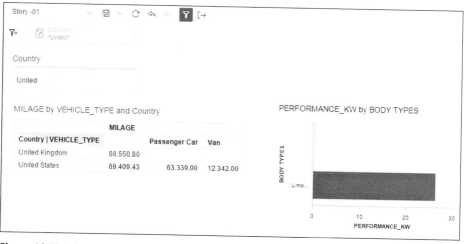

Figure 16.32 Interact with Text Box Control

6. Select the Text Box control and type "land". Confirm by pressing [Enter] or clicking outside of the control to apply the value. Due to the fact that we defined contains as the operator, each country with the string *land* is included in the story as well. The result is displayed in Figure 16.33.

Figure 16.33 Filter Using Text Box Control with the Operator Contains

7. Now add a second control to the story. Create a filter on **HOBBIES** and add a drop-down control to the canvas, as displayed in Figure 16.34.

Figure 16.34 Dropdown control

8. Click on ⌄ to expand the dropdown control, as shown in Figure 16.35. The scroll bar on the right side of the control allows scrolling through the complete list of members. A search field at the top can be used to reduce the members displayed by typing in one or multiple characters.

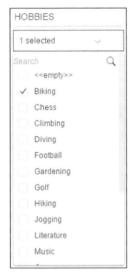

Figure 16.35 Using a Dropdown Control to Select Multiple Members

The choice control, as shown in Figure 16.36, is very similar to the dropdown control. The main difference is that it permanently displays the available filter members on the canvas. This type of control works best with a very limited list of members. It allows you to quickly interact without expanding the dropdown list.

The date control is only available for dimensions of data type **Date**. As mentioned, it allows you to filter the visualizations in your page or story based on a single date or a range defined by a start and end date depending on the operator of the filter. In

Figure 16.37, a start and end date can be selected by interacting with the date picker dialog box.

Figure 16.36 Example of Choice Control

Figure 16.37 Date Control with Date Picker Dialog Box

The slider control, as shown in Figure 16.38, is only available for dimensions with a numeric data type. In this example the slider is defined to filter on each value of the dimension **AGE**, which lies between 35 and 75.

You can interact with the slider in different ways. Drag and drop the circles which mark the start and end value, or click on the slider bar to adjust the range. Selecting the blue bar allows you to change the start and end value while keeping the range intact.

The behavior and available options of the slide control depend on the operator selected in the filter.

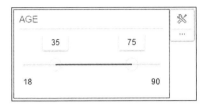

Figure 16.38 Slider Control

Besides interacting with the slider control to change the values, you can also change the minimum and maximum values of the slider and the interval via the dialog box shown in Figure 16.39. This option is available by clicking on the configure slider icon, which becomes visible when you select the slider control.

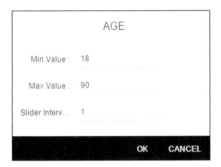

Figure 16.39 Configure Slider Dialog Box

The final control available in SAP Lumira, discovery edition is the complex filters control. Basically this control only lists the dimension and the filters specified. There is no interaction possible with this type of control. Figure 16.40 shows an example of a complex filter defined.

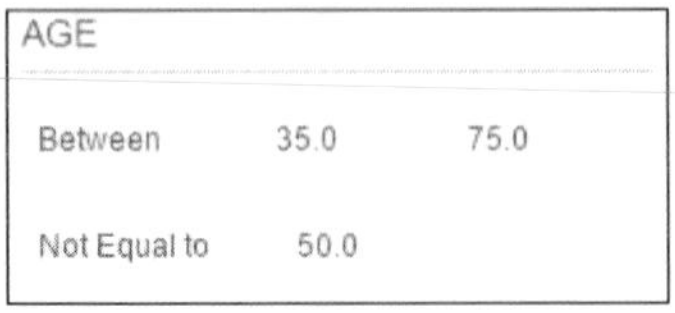

AGE		
Between	35.0	75.0
Not Equal to	50.0	

Figure 16.40 Example of Complex Filter Control

16.4.2   Edit Controls

In the **DesignView** mode, it's possible to edit a control by either clicking on the filter in the filter bar or selecting the input control on the canvas and selecting **Edit Filter**. Making changes to a filter, by adjusting for instance the operator or selected values, can also have an impact on whether the control remains applicable. Follow the next steps to familiarize yourself with the editing controls:

1. Select the **AGE** slider control on the canvas and click on **Edit Filter**. The filter dialog box, as shown in Figure 16.6, will be displayed.

2. Change the operator to **Equals**. As a result of this, the end value is automatically removed.

3. Select multiple values from the available members and click **OK**.

4. Because the slider control is not compatible with selecting multiple values combined with the **Equals** operator, the control type dialog box, as shown in Figure 16.31, is displayed. Please select one of other control types and click **OK**.

5. Clicking on the **Change Control Type** icon, as shown in Figure 16.41, is available when selecting the control on the canvas.

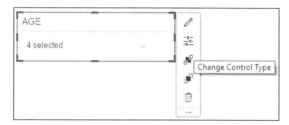

Figure 16.41 Change Control Type

16.4.3   Delete Controls

The final action discussed in this chapter is deleting a control. Select a control on the canvas and click on the **Delete** icon, displayed in the context menu, to remove it from your story. Please be aware that deleting a control from the canvas will not remove the filter on which the control is based.

If you delete a filter on which on control is based, the **Input Control Dependency Found** dialog box, as shown in Figure 16.42, is displayed. By clicking **OK** both the filter and the control will be removed.

16

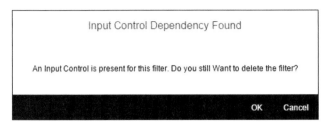

Figure 16.42 Input Control Dependency Dialog Box

16.5   Summary

In this chapter, we described all available options that SAP Lumira, discovery edition has to offer to apply filtering on datasets, visualizations, pages, and stories. You have familiarized yourself with applying filters on dimensions and measures using the filter dialog box. Furthermore, we explained how to use data point selection, hierarchies, ranking, and linked analysis to limit the data visible in your visualizations. Finally, we introduced the concept of using controls directly onto the canvas to create interactive pages and stories that you can share with your user community.

Besides filters, you can further enhance your pages and stories to efficiently communicate the information by adding text boxes, images, shapes, and illustrations. Chapter 17 focuses on the available options to format your story.

Chapter 17

Story Formatting

To create visually stunning stories that effectively communicate your message, you can format your story pages and add text boxes, images, illustrations, and images. Learn in this chapter how to create professional looking presentation-style documents.

Part III, so far, has explained how to create different visualizations, discussed when to use the different available chart types, and provided an overview of the various chart properties as well as how to apply filtering to hide data.

In addition to visualizations, which are the primary elements of your story, SAP Lumira, discovery edition offers elements such as text boxes, images, illustrations, and shapes to enhance your story and describe data.

In this chapter we focus on the options SAP Lumira, discovery edition offers to format and enhance your story pages to act as professional, presentation-style documents.

17.1 Story Pages

A story consists of one or multiple story pages. As you work on your storyboard you can add, duplicate, move and delete pages.

You can create a new page by clicking on the **+** on the next-to-last page. In our example, as shown in Figure 17.1, this is **Page -01**.

Figure 17.1 Add a New Story Page

When you click on the ≡ icon, a list of pages is displayed which can be used to directly jump to one of the pages in your story.

Other page settings available to interact with pages can be accessed by clicking on the ⁝ icon next to the name of page, as shown in the pane displayed in Figure 17.2.

Figure 17.2 Story Page Settings Pane

In Table 17.1, we explain in more detail the available options to interact with story pages.

Option	Description
Duplicate	When you have created a certain template with, for instance, default elements like a standard header and footer, company logo, etc., it can be very helpful to use the **Duplicate** option. This will add a new page as a duplicate with no reference to the original story page.
Rename	After duplicating or adding a new page to your story, you can use the **Rename** option to change the name of the page to reflect the content of the story page. Instead of using the **Page Options** menu, you can double-click on the page name and change it.
Move Left Move Right	Depending on the position of the story page, you can move a page to the left or right and rearrange the order.
Settings	The **Settings** option allows you to change the size of the selected page, depending on the preferred layout and type of device used for viewing the story. The following predefined options are available: ▪ Standard (4:3) ▪ Extended (16:9) ▪ BI Launchpad (20:7) ▪ Custom: Allows you to define the width and height in pixels. The selected size can be applied directly to the page or to all pages in your story.
Delete	If you want to delete a page, click **Delete**.

Table 17.1 Story Page Settings

17.2   Text Boxes

Text boxes can be placed anywhere on the page or can even overlay visualizations. They are ideal for titles, captions, paragraphs and sections, textual information, etc.

You can add a text box by selecting the **Choose Text (T)** icon on the **Design** tab in the left side pane. As shown in Figure 17.3, a number of predefined text boxes with different styles are available to directly drag-and-drop onto the canvas. Pick the one closest to the required layout to minimize the number of changes.

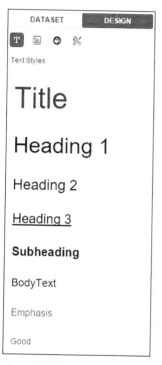

Figure 17.3 Text Styles

After adding a text box to the canvas, a context menu is displayed which offers shortcuts to the most common actions to change the layout of the text box. By either right-clicking on the text box or clicking on the **Show All** icon, you can display all available options, as shown in Figure 17.4.

By selecting the text box, you can move it around on the canvas. Optionally, resizing can be done by selecting an anchor of the blue bounding box and changing it to fit the required size.

Figure 17.4 List of Available Options to Change Appearance of Text Box

17.3   Images, Illustrations, and Shapes

In addition to text boxes, you can also enhance your story with images, illustrations, and shapes. These options are available via the **Choose Graphic** icon on the **Design** tab.

Before you can add an image to the canvas, you first have to upload the image by clicking on the **+**, as shown in Figure 17.5.

The uploaded image is displayed as a thumbnail and can be used on the canvas. If you hover over the thumbnail of the image, a cross appears in the upper-right corner, which allows you to delete the image from your SAP Lumira document.

To add an illustration or shape, select the applicable menu item and choose from the already available options. You can narrow the list of thumbnails by selecting a category. Furthermore, a similar option is available to add your own illustrations and shapes. A prerequisite, however, is that the file has to be in Scalable Vector Graphics (SVG) format with valid XML coding.

Figure 17.5 Upload Images

17.4 Background

Finally, we can also change the background color and set a background image for a story page. This option is available via the **Choose Background** icon on the **Design** tab, as shown in Figure 17.6.

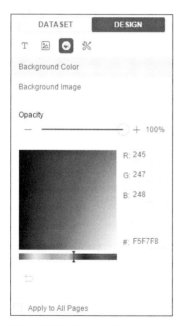

Figure 17.6 Choose Background

You can set the **Opacity** for both the background image as well as the background color. The **Reset** icon will revert all changes. If you check the **Apply to All Pages** option, each page within your SAP Lumira document will have the same defined background image and color.

17.5   Summary

In this chapter we described the options SAP Lumira, discovery edition offers to create presentation-style stories. By selecting the right size of your pages—depending on the layout and device used to consume the story—and adding text boxes, images, illustrations, and shapes, you are able to effectively communicate the message you want to send out with your data-bound visualizations.

The next and final chapter of Part III provides a deep dive into the capabilities of linking datasets. With data linking, it's possible to display data from different data sources into a single visualization without merging or appending the data sources.

Chapter 18
Linking Datasets

Being able to interact with datasets independent of your IT organization is key to quickly responding to questions from your stakeholders and performing the required analysis. Linking multiple datasets is one of the features that SAP Lumira, discovery edition offers to increase flexibility to perform such tasks.

SAP Lumira, discovery edition provides capabilities to link multiple datasets that contain related data and display the data in a single visualization without creating a new (merged) dataset first. Dataset linking lets you enrich datasets with, for instance, your own personal data, by adding columns your corporate datasets might not provide such as virtual teams, weighted factors, target data, etc.

The concept of linking datasets differs from merging. In this chapter, we explain the differences and the specific terms to dataset linking, as well as the available join types and limitations. Furthermore, we show how to create dataset links.

> **Note**
>
> The source files used for the exercises in this chapter are available for downloading via *www.sap-press.com/4511*.

18.1   Linking versus Merging

A visualization with linked datasets contains one or more links between dimensions from separate datasets and measure values of those datasets. Prior to displaying the data in the visualization, these datasets are not merged based on a join condition. Instead, data is aggregated for each dataset separately and joined on one or more common dimensions, to produce the result set visualized in a chart or table.

When performing a merge, a join operator is used to combine the datasets based on a key dimension. Furthermore, a key dimension needs to be present and only dimensions with similar data types can be merged. The result of a merge operation is that dimensions are added to the dataset and a new dataset is created. More information on merging datasets can be found in Chapter 8, Section 8.4.

If you want to restore the original dataset, you need to undo the merge operation, or remove the merged dataset and reacquire the original dataset. With traditional database merging you have to decide to which level you want to roll up your data, and then join the databases at that level.

The terms listed in Table 18.1 are specific in the context of linking datasets.

Terms	Description
Primary dataset	The dataset used when first creating a visualization.
Secondary dataset	Dataset that is added to the visualization based on the primary dataset. There is no limitation to the number of secondary datasets that can be added.
Primary (or secondary) dimension	A dimension from the primary or secondary dataset.
Link	Relationship between dimensions in different datasets. For example, an *<Account>* dimension in the secondary dataset can be linked with the *<Account>* dimension in the primary dataset. Please note that a secondary dataset always links to the primary dataset and not to other secondary datasets.
Active linked dimensions	The set of dimensions that the datasets are linked on.

Table 18.1 Terms Related to the Context of Linking Datasets

When linking datasets, you can choose between the different types of joins listed in Table 18.2.

	Join Type	Description
	Left outer join	Returns all rows from the primary dataset, even if there are no matches in the secondary dataset.
	Inner join	Returns all rows that match in both datasets.
	Full outer join	Returns all rows from both datasets.
	Exception	Only returns rows from the primary dataset that do not have a match in the secondary dataset.

Table 18.2 Available Join Types for Linking Datasets

When linking datasets, there are a number of limitations you need to keep in mind:

- **Online versus offline**
  When creating a link between two datasets, these datasets need to be either both added as live data sources or imported data sources. Currently there is no support to link live datasets with imported datasets.

- **Filtering**
  If you add a filter on a linked dimension, the list of values displays a combination (union) of the values available from all datasets used in the visualization.

- **Heap size**
  When linking datasets a message may be displayed that the default Java heap size is insufficient. Depending on the size of your result set you might need to increase the heap size. This can be done as follows:

  - Open the *SAPLumiraDiscovery.ini* file, located at *C:\Program Files\SAP Business-Objects Lumira\Lumira Discovery\Desktop*.
  - Find the heap size setting: -Xmx1024m (default value).
  - Change the setting to a larger value; for example, -Xmx2048m. The value must be no greater than the amount of physical memory you have in your machine, in megabytes. For example, 2048 = 2 GB.
  - Save the file and restart SAP Lumira, discovery edition.

18

18.2   Creating Dataset Links

Dataset links can be created in multiple ways. In the following sections, we show you how to link datasets through the menu bar and then create your visualization or link your datasets directly when creating a visualization.

18.2.1   Define Dataset Links

Let's start with an example where we already acquired two datasets containing demographic and healthcare data per neighborhood and want to create a link to visualize measures from both datasets in a single visualization:

1. Click on the menu bar and select **Data · Link Datasets** (Figure 18.1) or use Ctrl + Shift + L.

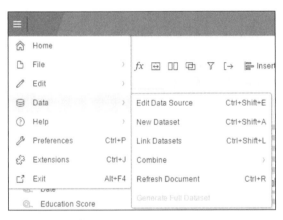

Figure 18.1 Link Datasets

2. If your SAP Lumira document doesn't contain two or more datasets that can be linked, an **Information** dialog (Figure 18.2) will be displayed as a reminder.

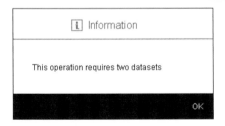

Figure 18.2 Dataset Linking Requires Two Datasets

3. In the **Link Datasets** dialog (Figure 18.3), select the primary dataset (left) and the secondary dataset (right). Please keep in mind that you can link multiple secondary datasets to one single primary dataset, but not vice versa. The dropdown boxes that contain the name of the datasets can be used to switch from primary to secondary.

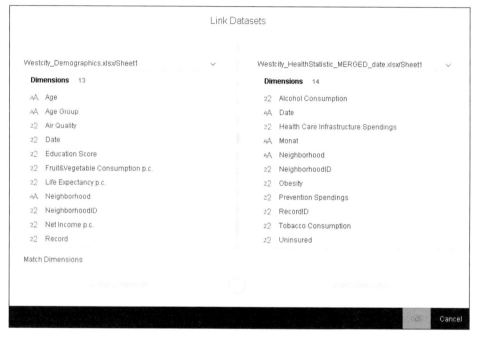

Figure 18.3 Link Datasets Dialog

4. To link the two datasets, select a dimension from the primary dataset and the secondary dataset. In this example, we select **Neighborhood**. Please note that selecting a dimension limits the list of available dimensions that can be selected for linking based on the type.

5. Select **Neighborhood** from the secondary dataset and, at the bottom of the dialog, the matched dimensions are visually represented (Figure 18.4).

6. Click **OK** to link the datasets.

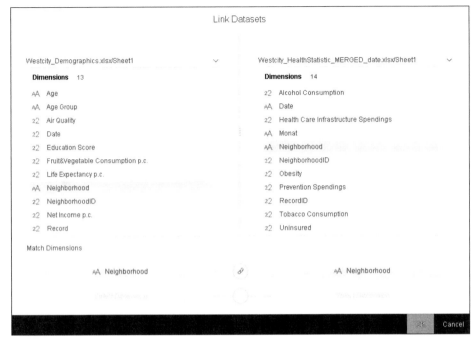

Figure 18.4 Matched Dimensions

Please note that you can delete or update any matched dimensions by hovering across the matched dimensions and clicking on the **X** to make changes. All visualizations based on matched dimensions are impacted when updating or deleting dataset links (Figure 18.5).

Figure 18.5 Update Dataset Links information Dialog

18.2.2   Create Visualization

Your next step is to create a visualization that combines multiple measures from two datasets based on the linked dimension, as follows:

1. Insert a column chart onto the canvas and maximize the chart.
2. Select a measure from the primary dataset, in our example **Alcohol Consumption**, and add this to the **Y Axis**.
3. Expand the secondary dataset and select a measure (**Life Expectancy**) and add this to the **Y Axis** as well.
4. As a result of adding a measure from another dataset into the same visualization, the linked dimension, in this case **Neighborhood**, is displayed under **Active Linked Dimensions** (Figure 18.6).

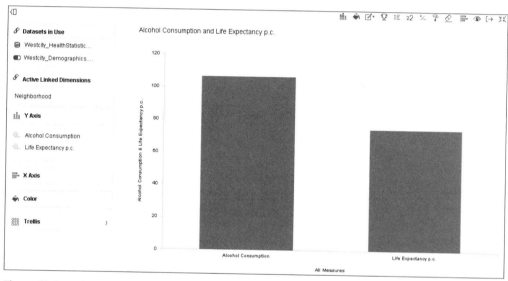

Figure 18.6 Active Linked Dimensions

5. If there are multiple linked dimensions defined, you can add them by clicking on the **+**, which is visible when hovering across the **Active Linked Dimensions** area in the feeding panel. You can also remove the linked dimension by deleting it from the visualization. In our example, there are no additional linked dimensions available (Figure 18.7).

Figure 18.7 Add Unused Linked Dimensions

6. In a similar way, additional datasets, if available, could be added by clicking the **+** in the **Datasets in Use** area of the feeding panel.

7. As shown in Figure 18.8, the type of join (as discussed in Section 18.1) between the primary and the secondary dataset is displayed by using different icons. By default, the **Left Outer Join** is selected. If required, you can change the type of join by clicking on the secondary dataset and selecting the join icon.

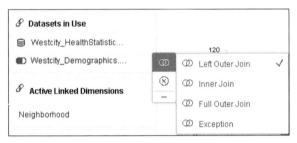

Figure 18.8 Select Join Type

8. Now let's add the **Neighborhood** to the **X Axis** to see the relationship between **Alcohol Consumption** and **Life Expectancy**. Please note that it's not possible to add the linked dimension from the secondary dataset (Figure 18.9).

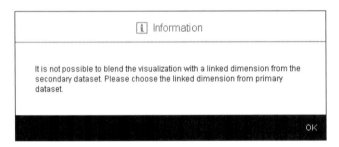

Figure 18.9 Not Possible to Blend with Linked Dimension

9. Figure 18.10 displays two measures from two different datasets combined in a single visualization based on a linked dimension.

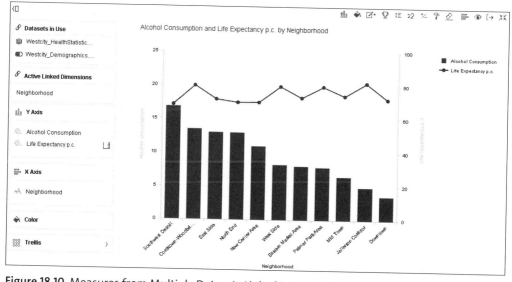

Figure 18.10 Measures from Multiple Datasets Linked in Single Visualization

18.2.3 Linking Dataset During Visualization Creation

The alternative way to define a link between multiple datasets is available when creating a visualization. In the following example, the same two datasets have been acquired but no link has been created.

1. Insert and maximize a column chart so the feeding panel is visible.

2. Drag and drop a measure from the dataset, which should act as primary, into the chart.

3. Add a second measure from a secondary dataset into the chart. The **Link Datasets** dialog will be displayed because no linked dimensions have been defined yet (Figure 18.11). Please note that the dropdown boxes available to select which dataset acts as primary and secondary are grayed out. If you want to swap them, please click **Cancel** and reverse the order in which the measures from the different datasets are added to the chart.

4. Select the dimensions that need to be linked and click **OK**. In the feeding panel, the **Active Linked Dimensions** are displayed.

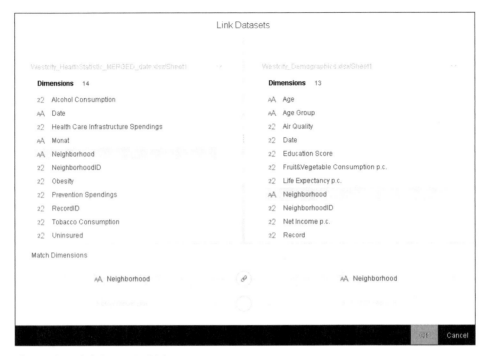

Figure 18.11 Link Datasets Dialog

18.3   Summary

In this chapter, we explained the concept of linking datasets to support you in creating visualizations that display measures from multiple datasets without the need to create a new, merged, dataset first. SAP Lumira, discovery edition will automatically detect if the necessary dimensions have already been linked. If not, a dialog is displayed and you can link dimensions even while creating visualizations.

Now that we have created multiple visualizations and stories, it's time to start sharing. The next chapter focuses on the possibilities SAP Lumira, discovery edition offers to share stories in different ways.

PART IV

Sharing

Chapter 19
Sharing Stories

Being able to share SAP Lumira documents is the key to delivering the right information to the right users on time. SAP Lumira documents can be easily distributed and shared using the local SAP Lumira document file or via the SAP BusinessObjects BI platform.

When you finalize a story that consists of multiple visualizations, filters, images, etc., it's time to share the information with other users. SAP Lumira, discovery edition offers two options for sharing stories:

- Locally
- SAP BusinessObjects BI platform

In the following sections, we show how you can share SAP Lumira documents, whether they are stored locally on the file system or saved on the SAP Business-Objects BI platform.

19.1 Local

The first option for sharing your SAP Lumira documents is by sharing a copy of the .lumx file, for instance via email. Let's first save our story to create the file:

1. Open an existing SAP Lumira document and click on **File · Save As** or use the shortcut combination `Ctrl`+`Shift`+`S` (Figure 19.1). A third option is provided through the menu bar (Figure 19.2).

2. The **Save Document** dialog will be displayed (Figure 19.3). By default, the **Local** tab is selected. Here you can enter a **Name** and **Description** or select an existing SAP Lumira document from the list. By selecting an existing document, you can replace or overwrite it with the current story. Use the **Find** option to limit the number of SAP Lumira documents displayed.

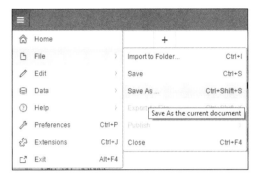

Figure 19.1 Save Current Document

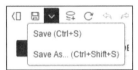

Figure 19.2 Save Option via the Menu Bar

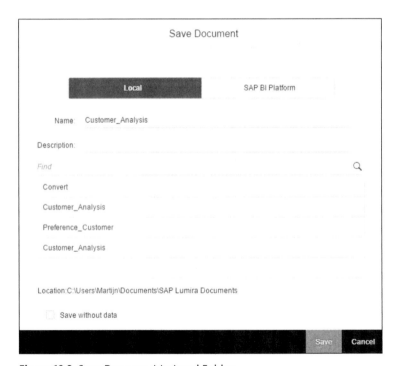

Figure 19.3 Save Document to Local Folder

3. Enter or change the **Name** of the SAP Lumira document and optionally add a **Description**.

> **Save Without Data**
>
> There is an option provided to save the document without data (**Save without data**). This option is relevant for documents based on imported datasets and useful when your data sources have row-level restrictions applied that limit the dataset for each user. In this way, you prevent sharing confidential or restricted data to unauthorized users.

4. Click **Save** to save the document to the default SAP Lumira folder: *C:\Users\<user-name>\Documents\SAP Lumira Documents*. If you have selected an existing document, a **Confirmation** message will be displayed (Figure 19.4) asking for confirmation to replace the SAP Lumira document.

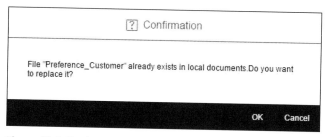

Figure 19.4 Replace Existing SAP Lumira Document

5. Now let's browse to the default folder (Figure 19.5) to view the SAP Lumira documents. From here, you can select a file and use the menu items available to copy and share it using email, a shared drive, etc.

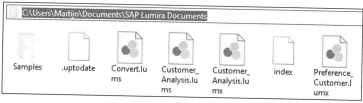

Figure 19.5 Default SAP Lumira Documents Folder

Change the Default Location of SAP Lumira Documents Folder

You can change the location of the default SAP Lumira documents folder by adding the following parameter to the *SAPLumiraDiscovery.ini* file:

`-Dhilo.document.dir=<folder path>`

The *SAPLumiraDiscovery.ini* file can be found in the install directory: *C:\Program Files\SAP BusinessObjects Lumira\Lumira Discovery\Desktop*.

Please keep in mind that in all cases SAP Lumira documents are stored at one location.

Sharing an SAP Lumira document by making a copy of the file and distributing it via email has a number of cons:

- To be able to view the SAP Lumira document, a user needs to have an SAP Lumira, discovery edition client installed.

- You cannot track who has access to this document once it's distributed. If you save the document containing data, this may result in unauthorized and unintended access.

- There is no way to recall or revoke the document once it's been shared.

- It is almost impossible to correctly manage versions.

- There is no scheduling functionality available (see Chapter 22, Section 22.2).

- You cannot control any edit or view rights (see Chapter 21, Section 21.8).

- It is difficult to share an update of the document.

In the next section, we show you how you can leverage the SAP BusinessObjects BI platform to mitigate these drawbacks.

19.2   SAP BusinessObjects BI Platform

In addition to sharing locally stored SAP Lumira documents, you can utilize the capabilities of the SAP BusinessObjects BI platform to securely save, share, and manage your stories. Furthermore, you can leverage the existing authentication and authorization of the SAP BusinessObjects BI platform as well as monitor usage through auditing of events.

Based on the authorizations, users can log in to the SAP BusinessObjects BI platform from their SAP Lumira, discovery edition client or from the BI Launchpad (see Chapter 22), and open and interact with an SAP Lumira document.

To be able to use the SAP BusinessObjects BI platform to share your stories and allow other users to retrieve them, the following prerequisites have to be met:

- Make sure that SAP BusinessObjects BI platform version 4.1 SP 3 or higher is available.

- Make sure that the SAP Lumira, server edition for the SAP BusinessObjects BI platform add-on is installed.

More details about the integration between SAP Lumira, discovery edition and the SAP Lumira, server edition can be found in Chapter 21.

Please ensure that the versions of your SAP Lumira, discovery edition client and the SAP BusinessObjects BI platform add-on are the same to avoid that some features might not be compatible.

The following two sections provide step-by-step instructions on how to save and open an SAP Lumira document from the SAP BusinessObjects BI platform.

19.2.1   Saving a Document

To save an SAP Lumira document to the SAP BusinessObjects BI platform, please follow these steps:

1. Open an existing SAP Lumira document and click on **File · Save As** or use the shortcut combination Ctrl+Shift+S (Figure 19.1). You can also use the menu bar.

2. Switch from **Local** to **SAP BI Platform** in the **Save Document** dialog (Figure 19.6). If you are already logged in to the SAP BusinessObjects BI platform during an earlier workflow, you will not be prompted to provide your credentials (unlike SAP Lumira 1.x).

19

Figure 19.6 Save Document to the SAP BusinessObjects BI Platform

3. Provide your SAP BusinessObjects BI platform **Server** details (IP address or host-name) along with the **Authentication** type and your **Username** and **Password**.

4. Click on **Connect**.

5. The next step is to browse to the folder where you want to store your SAP Lumira document (Figure 19.7).

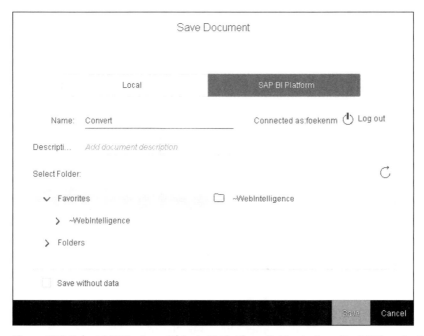

Figure 19.7 Select SAP BusinessObjects BI Platform Folder to Save the SAP Lumira Document

6. Provide a **Name** and optionally a **Description**.

> **Note**
>
> You can save the document without data (**Save without data**). This option is relevant for documents based on imported datasets and useful when your data sources have row-level restrictions applied that limit the dataset for each user. In this way, you prevent sharing confidential or restricted data to unauthorized users.

7. Click **Save**. To be able to successfully save your SAP Lumira document, you need to have write access to the selected folder.

8. A confirmation is displayed to indicate that you successfully saved the SAP Lumira document to the SAP BusinessObjects BI platform.

Once an SAP Lumira document is saved to the SAP BusinessObjects BI platform, you can also generate **OpenDocuments** links and share those with other users via email or embed these links within other applications. See Chapter 22, Section 22.1.6 for more information on **OpenDocument** links.

19.2.2   Opening a Document

To open an SAP Lumira document stored on the SAP BusinessObjects BI platform, please follow the next steps:

1. On the **Home** screen, click on **SAP BI Platform** below the **Data Source** area (Figure 19.8).

Figure 19.8 Connect to SAP BusinessObjects BI Platform from the Home Screen

2. Provide your SAP BusinessObjects BI platform server details (IP address or hostname) along with the **Authentication** type and your **Username** and **Password**. If you are already logged in to the SAP BusinessObjects BI platform during an earlier workflow, you will not be prompted to provide your credentials (unlike SAP Lumira 1.x).

3. Click on **Connect**.

4. Browse to the folder where the SAP Lumira document you want to open is stored (Figure 19.9). Only users with appropriate authorizations are able to open and view the documents.

Figure 19.9 Select SAP BusinessObjects BI Platform Folder to Open the SAP Lumira Document

5. Select the SAP Lumira document that you want to open.

19.3 Summary

SAP Lumira, discovery edition offers multiple options to share SAP Lumira documents with other users, either through the local file system or by utilizing the benefits of the SAP BusinessObjects BI platform.

In the next chapter, we discuss how you can export and share the datasets in SAP Lumira documents to different formats and destinations.

Chapter 20
Exporting Data

Besides sharing and publishing stories either offline or through the SAP BusinessObjects BI platform, SAP Lumira, discovery edition offers the capabilities to export datasets and visualizations into multiple formats, like PDF, CSV, Microsoft Excel, and SAP HANA.

Datasets and visualizations created with SAP Lumira, discovery edition can be exported into multiple formats like PDF, CSV (comma-separated values), Microsoft Excel, and SAP HANA. During the export, the data and visualizations (PDF only), which are in .lumx format, are translated into the new target format, which can be easily shared and reused in other applications.

In the following sections, we explain how you can export your stories and all data values from a visualization and how to share and publish datasets created with SAP Lumira, discovery edition.

20.1   Export to PDF

Sharing visualizations can be done by generating a PDF file, which can be distributed, for example, via email. Users without access to an SAP Lumira, discovery edition desktop client or the SAP BusinessObjects BI platform will still be able to view the story.

Please follow these steps to export your story to a PDF file:

1. Open your story and click on **Export to PDF** in the toolbar (see Figure 20.1).

Figure 20.1 Export to PDF

2. The **Export as PDF** dialog, as shown in Figure 20.2, is displayed. Here you can select if you want to export all pages in your story or select a range. A range can be defined by separating page numbers using a comma or combined with sequential pages separated by a dash (-). An example of the syntax to include pages 2 and 5 through 8 would be "2, 5-8".

Figure 20.2 Export Story as PDF

3. Select whether to **Show Filters** in the appendix or to not display any applied filters.

4. Another option is to **Show Crosstabs** in the appendix when exporting as a PDF. This means that the full crosstab will be included in the appendix instead of displaying only the columns and rows visible in the story. As displayed in Figure 20.3, you need to decide if you want **All Crosstabs** or only a selection of crosstabs to be exported.

Figure 20.3 Select Which Crosstab to Export

5. Click **Done** to export the story as a PDF file.

6. SAP Lumira, discovery edition will open a **Save File** dialog box.

7. Navigate to the destination folder using the file tree.

8. Enter a file name and click on **Save** to generate the file and close the dialog box. You can now open the generated PDF file and start sharing.

20.2 Export Records

In addition to exporting a story or story pages to PDF, you can also select a visualization and export the underlying data values into a CSV or Microsoft Excel file. Let's assume that your visualization, a bar chart, shows sales revenue per city from a dataset that also contains the measures **Customer Satisfaction** and **Number of Issues Reported**. These two measures are not easily accessible from the visualization, but are useful for further analysis. Instead of creating a new visualization, for instance a crosstab, you can export and share the records by following these steps:

1. Open the story and select the visualization for which you want to export the records in the design view.

2. Click on **Export Records** from the context menu. Alternatively, you can first maximize the visualization before selecting the **Export Records** option in the upper-right corner of the toolbar.

3. The **Export as File** dialog box, shown in Figure 20.4, is displayed. There are two export types available:

   – **Aggregated**
   Exports only the data values that are included in the selected visualization.

   – **Detailed**
   Exports each selected dimension and measure from the available dataset(s).

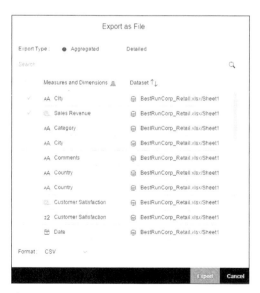

Figure 20.4 Export Records from Visualization as File

The **Search** field allows filtering on the list of **Measures and Dimensions** displayed by entering a search string. Another option to view and scroll through the available **Measures and Dimensions** is to change the sort order of both available columns (**Dataset**).

4. In this example, select **Detailed** as **Export Type** and select the measures **Customer Satisfaction** and **Number of Issues Reported**.

5. Select the file format, in this example **XLSX**.

6. Click on **Export** to open the **Save As** dialog box.

7. Navigate to the destination folder using the file tree.

8. Enter a file name and click on **Save** to generate the file and close the dialog box.

9. Open the Microsoft Excel file to review the results.

20.3   Export Datasets

Instead of exporting records from a visualization, you can export complete datasets created with SAP Lumira, discovery edition as files to your local system, either as CSV files or Microsoft Excel files.

20.3.1   Export as File

Exporting datasets can be useful if you, for instance, want to reuse the enrichments applied to your dataset in a different context or application.

To export the dataset, follow these steps:

1. Open the SAP Lumira document and switch to the data view.

2. Click on the **Export as File** icon in the toolbar. This function is also available via the menu: **File • Export as File** (Figure 20.5) or using the following shortcut: Ctrl + Shift + X .

3. In the **Export as File** dialog box, you may select the following options:

   - **Export hidden dimensions**
     Select this checkbox if you want to export hidden dimensions in the export.

– **Export hidden dimensions derived from dataset enrichment**
Select this box if you want to include hidden dimensions that are a result of enrichment of the dataset. Examples of these hidden dimensions are the **Longitude** and **Latitude** columns, which are generated when creating a **Geo Hierarchy by Names**.

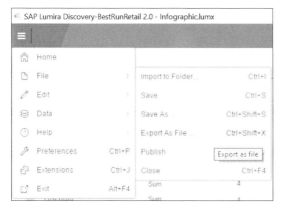

Figure 20.5 Menu—Export As File

4. Click on **Export** to open the **Save As** dialog box.
5. Navigate to the destination folder using the file tree.
6. Enter a file name and select the file format: CSV files or Excel.
7. Click on **Save** to generate the file and close the dialog box. A message will be displayed to confirm that the dataset has been exported.

20.3.2   Publish to SAP HANA

A final option to export a dataset is to publish the data to SAP HANA. When publishing a dataset to SAP HANA, only the data is published without any of the visualizations.

Please follow the next steps to publish a dataset to SAP HANA:

1. Switch to data view mode and click on **File** · **Publish** · **SAP HANA** (Figure 20.6). The option to publish data to SAP HANA is only available in data view mode.

20

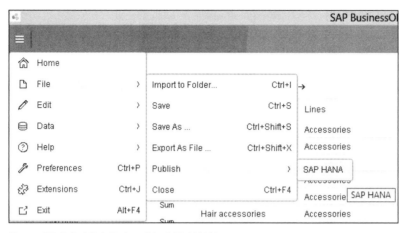

Figure 20.6 Publish Dataset to SAP HANA

The **Publish to SAP HANA** dialog box is displayed (Figure 20.7). Enter the **Server** name, **Instance** number, **User Name**, and **Password** and then click on **Connect**.

Figure 20.7 Publish to SAP HANA Dialog Box

2. The next step is defining in which **Schema** the table will be created. By default, the schema of the logged-in user is selected. Click on the **Schema** dropdown list to select a different **Schema** if required. Please note that the user needs to have the proper authorizations in SAP HANA to create a table in the selected schema.

3. In Figure 20.8, the available package structure on the SAP HANA system is displayed. You can either choose to create a new package or use an existing package to create the analytic view.

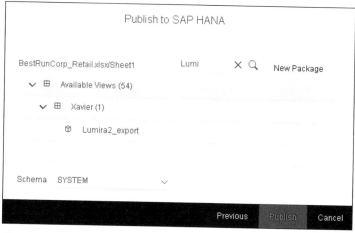

Figure 20.8 Select Schema and Package to Publish

4. Click on **New Package** and enter a name, in our example "Lumira Export" (Figure 20.9).

Figure 20.9 Create New Package

5. Click on **New View** next to the created package, enter the name of the view, and click on **Publish** (Figure 20.10).

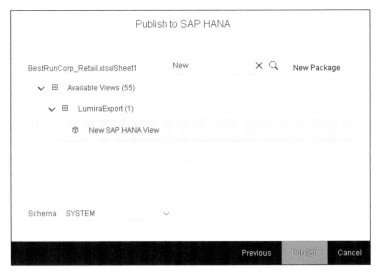

Figure 20.10 Create a New View and Publish

6. A message is displayed when the dataset is successfully published to SAP HANA (Figure 20.11).

Figure 20.11 Dataset Successfully Published

7. Now let's create a new SAP Lumira document based on the SAP HANA Live connection. Log in to SAP HANA directly or use a managed connection on the SAP BusinessObjects BI platform.

8. Search or browse through the folder structure and locate the package and the analytic view that you just created (Figure 20.12).

If you want to replace or update the data in the table on SAP HANA, you need to republish the dataset. Select an existing view to overwrite. A dialog message reading **Do you really want to replace the existing view?** will be displayed. To confirm, click **Yes**.

Please note that re-publishing the dataset by overwriting an existing view will add a new table to the selected schema. The analytic view is updated to point to the new table, which leaves the previous table orphaned.

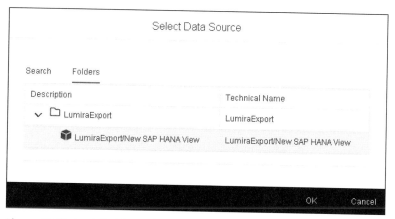

Figure 20.12 Analytic View of Published Dataset

In our example, the dataset contains two hierarchies:

- **Time_Date**
- **Geography_Country_City**

If you open the analytic view in SAP HANA Studio, it becomes clear that these hierarchies have been converted to their own attribute view and modeled using a star join, as shown in Figure 20.13.

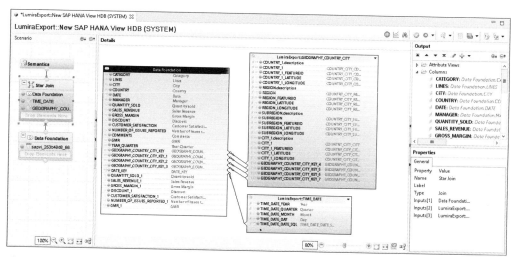

Figure 20.13 Analytic View in SAP HANA Studio

20.4   Summary

In this chapter we described how to use the different export functionalities available in SAP Lumira, discovery edition to share stories, records, and datasets that can be consumed and reused in other applications.

Our next chapter is a deep dive into how to integrate SAP Lumira, discovery edition into your existing SAP BusinessObjects BI 4.2 deployment.

Chapter 21
Integrating SAP Lumira with SAP BusinessObjects BI Platform

Being able to securely distribute, manage, and share your SAP Lumira stories is key for user adoption. With SAP Lumira, server edition, SAP Lumira, discovery edition offers these capabilities via an in-memory component deployed on the SAP BusinessObjects BI platform.

Sharing, securing, and scaling are the three main points when it comes to defining trusted data discovery and self-service BI. Within the SAP analytics portfolio, the SAP BusinessObjects BI platform delivers all of these capabilities and even more. With the SAP Lumira, server edition deployed, users can bring their SAP Lumira, discovery edition content to the SAP BusinessObjects BI platform.

This chapter describes how to integrate SAP Lumira, discovery edition into your existing SAP BusinessObjects BI platform deployment—from installing, configuring, and sizing the SAP Lumira, server edition, to managing the SAP Lumira, discovery edition client and securing the SAP Lumira, discovery edition content using the SAP BusinessObjects BI Central Management Console (CMC).

21.1 Overview

SAP Lumira, server edition hosts the execution runtime that makes it possible perform the following actions:

- View and create (limited to SAP BW and SAP HANA live connectivity) SAP Lumira documents
- Interact with data (filtering, sorting, and ranking, for example)
- Change visualizations
- Create and share bookmarks, etc. using the SAP BusinessObjects BI Launchpad (see Chapter 22) or on mobile devices through SAP BusinessObjects Mobile (see Chapter 23).

By installing the SAP Lumira, server edition, SAP Lumira stories can be published from the SAP Lumira, discovery edition client to the SAP BusinessObjects BI platform. Integration with the SAP BusinessObjects BI platform offers existing capabilities to seamlessly adopt SAP Lumira documents within your organization:

- Security: Access to the SAP Lumira documents is restricted based on the user authentication and authorization applied on folders and categories.
- Lifecycle management: Using promotion management, you are able to promote SAP Lumira documents from, for instance, a development to a productive SAP BusinessObjects BI platform.

As shown in Figure 21.1, the solution contains four essential components:

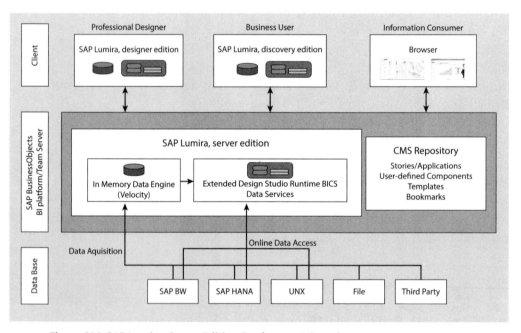

Figure 21.1 SAP Lumira, Server Edition Deployment Overview

- **SAP Lumira, server edition**
  The add-on installs an SAP Lumira server on each host, which acts as the processing service for SAP Lumira content. It contains the in-memory data engine (Velocity), which is utilized when working with imported datasets. It also makes it possible to display and execute SAP Lumira documents in the BI Launchpad as well

as allow communication between the SAP Lumira, discovery edition client and the SAP BusinessObjects BI platform to save and launch documents.

- **SAP Lumira, discovery edition client**
  This is the client tool for creating visualizations and stories saved as SAP Lumira documents. It has to be installed on client machines (see Chapter 2 for more details) of business users who create stories.

- **SAP Lumira web applications**
  This application is embedded within both the BI Launchpad and CMC to allow access and create (only based on live data sources) and edit SAP Lumira documents.

- **SAP BusinessObjects BI platform**
  Prerequisite to enabling users to interact with SAP Lumira documents via the BI Launchpad and SAP BusinessObjects Mobile. It's also used as a platform for managing universes and OLAP data source connections required to communicate with, for example, SAP HANA and SAP BW systems (more information in Section 21.5).

Before describing how to install the SAP Lumira, server edition, we look at different deployment scenarios in the following section.

21.2   Deployment Scenarios

Before deploying the SAP Lumira, server edition, there are factors you need to take into consideration, including the following:

- **Actions users will typically perform when interacting with SAP Lumira documents**
  Depending on the number and type of users and the type of data access used in SAP Lumira documents (live versus imported), the SAP BusinessObjects BI platform needs to be sufficiently sized. If users primarily use the SAP HANA Live connectivity via the SAP Lumira, discovery edition client, the impact on your SAP BusinessObjects BI platform will be limited compared to a scenario where Lumira documents with imported datasets are published to the BI Launchpad and consumed by a large user community. In Section 21.6, we focus specifically on sizing to support different scenarios.

- **Architecture of the current SAP BusinessObjects BI platform**
  The SAP Lumira, server edition needs to be installed on each SAP BusinessObjects

21

BI platform server that should provide an SAP Lumira server runtime. It is not required to run an SAP Lumira server on each node if the SAP BusinessObjects BI platform is running on multiple nodes. However, you do need to install the SAP Lumira, server edition to each node hosting the web applications.

Furthermore, the convergence of SAP Lumira 1.x and SAP BusinessObjects Design Studio 1.x into SAP Lumira 2.1 introduces different installation and upgrade scenarios. As explained in Chapter 1, the two existing 1.x server components are replaced with a single SAP Lumira, server edition.

When you install the product for the first time, you must run a full installation of the SAP Lumira, server edition. However, if you have already deployed SAP Lumira server 1.x or SAP BusinessObjects Design Studio server 1.x to your SAP BusinessObjects BI platform, or both, there are three upgrade scenarios:

- SAP Lumira server 1.x installed: Upgrade to 2.x SAP Lumira, server edition by installing the patch.
- SAP BusinessObjects Design Studio server 1.x installed: Run a full installation of the 2.x SAP Lumira, server edition, as described in Section 21.4.2.
- Both SAP Lumira server 1.x and SAP BusinessObjects Design Studio server 1.x installed: Upgrade to 2.x SAP BusinessObjects BI platform by installing the patch.

When you do a full installation, there is no need to uninstall the existing SAP BusinessObjects Design Studio server 1.x add-on. Of course, like with all patches and Support Packs, you can uninstall it to clean up your system.

21.3   System Requirements

After deciding which nodes you want to install on the SAP Lumira, server edition, you need to check if the supported platforms are consistent with your environment. A list of supported platforms and specific supported configurations can be found in the Product Availability Matrix (PAM), available on the SAP Support Portal at *https:// apps.support.sap.com/sap/support/pam*.

To be able to install the SAP Lumira, server edition, your system needs to meet the following prerequisites:

- The operating system must be 64-bit.
- Your account needs to have Administrator rights on your operating system.

- You have correctly installed and configured either the SAP BusinessObjects BI platform version or above:
    - 4.1 SP 08
    - 4.1 SP 09
    - 4.1 SP 10
    - 4.2 SP 03
    - 4.2 SP 04 Patch 1
    - 4.2 SP 05

    Due to the introduction of the .lumx object type, only the listed versions including the patch level or above can recognize the new object necessary for the Promotion Management (SAP KBA 2437742) and Translation Manager (SAP KBA 2515265) functions.

- The required ports are open. The SAP Lumira, server edition will use the same content management system (CMS), RESTful web services (RWS) and app server ports as the SAP BusinessObjects BI platform.

- There is a minimum of 8 GB of free space available.

- You have a system with a minimum of 16 GB RAM. It's recommended to have at least 32 GB RAM depending on your sizing.

- Microsoft redistributable runtime VS 2015 DLL(X64) is installed. If this is not the case, this component will be automatically installed.

These prerequisites will be checked by the SAP Lumira, server edition installation wizard.

21.4   Installing SAP Lumira, Server Edition

In the following sections, we describe step-by-step how to download, install, and modify SAP Lumira, server edition.

21.4.1   Downloading SAP Lumira, Server Edition

The SAP Lumira, server edition installation file can be downloaded from the SAP Software Download Center on the SAP Support Portal at *https://launchpad.support.sap.com/#/softwarecenter*. To begin the download, perform the following steps:

1. Use your web browser to go to the SAP Software Download Center on the SAP Support Portal (Figure 21.2) at *https://support.sap.com/en/index.html*.

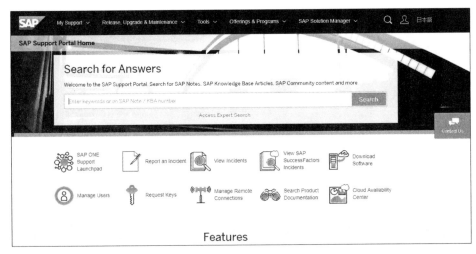

Figure 21.2 SAP Support Portal Home

2. Click on **Download Software**.

3. Log on with your SAP Support Portal account.

4. Click **By Alphabetical Index (A-Z)** (Figure 21.3) to navigate in the alphabetical list of available products and click **L**.

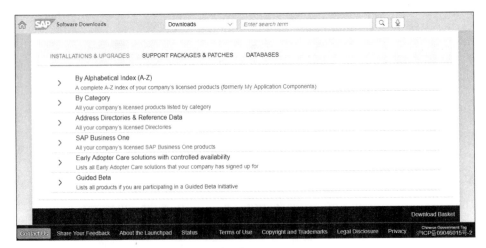

Figure 21.3 Select By Alphabetical Index (A-Z)

5. Under **INSTALLATIONS AND UPGRADES - L**, select **SAP LUMIRA SERVER 2.1** (Figure 21.4). Please note that when executing an upgrade scenario, you first click on **SUPPORT PACKAGES & PATCHES**.

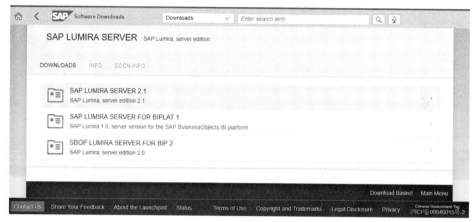

Figure 21.4 Select SAP Lumira Server 2.1

6. Click on **Installation and Upgrade** (Figure 21.5).

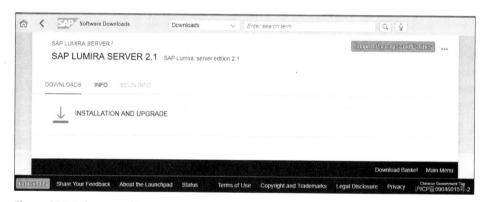

Figure 21.5 Select Installation and Upgrade

7. Select the required operating system, in this example **Windows**, from the drop-down menu.

8. Click on the name of the installation file (Figure 21.6), in this example **51052699**, to start downloading the ZIP file.

Figure 21.6 Select the SAP Lumira Server 2.1 File

9. After the download is complete, unpack the installation file.

The installation workflow depends on the platform.

21.4.2   Installation on a Windows Platform

SAP Lumira, server edition must be installed on each node of the cluster that should host an SAP Lumira server runtime, including the nodes hosting the web server. Before you start the installation, make sure you make a note of the required CMS credentials of the SAP BusinessObjects BI platform installation. This includes:

- CMS name
- Port number
- User name (administrator)
- Password

To install the full SAP Lumira, server edition on a Windows platform please perform the following steps:

1. Browse to the location where you unpacked the installation file.
2. Right-click on *setup.exe* and choose **Run as Administrator**. The file is located in the following folder: *\51052699\DATA_UNITS\SAP_LUMIRA_SERVER_21_WIN_SPOO*.

During the launch of the SAP Lumira, server edition installation wizard, the installer verifies if all the prerequisites listed in Section 21.3 are met. If a prerequisite is missing, a dialog screen will appear with a list of the missing components. You can click on such an item for detailed information on the action required. To be able to continue with the installation you have to resolve the issues related to the prerequisites first.

3. You can read the software license agreement or simply skip it and accept the **License Agreement**. Click **Next** to continue.

4. Please select which features you want to install (Figure 21.7). When you perform an update using the patch instead of the full installation, this part of the installation is skipped. By default, when performing a full install, all options are selected.

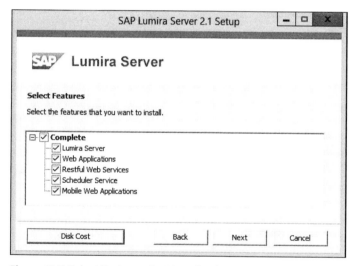

Figure 21.7 Select Features that Need to be Installed

5. Click **Next** to continue.

6. The next step is to specify the CMS and administrator logon information (Figure 21.8).

7. Enter the **CMS Name**, **CMS Port**, and the password of the **Administrator** account and click **Next**.

8. If your installation is completed successfully, click **Finish** to complete the installation (Figure 21.9).

21

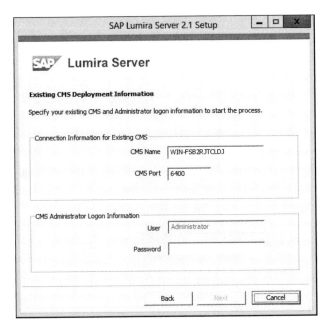

Figure 21.8 Enter CMS Deployment Information

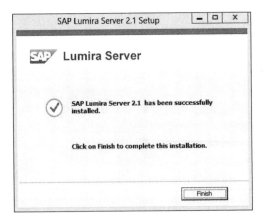

Figure 21.9 SAP Lumira, Server Edition Is Successfully Installed

Installation on Linux, AIX, or Solaris

For more information on how to install the SAP Lumira, server edition on a Linux, AIX or Solaris operating systems, please check the *Administrator Guide: SAP Lumira* on *https://help.sap.com*.

21.4.3   Modifying, Repairing, or Removing the Server

Before you try to modify or remove the server, please validate whether removing SAP Lumira, server edition is supported for your deployment scenario described in Section 21.2. More information can be found in the following SAP Notes:

- 2506102: Failed to revert Lumira 2.0 BI platform add-on installation, to allow reinstallation of Design Studio 1.6

- 2458018: Uninstallation and re-installation is not supported if you have SAP Design Studio add-on 1.6 and SAP BusinessObjects Lumira, server edition on the same box

To modify, repair, or remove SAP Lumira, server edition, please follow the next steps:

1. Choose **Programs and Features** from the Windows Control Panel (Figure 21.10).

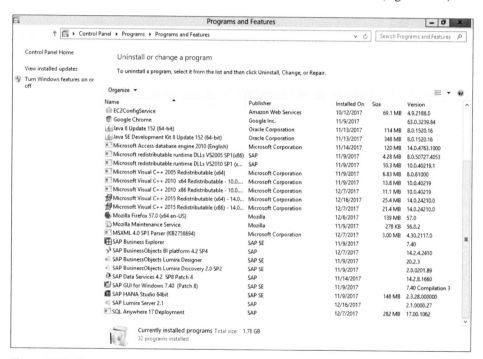

Figure 21.10 Programs and Features

2. Double-click on **SAP Lumira Server 2.1** or right-click and select **Uninstall/Change**.

3. The **Application Maintenance** dialog is displayed. Select one of the following required options and choose **Next**:

- **Modify**: Provides capabilities to add or remove components.
- **Repair**: Replaces corrupted binaries or files.
- **Remove**: Uninstalls the add-on.

4. Depending on the selection in the **Application Maintenance** dialog, proceed as follows:
   - **Modify** or **Repair**: Enter the CMS logon credentials and proceed with the installation steps.
   - **Remove**: Choose **Next**, enter the CMS logon credentials, and click **Finish**.

The SAP Lumira server edition will either be modified, repaired, or removed.

21.5 Configuring the SAP BusinessObjects BI Platform

In this section, we explain how to enable (in case of SAP HANA) and create OLAP connections on the SAP BusinessObjects BI platform. These connections, for both SAP HANA and SAP BW, are the preferred connection type when you want to share your SAP Lumira documents via the BI Launchpad.

21.5.1 Enable SAP HANA HTTP Connection

To be able to create an OLAP connection in the CMC that allows connecting through SAP HANA Live, the SAP BusinessObjects BI platform needs to have the SAP HANA HTTP connection type enabled. This can be done by editing the *mdas.properties* file on the SAP BusinessObjects BI platform server(s) and set the following property:

```
multidimensional.services.enable.hana.http.connections = true
```

The location of the *mdas.properties* file on a Windows server is:

<BI platform install directory>\SAP BusinessObjects Enterprise XI 4.0\java\pjs\services\MDAS\resources\com\businessobjects\multidimensional\services

Please ensure that in a multi-server environment or cluster, the *mdas.properties* file is changed on each node.

After changing the property, restart each adaptive processing server, which hosts the multi-dimensional analysis service (MDAS), to ensure that the SAP HANA HTTP connection type will appear in the **Provider** list (Figure 21.11).

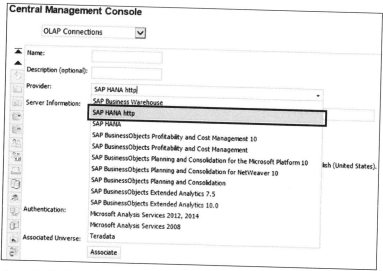

Figure 21.11 List of Available Data Sources to Create an OLAP Connection

To be able to use the SAP HANA HTTP connection, the following prerequisites need to be met:

- SAP HANA platform SPS 10 (revision 100 or higher recommended) or 2.0 SPS 01 or higher (including SAP HANA EPMS-MDS 1.0).
- SAP BusinessObjects BI platform 4.1 SP 5 or higher.
- SAP HANA Info Access Service (InA) with delivery unit HCO_INA_SERVICE is deployed on the HANA platform.
- `sap.bc.ina.service.v2.userRole::INA_USER` is assigned to SAP HANA user. Verify that the following authorizations are selected: Schema _SYS_BIC, schema _SYS_BI, and schema _SYS_RT.

More information can be found in SAP KBA 2182187. If you are facing issues with the SAP HANA HTTP connection on the SAP BusinessObjects BI platform, please check SAP KBA 2307199. This article contains a number of troubleshooting options.

21.5.2   Creating an SAP HANA HTTP OLAP Connection

Now that we have the SAP HANA HTTP connection enabled, an SAP HANA (HTTP) OLAP connection can be created on the SAP BusinessObjects BI platform. To set up such an OLAP connection, follow these steps:

1. Log in to the CMC.
2. Go to **OLAP Connections** and click **New Connection**.
3. Enter a **Name** and a **Description** (optional) for the connection.
4. Choose **SAP HANA HTTP** as the **Provider** for this OLAP connection (Figure 21.12).

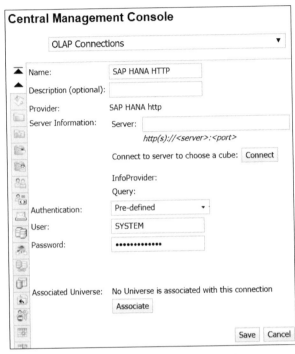

Figure 21.12 Create SAP HANA HTTP Connection

5. Enter the **Server** address and port of your SAP HANA XS engine in the **Server Infor-mation** area.
6. Select the **Authentication** type and click on **Save**.

If you want to create an **SAP HANA** connection, please follow the next steps:

1. Enter a **Name** and a **Description** (optional) for the connection.
2. Choose **SAP HANA** as the **Provider** (Figure 21.13).

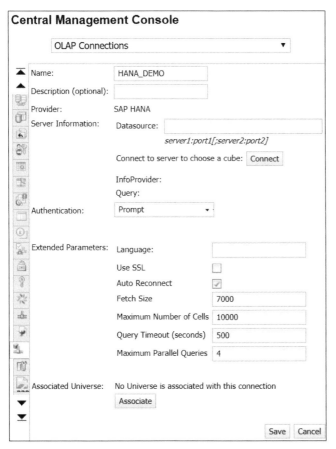

Figure 21.13 Create SAP HANA Connection

3. Enter the **Datasource** server and port information of your SAP HANA SQL service in the **Server Information** area.

4. Select the **Authentication** type and click on **Save**.

21.5.3   Creating an SAP BW OLAP Connection

Setting up an OLAP connection to SAP BW requires most of the same steps as in the previous section. To set up such an SAP BW to OLAP connection, follow these steps:

1. Log in to the CMC.

2. Go to **OLAP Connections** and click **New Connection**.

3. Enter a **Name** and a **Description** (optional) for the connection.

4. Choose **SAP Business Warehouse** as the **Provider** for this OLAP connection (Figure 21.14).

Figure 21.14 Create SAP Business Warehouse Connection

5. Enter the **SAP Business Warehouse** server information of the server to which you want to connect.

6. Finally, define the **Authentication** method.

7. Click **Save** to save the new OLAP connection. The OLAP connection is now added to the list of available connections.

21.6   Sizing

Making sure that your SAP Lumira, discovery edition deployment is effectively and accurately sized is key to ensuring that end users have the best possible user experience when interacting with and creating SAP Lumira documents. In order to do that, you should estimate the following:

- The number and types of users who will use the system: information consumers, business users and/or expert users.
- Type of data sources: live or import.
- Complexity of the SAP Lumira documents created: the dataset size.
- Ratio between documents that are scheduled and processed overnight versus refreshed on demand.

In the following sections, we explain how to estimate and use this information to properly size your SAP Lumira deployment using the Quick Sizer.

21.6.1   Users

Users interacting with your SAP Lumira, discovery edition deployment can be classified into the following user types based on the average idle time between navigation steps and actions:

- Information consumers: Spend an average of 300 seconds (5 minutes) between navigation steps. These users typically view predefined and static content with relatively little drilling and filtering.
- Business users: Spend an average of 30 seconds between navigation steps and perform some moderate amount of drilling and filtering on their own.
- Expert users: The most active users who spend an average of 10 seconds between navigation steps. These type of users will most likely perform resource intensive operations like customization of reports, retrieving large number of rows, client side filtering, and ad hoc analysis.

The number of these user types and their expected concurrency can be used to predict the expected load on the system.

When sizing your SAP Lumira, discovery edition deployment, the first step is to estimate the total number of users who will be granted access to interact with SAP

21

Lumira documents. Let's assume that your SAP BusinessObjects BI platform has a total number of 5,000 users and 30% will be using SAP Lumira, discovery edition, so 1,500 estimated users.

The next step is to determine how many of the 1,500 users will be logged in to the system at the same time. The best way to determine this is to understand the usage patterns of the user community. If you can't get a clear indication, it's common to estimate 10% as a minimum. In our example, we estimate that 150 users are active at any one time.

As mentioned, most users spend much of their time being idle after logging in. So to get a clear estimation, we have to decide how many of the active users will be concurrently generating load. Again a common estimate is 10%. In our example, we expect that 15 concurrent active users will be generating load on our SAP Lumira, discovery edition deployment.

The expected concurrency in our example translates into 1% of the number of users. Please keep in mind that these estimations can heavily vary and should be monitored. If you expect or experience higher concurrency than these ratios, adjust your sizing accordingly.

In the next section, we describe how to use the active concurrency for each user type as input to estimate your sizing.

21.6.2 Quick Sizer

With the Quick Sizer, SAP offers a web-based application designed to support sizing exercises for a large number of SAP products. The Quick Sizer will calculate CPU, disk, and memory requirements based on the number of active concurrent users for each user type (information consumers, business users, and expert users).

The following steps guide you through the process of using the Quick Sizer specifically for SAP analytic solutions to estimate your SAP Lumira, discovery edition deployment as part of the SAP BusinessObjects BI platform:

1. Browse to the **Quick Sizer** on the **SAP Service Marketplace** using the following URL (Figure 21.15): *http://service.sap.com/quicksizer*.

2. Start the Quick Sizer by clicking on **HANA version** (Figure 21.16).

3. Your **customer no** is listed by default. Enter a **Project Name** and click on **Create Project** (Figure 21.17).

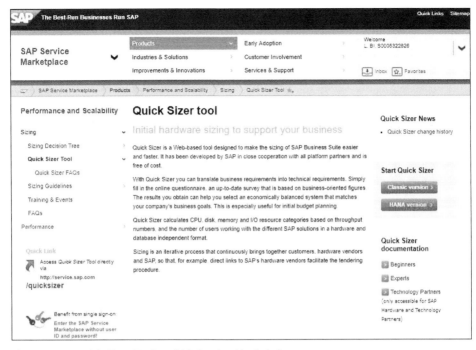

Figure 21.15 Quick Sizer Tool on SAP Service Marketplace

Figure 21.16 Start HANA Version of Quick Sizer

Figure 21.17 Create a Project

4. Enter **Analytics Solutions** in the search bar to limit the number of results and click on **Search in Tree** (Figure 21.18).

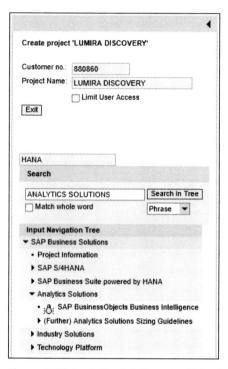

Figure 21.18 Analytics Solutions Available in Quick Sizer

5. Click on **SAP BusinessObjects Business Intelligence**. The Quick Sizer template, as shown in Figure 21.19, is displayed. Enter the information requested for the following elements/scenarios:

   - **LUMIRA** (for all users working with documents using imported datasets)
   - **LUMIRA-BW-LIVE**
   - **LUMIRA-HANA-LIVE**

Furthermore, you should do the same for all other elements/scenarios relevant to your current SAP BusinessObjects BI platform deployment to get a complete overview of the required CPU and memory.

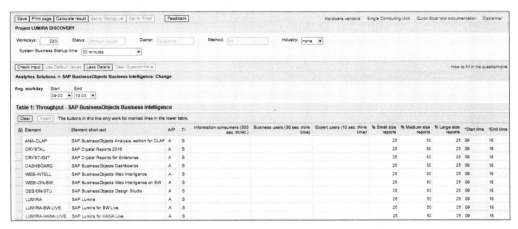

Figure 21.19 Quick Sizer Template for SAP BusinessObjects Business Intelligence

---

Sizing of Backend Systems

Refreshing an SAP Lumira document based on imported data or interacting with a document based on a live connection has an impact on the backend system of the particular data source in terms of that host's CPU, memory, and I/O consumption. For example, viewing SAP Lumira documents based on a live SAP BW connection needs a sufficient amount of available work processes and resources to handle the request.

The scope of this chapter is limited to the sizing of the SAP BusinessObjects BI platform. However, please consult your system administrators for the various backend systems to create an end-to-end sized system capable of handling all requests.

---

6. Enter the number of expected concurrent active information consumers, business users, and expert users along with the distribution of the estimated average document size. You can also specify the start and end time of an average workday, also per element.

7. Click on **Calculate Result**.

8. The results of the Quick Sizer exercise are displayed (Figure 21.20). Based on the outcome you can validate if the SAP BusinessObjects BI platform hosting the SAP Lumira, discovery edition deployment is sufficiently sized based on the calculated CPU and memory requirements.

21

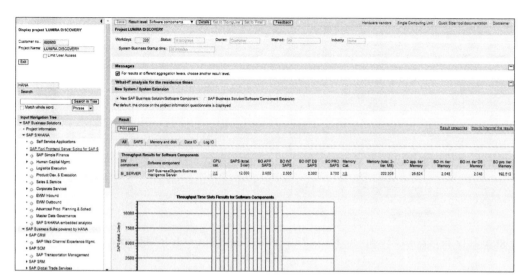

Figure 21.20 Quick Sizer Results

At startup, the SAP Lumira, server edition allocates a maximum of 85% of the available free memory of the host machines to the in-memory data engine. The actual memory consumption varies based on document memory requirements. For large enterprise deployments it is recommended to deploy the SAP Lumira, server edition on dedicated machines to handle and allocate memory without interfering with other SAP BusinessObjects BI platform workflows.

If your deployment involves more than 50 concurrent active users, we recommend adding more nodes rather than adding more SAP Lumira servers to an existing node. This will avoid potential memory allocation conflicts. Furthermore, if one of the SAP Lumira server services fails, another node can start handling requests.

21.7   Single Sign-On

SAP Lumira, discovery edition supports X.509 authentication from the client to the SAP BusinessObjects BI platform via the Secure Login Client. After you authenticate X.509 it stores the certificate and SAP Lumira, discovery edition uses the certificate to log on to the SAP BusinessObjects BI platform without providing a password.

In order to enable this, the following prerequisites have to be met:

- Secure Login Client is set up on your desktop machine for authentication. It has a valid X.509 certificate stored. For more information on Secure Login Client, refer to the blog, "Why Secure Login Web Client" at *https://blogs.sap.com/2013/11/12/why-secure-login-web-client/.*

- SAP BusinessObjects BI platform is configured to accept X.509-based logon requests via a RESTful connection. For more information on how to set up X.509 authentication, refer to "X.509 Authentication" in the *Business Intelligence Platform Administrator Guide* on the SAP Help Portal at *https://help.sap.com.*

- The SAP BusinessObjects BI platform is version 4.2 SP 05 and above.

To enable using Secure Logon Client to directly log on to the SAP BusinessObjects BI platform from the SAP Lumira, discovery edition client, please follow the next steps:

1. On the home page, click on the menu bar in the top-left corner and select **Preferences**.

2. Click on **Network** (Figure 21.21). Under **SAP BI Platform**, enable both the **RESTful Logon** and the **Secure Logon Client**. You can also set the default SAP BusinessObjects BI platform server URL.

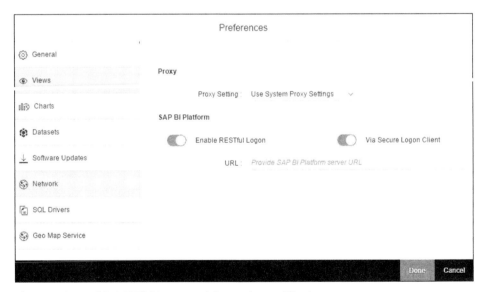

Figure 21.21 Enable RESTful Logon and Secure Logon Client

3. An information dialog is displayed to inform you that SAP Lumira, discovery edition needs to be restarted to apply the changes (Figure 21.22). Click **OK** and restart the SAP Lumira, discovery edition client.

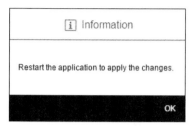

Figure 21.22 Restart SAP Lumira, Discovery Edition Client to Apply Changes

4. After the restart, click on **SAP BI Platform** on the home screen (Figure 21.23). The option to select **SSO Authentication** is now visible.

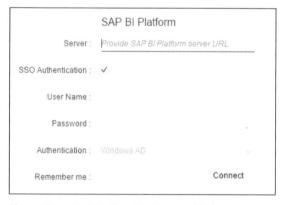

Figure 21.23 SSO Authentication Enabled

5. Click on **Connect** after providing the SAP BusinessObjects BI platform server URL and you will be authenticated to the SAP BusinessObjects BI platform without providing your **User Name** and **Password**.

21.8 Managing Content on the SAP BusinessObjects BI Platform

The SAP BusinessObjects BI platform offers a lot of functionality that SAP Lumira, discovery edition can seamlessly integrate with. In the following sections, we explain how to utilize this.

21.8.1   Authorization

One of the main advantages of integrating SAP Lumira, discovery edition with the SAP BusinessObjects BI platform is the ability to use the existing authorization framework to specify which user (group) can view, refresh, edit, or perform other available actions for specific types of content based on the assigned rights. Without these rights, users are unable to interact with SAP Lumira documents, both on the BI Launchpad and from the SAP Lumira, discovery edition client.

In the following sections, we briefly highlight some of the areas where you should assign rights. For a complete overview of all SAP Lumira specific rights, please check out the *Administrator Guide: SAP BusinessObjects BI Platform* on *https://help. sap.com*.

Application

To enable SAP BusinessObjects BI platform users to acquire datasets via the BI Launchpad (supported for both SAP HANA and SAP BW online data sources), you have to assign the application right **Acquire Data in SAP Lumira Server**. You can assign this right by browsing to the CMC and selecting **Applications**. Right-click on **SAP Lumira** and select **User Security** (Figure 21.24).

Figure 21.24 Assign Security to the SAP Lumira Application

This dialog allows you to view and manage the access levels assigned to users and groups (principals). The right can be assigned by selecting a principal and clicking on **Assign Security**. Next, click on **Advanced** and select **Add/Remove Rights** (Figure 21.25).

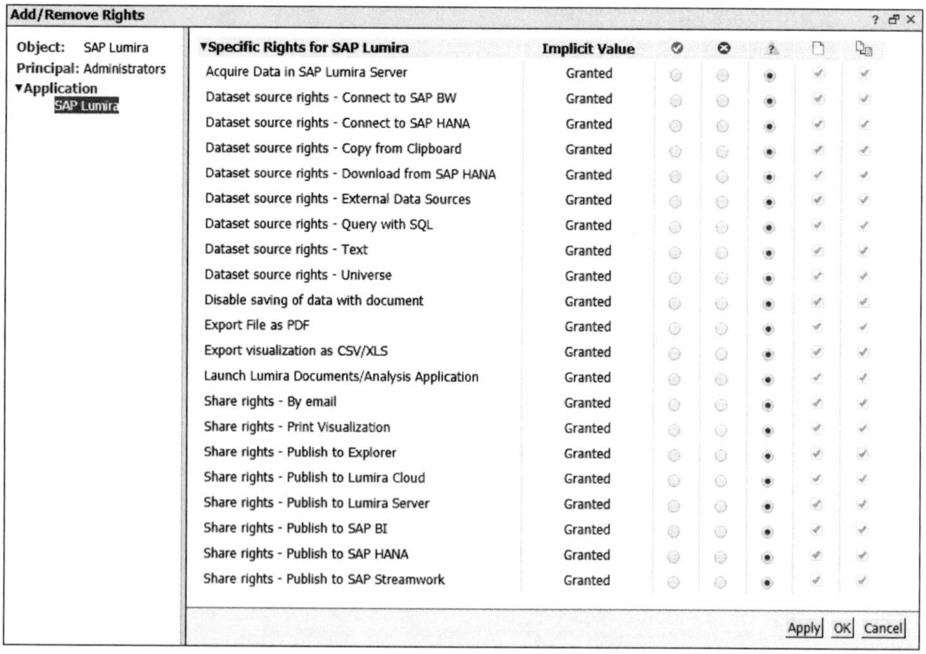

Figure 21.25 Add/Remove Rights to the SAP Lumira Application

Another important right we want to highlight is **Disable saving of data with document**. This can be used to ensure that users cannot uncheck the option to save an SAP Lumira document with data to the SAP BusinessObjects BI platform. Saving with data might lead to unwanted and unauthorized access to data.

Furthermore, the right **Launch Lumira Documents/Analysis Application** has to be assigned to allow SAP BusinessObjects BI platform users to view SAP Lumira documents from the BI Launchpad.

Migration of Application Object User Rights

Depending on the deployment scenarios described in Section 21.2, existing application rights (based on the Design Studio 1.x or Lumira 1.x add-on) are migrated. However, when a Design Studio 1.x add-on is installed (scenario 2 and 3), the user rights on the application must be checked manually. This is related to the SAP BusinessObjects BI platform specific right **Modify the rights users have to this object**. For more information, please check out the *Administrator Guide: SAP Lumira* on *https://help.sap.com*.

Documents

To assigns rights to specific folders, right-click on a folder in the CMC and select **User Security**, similar to setting application rights.

As shown in Figure 21.26, there are limited rights (refresh) specific to .lumx documents. All other rights are general rights applicable to most objects stored on the SAP BusinessObjects BI platform. Please ensure that you specify **Copy to Another Folder** and **Scheduling** rights as well, if applicable.

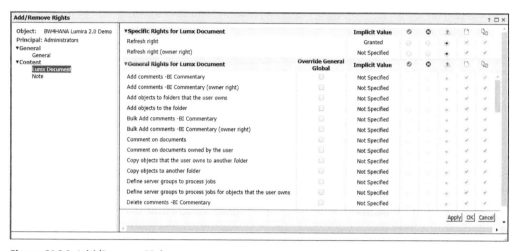

Figure 21.26 Add/Remove Rights

Connections

Besides specifying rights on the application and folders, the same concept applies to managed connections. To ensure that other users can, for example, open an SAP Lumira document based on a live SAP HANA connection defined on the SAP BusinessObjects BI platform, you need to ensure that:

- The SAP BusinessObjects BI platform user is allowed to view and use the SAP HANA connection.
- The user has a valid user account in the data source system (SAP HANA) that allows access to the related objects, including authorization on data retrieval (through analytic privileges).

21

Extensions

Before users can add or remove SAP Lumira extensions (Section 21.8.5 for more information) on the SAP BusinessObjects BI platform, you need to add those users to the SAP Lumira SDK administrators group. By default, only SAP BusinessObjects BI administrators are allowed to add or remove extensions. To add or remove users to the SAP Lumira SDK administrators group, please follow the next steps:

1. Browse to the CMC and click on **Users and Groups · User List**.

2. Double-click on the required user and select **Member of** (Figure 21.27).

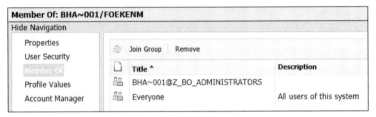

Figure 21.27 Join Group

3. Select **Join Group** and add **Lumira SDK Administrators** to **Destination Groups** (Figure 21.28). Choose **OK**.

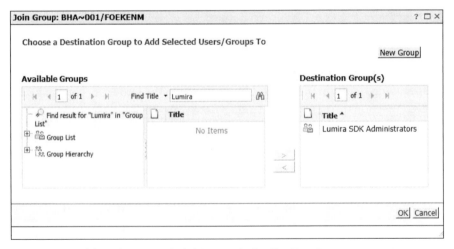

Figure 21.28 Add Lumira SDK Administrators to Destination Group

4. The selected user should now be able to manage SAP Lumira SDK extensions via the CMC.

Setting Rights in the CMC

To learn more about the authorization framework of the SAP BusinessObjects BI platform and setting rights in the CMC, refer to *SAP BusinessObjects BI Security* (SAP PRESS, 2013) or see "Setting Rights" in the *Business Intelligence Platform Administrator Guide* at *https://help.sap.com*.

21.8.2   Bookmarks

Bookmarks, which store a specific state of an SAP Lumira document (see Chapter 22, Section 22.1.7), can be managed in the same way as other objects stored on the SAP BusinessObjects BI platform. The SAP Lumira, server edition provides a bookmark administration feature within the CMC (Figure 21.29), available under **Applications · SAP Lumira**.

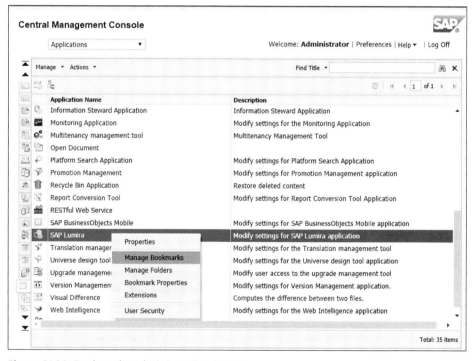

Figure 21.29 Bookmarks Administration in CMC

Manage Bookmarks

Click on **Manage Bookmarks** to navigate to the **Bookmarks Administration** dialog (Figure 21.30). At the bottom, a list of available bookmarks stored on the SAP BusinessObjects BI platform is displayed. The top half of the dialog provides filtering capabilities based on type, user, and usage. When you select a bookmark, you can either delete it or move the bookmark to a specific folder.

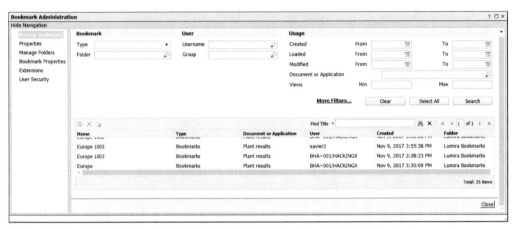

Figure 21.30 Bookmarks Administration

Manage Folders

The **Manage Folders** option allows you to create, rename, and delete a folder structure (including security) as a way of organizing your bookmarks, for instance per area of business. Figure 21.31 displays the **Bookmark Folder Administration** dialog.

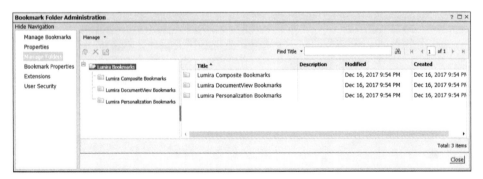

Figure 21.31 Bookmark Folder Administration

SAP Lumira, discovery edition bookmarks on the document level are stored in the root folder: **Lumira Bookmarks**. Under this root folder, three pre-delivered technical folders are available (please do not delete them):

- **Lumira Composite Bookmarks**: Contains for each story of an SAP Lumira document a link to the document's main bookmark.

- **Lumira DocumentView Bookmarks**: While users are exploring and bookmarking an SAP Lumira document, the document's original document state is temporarily stored in this folder. Closing the document clears the folder.

- **Lumira Personalization Bookmarks**: This folder holds user-specific bookmark settings, such as recently used bookmarks or default bookmarks.

Bookmark Properties

The **Bookmark Properties** dialog (Figure 21.32) can be used to:

- Set the number of items displayed per page.
- Upgrade the bookmark metadata.

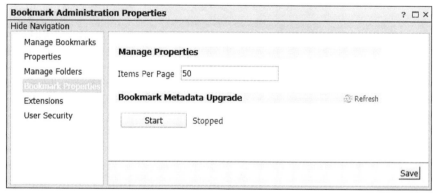

Figure 21.32 Bookmark Administration Properties

Upgrading Bookmark Metadata

If your SAP BusinessObjects BI platform deployment contains Design Studio bookmarks created prior to Design Studio 1.5, you include these bookmarks and make them searchable using this feature. For more information, please see "Upgrading Bookmark Metadata" in the *Administrator Guide: SAP BusinessObjects Lumira*, at *https://help.sap.com*.

21.8.3   Auditing

Another benefit of using the SAP BusinessObjects BI platform to distribute and manage your SAP Lumira documents is auditing. By using the auditing capabilities, you can track a number of events. This information can be valuable to determine system usage as input for sizing or to track user activity.

In Table 21.1, an overview is provided of the events that can be audited for all content accessed on the SAP BusinessObjects BI platform. Local actions are not audited.

Event	Event ID	Description
Document created	1005	User creates a document using the BI Launchpad.
Document refreshed	1003	<ul><li>User refreshes SAP Lumira document.</li><li>User opens SAP Lumira document that is set to **Refresh On Open**.</li><li>User schedules an SAP Lumira document.</li></ul>
Document saved	1008	User saves SAP Lumira document.
Document modified	1007	User modifies a property of an object, deletes, and enters **Edit Document** mode for an existing SAP Lumira document.
User login	1014	User logs in to the system.
User logout	1015	Users logs out of the system.
Document viewed	1002	User views an SAP Lumira document.
Document sent	1012	User sends an SAP Lumira document to the required destination.
Document scheduled	1011	A job has been successfully scheduled.

Table 21.1 Events That Can Be Audited

You can configure which events will be audited in the Central Management Console:

1. Browse to the CMC.

2. Under **Manage**, click on **Auditing**.

3. The **Auditing** page will be displayed (Figure 21.33). Scroll down to view which events are currently monitored along with the current Audit status and configuration settings.

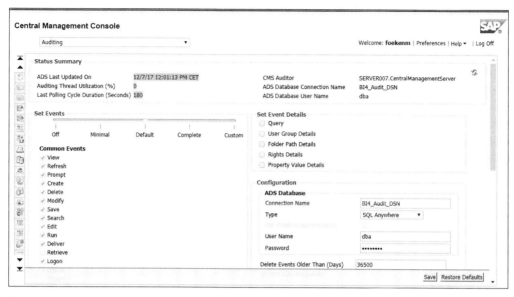

Figure 21.33 Auditing in the Central Management Console

4. By using the slider, you can change which events will be monitored.

5. Please keep in mind that the events selected impact each type of content to which it is applicable on the SAP BusinessObjects BI platform. Furthermore, the auditing of events can impact the overall performance of your deployment.

Auditing Content

The information stored in the Audit database can be accessed by using a universe and a set of Web Intelligence documents available for SAP BusinessObjects BI platform 4.1 SP 5 or greater and 4.2. Please visit the following URL for more information how to download, import, and configure this content into your SAP BusinessObjects BI platform:

https://blogs.sap.com/2015/07/15/unlock-the-auditing-database-with-a-new-universe-and-web-intelligence-documents-for-bi41/

For more information on auditing, please consult the "Auditing" chapter in the *Business Intelligence Platform Administrator Guide* on the SAP Help Portal at *http:// help.sap.com*.

21.8.4   Lifecycle Management

If you are running multiple SAP BusinessObjects BI platform instances in your landscape (for example, for development, testing, and productive usage), you can transport objects from one SAP BusinessObjects BI platform system to another using promotion management.

To promote SAP Lumira documents using the promotion management tool, please follow next steps:

1. Browse to the CMC and select **Promotion Management** under **Manage**. The Promotion Management application will be displayed (Figure 21.34).

Figure 21.34 Promotion Management Tool in CMC

2. Click on **New Job** to create a promotion job, enter a **Name**, and select the **Source** and **Destination** system (Figure 21.35). Click on **Create**.

3. Add the SAP Lumira document(s) by browsing through the SAP BusinessObjects BI platform folder structure and selecting the checkbox followed by **Add** or **Add & Close** (Figure 21.36).

Figure 21.35 Create New Promotion Management Job

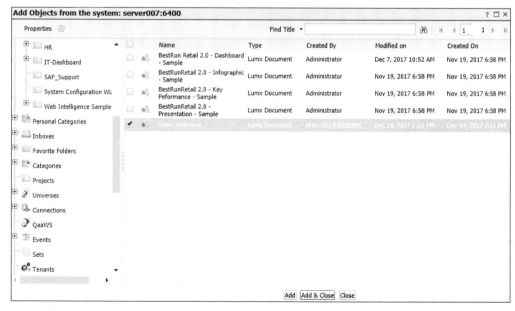

Figure 21.36 Add Objects to Promotion Management Job

4. Click on **Promote**.

5. A summary of the promotion job is displayed (Figure 21.37). Here you can change the security settings, test the promotion, etc. Click **Promote** to create a job that will promote the selected SAP Lumira document(s) from the source to the destination.

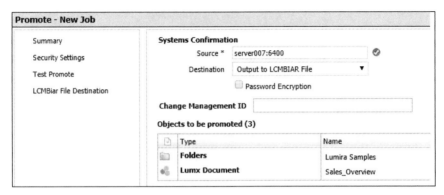

Figure 21.37 Summary of Promotion Job

Promotion Management

The Promotion Management application offers many more functionalities than discussed. To learn more about promotion management on the SAP BusinessObjects BI platform, please consult the *Business Intelligence Platform Administrator Guide*, available at *https://help.sap.com*.

21.8.5   Managing Extensions

The functionality of SAP Lumira, discovery edition can be extended by using data access and visualization extensions (see Chapter 3, Section 3.2.7 for more information). SAP Lumira documents stored on the SAP BusinessObjects BI platform that use extensions can only be viewed via the BI Launchpad if these extensions are installed on the SAP BusinessObjects BI platform as well.

To add or remove SAP Lumira extensions on the SAP BusinessObjects BI platform, please follow next steps:

1. Browse to the CMC and click on **Applications**.

2. Right-click on **SAP Lumira** and select **Extensions** (Figure 21.38).

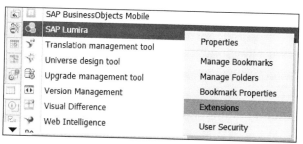

Figure 21.38 Select Extensions for SAP Lumira in CMC

3. The **Extension** dialog is displayed (Figure 21.39). Here you can upload or remove an extension. Now let's upload one of the extension samples located in the installation folder of the SAP Lumira, discovery edition client: *C:\Program Files\SAP Busi-nessObjects Lumira\Lumira Discovery\Desktop\samples\extensions\charts*.

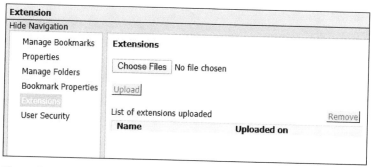

Figure 21.39 Extension Dialog

4. Click on **Choose Files** and browse to the *samples* folder.

5. Select one of the sample visualization extensions and click **Open**. The filename is now displayed next to the **Choose Files** button.

6. Click on **Upload**. The extension will be uploaded and becomes visible in the list (Figure 21.40). In some cases, when you upload a data access extension to the SAP BusinessObjects BI platform, the system prompts you to restart the SAP Lumira server.

7. If you select any uploaded extension (multiple selection supported) from the list, you can use the **Remove** button to delete the extension from the SAP Business-Objects BI platform.

21

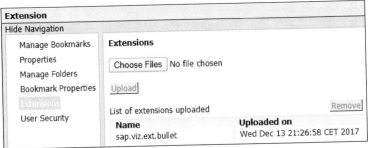

Figure 21.40 Sample Extension Uploaded to the SAP BusinessObjects BI Platform

8. Extensions cannot be promoted between SAP BusinessObjects BI platform systems (Section 21.8.4). If you are running multiple SAP BusinessObjects BI platform instances (for development, testing, and productive usage), you need to install the required extensions on each system through the CMC as described.

21.9   Summary

In this chapter we covered a wide variety of topics, all related to integrating SAP Lumira, discovery edition into the SAP BusinessObjects BI platform. We introduced the SAP Lumira, server edition, explained how to deploy it in certain scenarios, and covered the system requirements.

Furthermore, we described how to download and install the add-on as well as how to ensure that your SAP BusinessObjects BI platform is sufficiently sized based on the expected number of active concurrent users and user types. Finally, we explained how to utilize some key areas of the SAP BusinessObjects BI platform to securely manage and audit SAP Lumira documents access and usage.

In the next chapter, we explain how users interact with SAP Lumira documents on the BI Launchpad now that your landscape is integrated.

Chapter 22

Using SAP Lumira Content in the BI Launchpad

We are not limited to an installation of SAP Lumira, discovery edition to use our stories. The web-based BI Launchpad is capable of running SAP Lumira, discovery edition content as well.

The SAP BusinessObjects BI Launchpad is the web-based user interface of the SAP BusinessObjects BI platform. On this portal, business intelligence users can find their business intelligence content, regardless of which of SAP's BI tools was used to create this material. For example, the BI Launchpad can run SAP BusinessObjects Web Intelligence or SAP Crystal Reports documents, as well as launch SAP Analysis for Microsoft Office workbooks. Of course, SAP Lumira documents are also included.

As you saw in Chapter 19, you can share SAP Lumira documents from the SAP Lumira, discovery edition client tool to the SAP BusinessObjects BI platform. The platform acts as a centralized place for storing content, eliminating the need to store documents locally (on the hard drive of the user's computer). In addition, the SAP Lumira documents can also be run within the BI Launchpad! In that way, users who don't have the SAP Lumira, discovery edition client tool installed are still able to run and interact with these reports. The SAP BusinessObjects BI platform administrators can use different folders, user groups, access rights, and other security settings to specify which user can perform what kind of actions on these documents (see Chapter 21 for more detail).

In this chapter, we see how we can use SAP Lumira documents to view and alter stories within the BI Launchpad. We also look at some of the standard SAP BusinessObjects BI platform features that we can use with SAP Lumira documents, like scheduling.

In addition to using existing SAP Lumira documents, we can even create completely new SAP Lumira documents on the BI Launchpad, without the need for an SAP Lumira, discovery edition client tool installation, as is discussed in the final section.

22

22.1 Interacting with Stories

The BI Launchpad supports a lot of SAP Lumira, discovery edition features that we discussed in most parts of this book up until now. We can not only view the SAP Lumira documents in the BI Launchpad, but also interact with them, and even make changes. This section gives you an overview, by showing you how to open stories and interact with them, what the options for (new) data sources are, and how to save a document on the SAP BusinessObjects BI platform. Furthermore, we look at the **Data Refresh** option, how to create OpenDocument URLs, and how to use bookmarks.

22.1.1 Opening an SAP Lumira Document

You can run an SAP Lumira document on the BI Launchpad, simply by browsing to the folder where the document was stored and double-clicking the object document. You can recognize the SAP Lumira documents from the SAP Lumira icon in front of the document, and by the **Lumx Document Type** (Figure 22.1). Make sure your user account has sufficient access rights to view (and edit) the document.

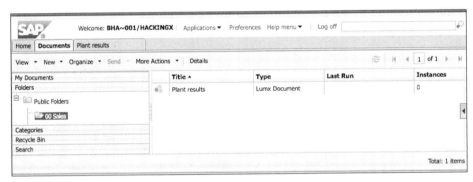

Figure 22.1 .lumx File on the BI Launchpad

As you can see in Figure 22.2, the look of SAP Lumira, discovery edition in the BI Launchpad is very familiar. It is almost completely the same as the **Preview** mode in the SAP Lumira, discovery edition client tool (Figure 22.3).

The BI Launchpad contains three additional buttons, which we discuss later in this section:

- **Generate OpenDocument Link**
- **Create Bookmark**
- **Manage Bookmark**

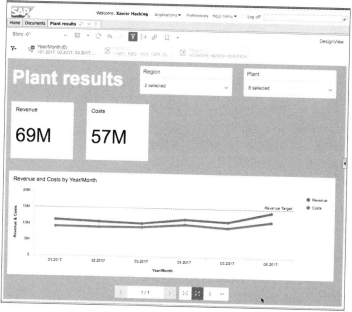

Figure 22.2 Running an SAP Lumira Document on BI Launchpad

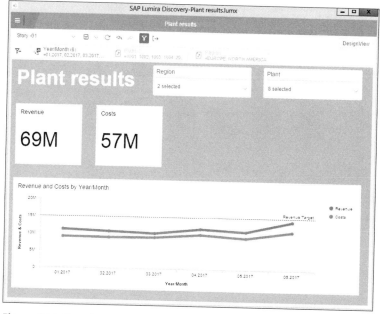

Figure 22.3 Running a Report in the SAP Lumira, Discovery Edition Client Tool

22

22.1.2   Interacting with an SAP Lumira Document

All the interactivity options that SAP Lumira, discovery edition offers in its stories, and which we are familiar with from the SAP Lumira, discovery edition tool, are available in the BI Launchpad as well. To start, we can use the filters and controls to adjust the data that is displayed. Furthermore, we have all the context menu options on all objects in the SAP Lumira story. That means that we can easily do analyses by applying sorting, ranking, and charting specific filters, but also completely change the chart itself. For this last option, we have to switch to the **DesignView** mode (Figure 22.4). We have the option to set up conditional formatting, include reference lines, add calculations, change the chart type and formatting, and even export the data here.

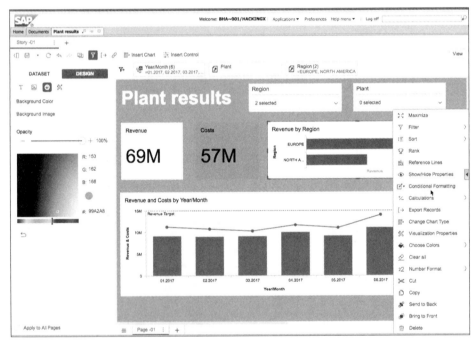

Figure 22.4 Adjusting a Story in BI Launchpad

In the design view, both the **Dataset** and **Design** tabs are available. You can add new charts or other design objects like images and shapes, and add stories and pages. Figure 22.5 shows the maximized chart mode, where you can set up a chart in the most detailed form.

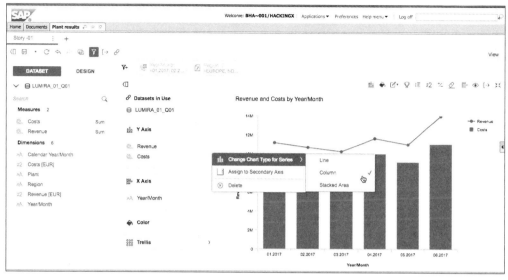

Figure 22.5 Adjusting a Chart in BI Launchpad

22.1.3 Working with Data Sources

A major limitation of the SAP Lumira, discovery edition solution in the BI Launchpad is the lack of the **DataView** tab in documents that were created in the SAP Lumira, discovery edition client tool on top of offline data sources. This means we cannot add or edit the data sources, browse the dataset within the grid or facet view, or perform any of the data actions.

This is something to take into account when offering the BI Launchpad instead of the SAP Lumira, discovery edition client tool, as it provides a solution to view and interact with SAP Lumira documents in a self-service kind of approach, where the end users are encouraged to create their own SAP Lumira documents. All the necessary data should be available in the initial versions of the SAP Lumira documents that are created with the SAP Lumira, discovery edition client tool and made available on the SAP BusinessObjects BI platform.

For live SAP HANA and SAP BW data sources, we do have the option to add and remove data sources. In Section 22.3, we explain that it is even possible to create SAP Lumira documents from scratch on the BI Launchpad, when using a live SAP HANA or SAP BW data source.

22

425

22.1.4   Saving a Document

After you made changes to an SAP Lumira document, you can save it with the **Save** button or create a copy by using **Save As**.

Root Folder

It is not possible to store SAP Lumira documents in the root folder of the SAP BusinessObjects BI platform folder structure (public folders).

Be aware that saving a document in a public folder on the SAP BusinessObjects BI platform means that other users may have access to this SAP Lumira document and can use it when they have sufficient access rights. If your SAP Lumira document contains an offline data source, it may be wise to check the **Save without data** box in the **Save As Document** dialog box. This will ensure that the document refreshes each time it is opened, based on the user account's access rights. This way, you won't run into a situation where people accidentally get to see data that they are not supposed to see. See Chapter 21 for more information on how to enforce this option.

Multiple Users

Multiple users can use and change an SAP Lumira document at the same time. Only the version of the SAP Lumira document that is saved last will remain. All previous changes that may have been saved will be overwritten by the version of the last user who saved it. SAP Lumira, discovery edition and/or BI Launchpad won't notify you in such a situation.

22.1.5   Refreshing Data

If your SAP Lumira document contains an offline data source, like an offline SAP BW query or a text file, the user may have the need to refresh the document to see the latest version of the data. The user can do this at any time by clicking the **Refresh** button. Depending on the source type and the way the data source connection was set up, a login screen and/or a variable prompt window will appear.

If you checked the option **Save without data** when saving the document on the SAP BusinessObjects BI platform, the document obviously doesn´t contain any data and automatically has to load this at the startup of the document.

For the different data source types, the following specific remarks have to be made:

- **Microsoft Excel or text files**
  The Microsoft Excel or text files that act as a data source in your SAP Lumira document must be accessible by the SAP BusinessObjects BI platform. This means that the files should be stored in a shared location, and an UNC path needs to be used to refer to the source file (for example, \\source_files\mydata.xlsx).

- **SAP BW**
  SAP Lumira documents with offline SAP BW data sources that use a managed OLAP connection on the SAP BusinessObjects BI platform are supporting data refresh on the BI Launchpad. Depending on the setup of the authentication mode of the managed OLAP connection, a popup may ask you to log in. In case there are input variables included in the SAP BEx query, a popup window will display these.

- **SAP HANA**
  For SAP Lumira documents with offline SAP HANA data sources, the same comments are valid as for the offline SAP BW data sources. In addition, it is possible to use a direct connection to an SAP HANA system instead of a managed OLAP connection. In that case, a popup will be shown where the connection details and user credentials have to be entered (Figure 22.6).

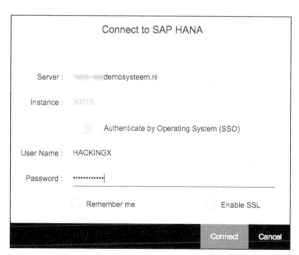

Figure 22.6 Refreshing an SAP Lumira Document with a Direct SAP HANA Connection

- **Universe**
  SAP BusinessObjects UNX universes are supported as refreshable data sources. If there are any prompts available, a popup window will display these.

- **Query with SQL**

  Refreshing documents with a non-SAP data source that is set up via the Query with SQL feature is also supported. Note here, that the drivers for the used data sources must be installed on the server that runs the SAP BusinessObjects BI platform.

22.1.6 Generating OpenDocument Links

OpenDocument is an SAP BusinessObjects BI platform technology that allows you to link directly to specific documents or locations on the SAP BusinessObjects BI platform. Furthermore, it is possible to pass parameter values via this link. When you execute an OpenDocument link on a browser, the document will load without the BI Launchpad interface around it. This means that there is no **Home** or **Documents** tab, and the **Preferences** and other menus are not visible.

You can find the OpenDocument link of an SAP Lumira document either by browsing the BI Launchpad and using the context menu option **Document Link** (Figure 22.7) or by using the **Generate OpenDocument Link** button in the SAP Lumira, discovery edition report on the BI Launchpad (Figure 22.8). In both situations, a link will be provided that points to the document. The difference between the two options is that in the second option, parameters for the story and page are also included, as well as the **Refresh** setting of the document.

Figure 22.7 Document Link in BI Launchpad

Figure 22.8 Generating an OpenDocument Link

The basic syntax for an OpenDocument link looks as follows:

*http(s)://<servername>:<port>/BOE/OpenDocument/opendoc/OpenDocument.jsp?
sIDType=CUID&iDocID=<cuid>&<parameter1>&<parameter2>*

An OpenDocument URL could for example look like this:

*http://server007:8080/BOE/OpenDocument/opendoc/openDocument.jsp?sIDType=
CUID&iDocID=AXmgBH14oqZLi2xcU89BWjA&sStoryName=Story -01&sPageNumber=
1&sRefresh=false*

Table 22.1 shows some OpenDocument parameters that can be used. As you can see, it is also possible to pass prompt values via OpenDocument.

> **OpenDocument Syntax**
>
> For more details on the complete OpenDocument syntax, check out the guide *Viewing Documents Using OpenDocument* at *http://help.asp.com/*.

Parameter	Description	Example
iDocID	Unique identifier of the document on the SAP BusinessObjects BI platform.	AXmgBH14oqZLi2xcU89BWjA
sDocName	Title of the document on the SAP Business-Objects BI platform.	Plant results

Table 22.1 OpenDocument Syntax

22

Parameter	Description	Example
sStoryName	Title of the story in the SAP Lumira document.	Story -01
sPageNumber	Number of the page in the SAP Lumira document.	1
sPageName	Title of the page in the SAP Lumira document.	Page -01
sRefresh	Forces a data refresh when the document is opened.	True, False
lsI[NAME]	Specifies the index or key value(s) and must be associated with one of the prompt parameters (lsS, lsM, or lsR). This is necessary when using SAP HANA online prompts. [NAME] is the prompt name.	Simple [S], multiple [M] or range [R].
lsS[NAME]	Single prompt value, where [NAME] is the prompt name.	1000
lsM[NAME]	Multiple prompt values, where [NAME] is the prompt name. Values need to be separated by a semicolon (;).	1000;1001;1002
LsR[NAME]	Range of prompt values, where [NAME] is the prompt name. Beginning and end value need to be separated by two points (..) and put between brackets ([ ]).	[1000..1010]

Table 22.1 OpenDocument Syntax (Cont.)

22.1.7   Using Bookmarks

Bookmarks are a handy and fast way to store a specific state of an SAP Lumira document. In the view mode of the SAP Lumira document, you can apply filters for the areas that you are interested in and save those in a bookmark. The next time that you view the document, you can choose this bookmark and quickly go back to the view that shows your areas of interest. It is also possible to set a bookmark as a default view and load it automatically when starting the SAP Lumira document.

To create a bookmark, click the bookmark icon or use the option **New Bookmark** from the dropdown menu (Figure 22.9).

Figure 22.9 Bookmarks Menu

You must enter a **Name** for the bookmark and an optional **Description**. As shown in Figure 22.10, we can make this bookmark a **Personal** or **Global** bookmark. Personal bookmarks are only visible to the creator of the bookmark. Global bookmarks are visible for all users who have access rights to this document. Edit rights on the document are necessary to create global bookmarks. If you check the **Set as default view** option, each time you start this SAP Lumira document, instantly this bookmark will be used.

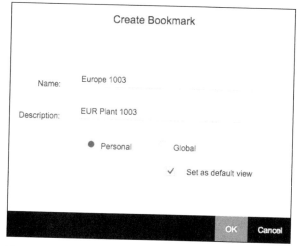

Figure 22.10 Create Bookmark

The dropdown menu that you saw in Figure 22.9 first shows the most recently used bookmarks. With the **View All Bookmarks** option, you open the bookmark manager. Here you can delete bookmarks and set a bookmark as the default (Figure 22.11). Furthermore, the bookmark dropdown menu has options to create a **New Bookmark**, remove the active bookmark to go **Back to the Original Document**, and **Clear the Default Bookmark** for the document.

Figure 22.11 Manage Bookmarks

22.2   Sharing and Scheduling

The SAP BusinessObjects BI platform comes with a lot of built-in features that can be used throughout the full BI toolset. Via the BI Launchpad, users can collaborate on BI reporting by creating, copying, sharing, and scheduling reports. SAP Lumira documents are no exception to this.

22.2.1   Sharing

Users can easily cooperate by sending each other documents on the SAP BusinessObjects BI platform. Besides the **Folders** area, where all the public folders are stored, has each user also has a **My Documents** area. Here you can find a personal **My Favorites** folder, in which each user can store his own documents.

Depending on the access rights that a user has on a folder, he is able to **Copy**, **Cut**, **Paste**, and **Delete** a document and create a **Shortcut in My Favorites** (Figure 22.12). In addition, there is the option to **Send** a document to another user of the SAP BusinessObjects BI platform (Figure 22.13). The document will end up in the user's **BI Inbox** in his **My Documents** area.

Using the BI Launchpad

For more information on the generic end user features of the BI Launchpad, please see the *Business Intelligence Launch Pad User Guide* on *http://help.sap.com/*.

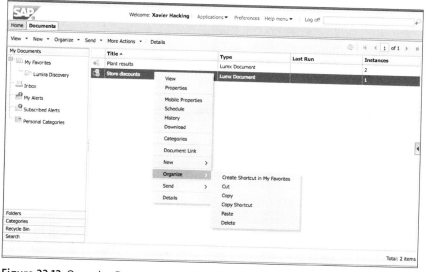

Figure 22.12 Organize Documents on the SAP BusinessObjects BI Platform

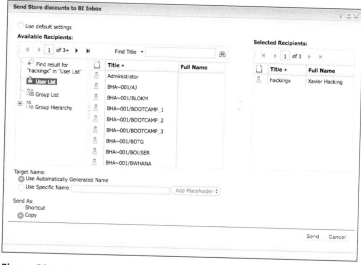

Figure 22.13 Sending a Document to a BI Inbox

22.2.2 Scheduling

With the scheduling feature on the SAP BusinessObjects BI platform, you can auto-matically distribute updated versions of a document, on a specific and/or recurring moment (Figure 22.14). Scheduling is supported for SAP Lumira documents that con-tain Microsoft Excel or text file, SAP BW, or SAP Universe data sources. Prompts are not supported.

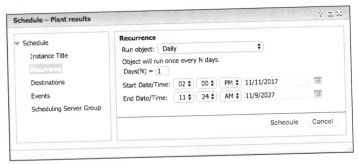

Figure 22.14 Scheduling an SAP Lumira Document

As shown in Figure 22.12, you can **Schedule** a document, see the scheduling **History**, and **Download** the file. For a new schedule, you have to determine the **Recurrence** of the schedule and its **Destinations**. This can be for example the BI inbox of one or more users. Figure 22.15 shows how the scheduled instances of the SAP Lumira docu-ment end up in such a BI inbox.

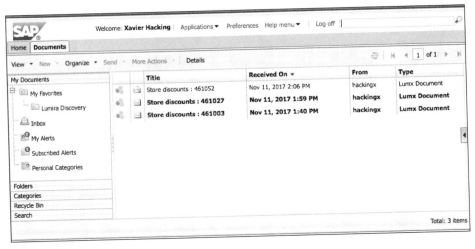

Figure 22.15 BI Inbox

The **History** option shows the previously run instances of the schedule (Figure 22.16). In case you scheduled a recurrence, an additional entry is shown here. The individual instances can be opened from here as well, but just clicking the title of the instance.

With the **Download** option, you can download the .lumx file from the BI Launchpad to a local drive.

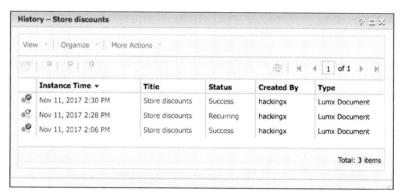

Figure 22.16 Scheduling History

22.3   Creating a New Story

We can not only open existing SAP Lumira documents on the BI Launchpad, we can even create new stories from scratch! You can find SAP Lumira, discovery edition under the **Applications** menu on the BI Launchpad (at least, if your account has the sufficient access rights for this), as shown in Figure 22.17.

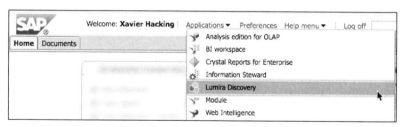

Figure 22.17 Starting the SAP Lumira, Discovery Edition Application on BI Launchpad

In the SAP Lumira, discovery edition application on the BI Launchpad, only live SAP HANA and SAP BW data sources via managed OLAP connections are supported when creating a new document. The steps to select a connection (Figure 22.18) and choose an SAP HANA view or SAP BW query are the same as in the SAP Lumira, discovery edition client tool. See Chapter 6 for more details.

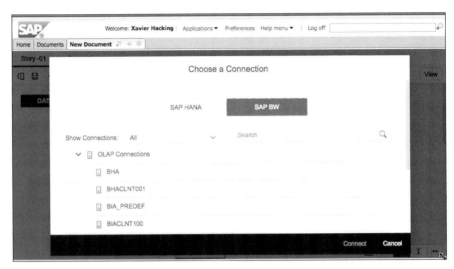

Figure 22.18 Select an OLAP Connection for SAP BW Live

After selecting the data source, the features of the BI Launchpad version for SAP Lumira, discovery edition are the same as in the desktop version. This also means that when you are using a live SAP HANA source, it is possible to add multiple datasets and set up linking between them. For the live SAP BW source, it is possible to add multiple datasets, but just as in the desktop version, linking is not available. See Chapter 18 for more information on this topic.

22.4   Summary

This chapter was all about using SAP Lumira, discovery edition content on the BI Launchpad. We discussed how to open, use, and interact with existing documents. We saw their specific features that aren't available in the desktop version of SAP Lumira, discovery edition, like the OpenDocument links and bookmarks. We also looked at the SAP BusinessObjects BI platform functions to share and schedule documents. Finally, we created a completely new SAP Lumira document in the BI Launchpad, without using the desktop client.

In the next chapter, we dive into the mobile possibilities of SAP Lumira, discovery edition, with the SAP BusinessObjects Mobile app.

Chapter 23

SAP Lumira, Discovery Edition on Mobile

With the SAP BusinessObjects Mobile app, users can access content from the BI platform on an iPhone, iPad, or Android device.

In this chapter, we introduce SAP BusinessObjects Mobile. With the SAP Business-Objects Mobile application, users of mobile devices can get access to several content types of the SAP BusinessObjects BI platform from a single mobile application. In addition to SAP Lumira stories and applications, this includes content from SAP Crystal Reports, SAP BusinessObjects Web Intelligence, and SAP BusinessObjects Dashboards.

In this chapter, we look at which devices are supported, how to set up a connection between the mobile app and the BI platform, and how to make SAP Lumira, discovery edition documents visible in the mobile app. Furthermore, we look into the different modes for SAP Lumira, discovery edition stories, and the native features of the mobile app.

> **Note**
> Please note that we are using version 6.7.6.18 for iOS in this chapter, and we are using an iPad (2017).

23.1 Supported Devices

The SAP BusinessObjects Mobile application is currently available for iOS devices (iPhone and iPad) and Android smartphones and tablets. The applications can be downloaded for free from the Apple App Store and the Google Play Store:

- SAP BusinessObjects Mobile 6.6.7 for iOS
  https://itunes.apple.com/us/app/sap-businessobjects-mobile/id441208302?mt=8
- SAP BusinessObjects Mobile 6.3 for Android
  https://play.google.com/store/apps/details?id=com.sap.mobi&hl=en

Although these apps are available for all device types (mobile phones and tablets), at the time of writing, SAP Lumira, discovery edition stories are only supported on iPad (iPad 3 or later) and Android tablets.

Windows Phone

At the moment, there is no SAP BusinessObjects Mobile app available for Windows Phone. In fact, there are no plans to release a Windows Phone version. As a work-around, SAP Lumira, discovery edition documents could be viewed in the Windows Phone native web browser, via OpenDocument URLs.

See also SAP KBA 2266517 - BI Mobile for Windows Phone: *https://launchpad.support.sap.com/#/notes/2266517.*

23.2   Connectivity

Connecting the SAP BusinessObjects Mobile application to an SAP BusinessObjects BI platform requires that you have set up a connection in the application. This can be done via **Browse · Settings** (the gear icon) · **Application Settings · Create New Connection**. In this screen, you can enter the connection name, provide the **Server URL** and **CMS Name**, and set the **Authentication Mode**. You can also enter your **User Name** and **Password** (Figure 23.1).

Mobile Server on the SAP BusinessObjects BI Platform

To connect to an SAP BusinessObjects BI platform and use its content on the mobile applications, the SAP BusinessObjects Mobile server needs to be installed and configured on the SAP BusinessObjects BI platform. More information about the Mobile server can be found at *https://help.sap.com/bomobilebi.*

Figure 23.1 Connection Setup

23.3   Setting Up the Mobile Category

Before you can use content from the SAP BusinessObjects BI platform in the SAP BusinessObjects Mobile app, you have to make sure that the content is available for mobile usage. This should be done by filing the content documents—for example, an SAP Lumira, designer edition application—in the **Mobile** category. In this section, we start by looking at the generic approach, where we use only a single category. After that, we explain how to make further specifications.

23.3.1   Generic Mobile Category

To set up a generic mobile category, follow these steps:

1. Log in to the Central Management Console (CMC) and go to **Categories** (Figure 23.2).

2. Check if there is a **Mobile** category available.

3. If not, select **Manage • New • Category**.

4. Enter "Mobile" as the new category name and click **OK** (Figure 23.3).

23

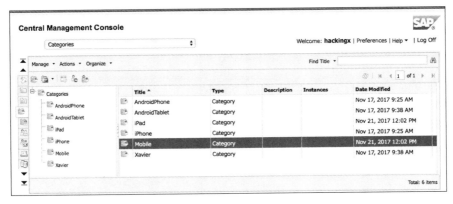

Figure 23.2 Mobile Categories

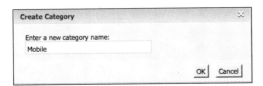

Figure 23.3 Create the Mobile Category

5. Browse to the document that you want to make visible in the mobile app (either in the CMC or in the BI Launchpad). Select the document, right-click it, and choose **Categories** from the context menu.

6. Select the **Mobile** category and click **Save & Close** (Figure 23.4). The document should now be visible in the mobile app.

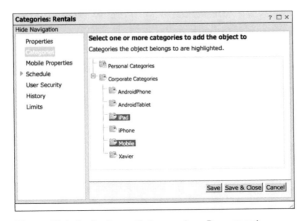

Figure 23.4 Assigning a Category to a Document

23.3.2   Specific Mobile Categories

The mobile category is an all-or-nothing type of scenario. All documents are displayed in the same group, on all devices types. For most of the usage scenarios this is sufficient, but you might need a more detailed approach if your BI platform hosts a lot of mobile documents, or if there are some documents that are specifically developed for a certain type of mobile device, such as an iPad.

Grouping

In addition to the mobile category, you can assign other categories as well. These additional categories are then visible in the mobile app under the **All Reports** area (Figure 23.5). All the documents that have this additional category assigned to it are shown in this group. This enables an easier way to browse for your documents, in case there are a lot of them.

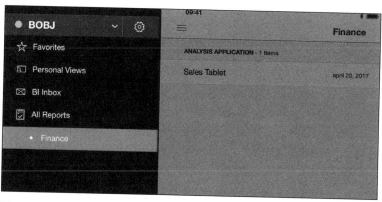

Figure 23.5 Additional Grouping

Device Specific

It is possible to further specify the mobile category itself. This can come in handy, for example, when you have documents that are specifically built for a mobile phone, which has a significantly different screen size than a tablet and is interacted with in a different way. You don't want that document to appear in the mobile app when using an iPad. For SAP Lumira, discovery edition, this won't be much of an issue of course, as currently, the SAP Lumira, discovery edition stories are only supported on tablets anyway.

1. Log in to the CMC and go to **Applications · SAP BusinessObjects Mobile · Properties**. By default, the mobile category is already defined for the `default.corporate`

Category key (Figure 23.6). Here, you can rename **Mobile** to a different value (make sure you also rename the mobile category in that case) and add specific categories for iPad, iPhone, Android tablet, and Android mobile phone devices.

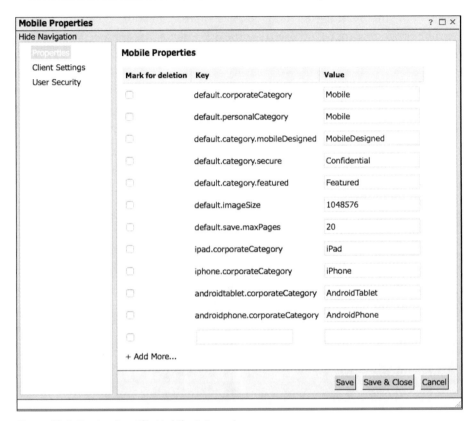

Figure 23.6 Device Specific Mobile Categories

2. Click **+ Add More**. An empty **Key** and **Value** field appear.

3. Enter the key and value for each device, as shown in Table 23.1. The value has to match the name of the category and can be any value that you like.

4. Click **Save & Close**.

5. Go to the **Categories** area in the CMC and add the new categories with the same names as the values you used (Figure 23.2).

6. Now you can either assign the generic mobile category to documents or use the device specific ones (Figure 23.4).

Key	Value
ipad.corporateCategory	iPad
iphone.corporateCategory	iPhone
androidtablet.corporateCategory	AndroidTablet
androidphone.corporateCategory	AndroidPhone

Table 23.1 Device Specific Properties

23.4   Native and HTML Modes

SAP Lumira stories can be viewed in a native and an HTML mode. By default, SAP Lumira, discovery edition documents are opened in the native mode. SAP Lumira, designer edition documents are opened in the HTML mode.

The native mode offers a better user experience, with an improved performance, better gesture and navigation support, and offline support of SAP Lumira stories. Unfortunately, not all components are supported yet. The components that are supported are as follows:

- Crosstab
- Line
- Line chart with two y-axes
- Bar
- Column
- Column chart with two y-axes
- Combined column line chart with two y-axes
- Pie
- Numeric
- Bubble
- Stacked bar
- Stacked column
- Area (100% stacked is not supported)
- Geo map

23

> **Extensions**
>
> Third-party extensions are currently not supported in both the native and HTML modes.

If you experience that some stories are not completely visualized in the mobile app, you can switch the default native mode to the HTML mode. The following must be done on the SAP BusinessObjects BI platform; the users cannot change this themselves in the mobile app:

1. Log in to the CMC and go to **Applications** · **SAP BusinessObjects Mobile** · **Client Settings** (Figure 23.7).
2. Click **+ Add More...**.
3. In the new **Key** field, enter "feature.lumira.view.mode".
4. In the new **Value** field, enter "Html".
5. Click **Save & Close**.

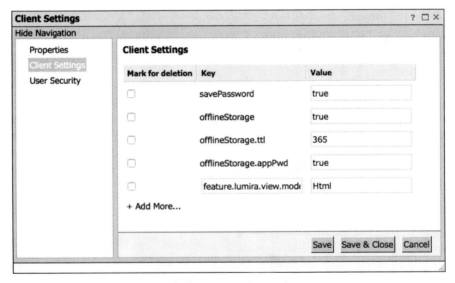

Figure 23.7 Switch to HTML Mode for SAP Lumira Stories

You can also modify the mode of individual SAP Lumira stories, as follows:

1. Browse to the document in the BI Launchpad or the CMC. Right-click it and select **Mobile Properties** for the BI Launchpad, and **Properties • Mobile Properties** for the CMC.

2. In the **Dynamic Properties** area, click **+ Add More....**

3. In the new **Key** field, enter "feature.lumira.view.mode".

4. In the new **Value** field, enter "Html" or "Native".

5. Click **Save & Close** (Figure 23.8).

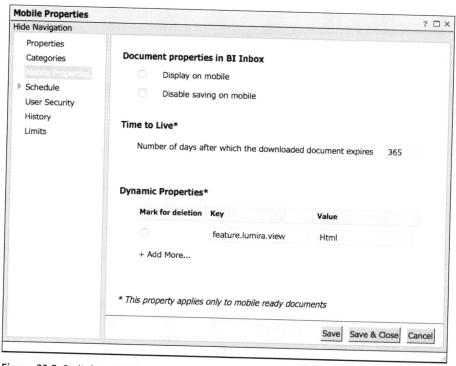

Figure 23.8 Switch to HTML Mode for a Specific SAP Lumira Document

23.5   Using Content in the Mobile App

After connecting to the SAP BusinessObjects BI platform, the available content shows up on the home screen of the mobile app (Figure 23.9). Here you can open a report, dashboard, an SAP Lumira, designer edition application or an SAP Lumira, discovery edition story. You can also view information about a document by tapping the **More Options** icon at the end of each row. With the **Search** and **Sort** options, you can quickly navigate to a document.

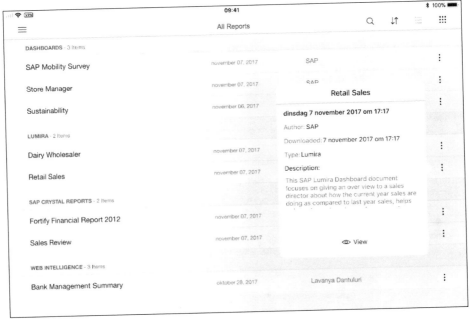

Figure 23.9 Content in the Mobile App

In the following sections, we walk through running an SAP Lumira, discovery edition story and some of the collaboration features offered by the app.

23.5.1   Running an SAP Lumira Story

When you run an SAP Lumira, discovery edition document on the mobile app, the first page of the first SAP Lumira, discovery edition story is displayed (Figure 23.10). From here, you can navigate to the other stories via the **Story List** icon ▧.

You can navigate between the pages by either swiping to the left or right, tapping the page numbers at the bottom of the screen, or clicking the **Stacked View** icon ⬭ (Figure 23.11).

Figure 23.10 SAP Lumira, Discovery Edition Story in the Mobile App

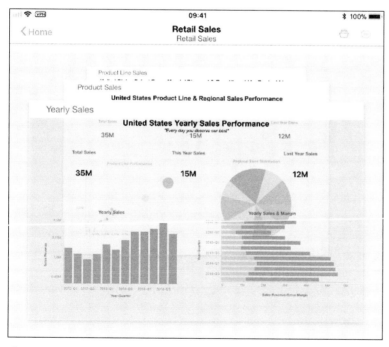

Figure 23.11 Stacked View

The filters can be found via the **Global Actions** menu. Tap the ☰ icon or swipe from the outer left side of the mobile device to the right to make it visible (Figure 23.12). Here you will see a list of all the available dimensions for each dataset, including a search option to quickly find a dimension. Just tap a dimension to create the filter on it. The **Applied Filters** will appear on top of the list and can be removed again from here. After setting one or more filters and closing the **Global Actions** menu again, the **Global Actions** icon will show a number, representing the number of applied filters (Figure 23.12). This number also includes filters based on input controls in the story itself.

Figure 23.12 Filters in the Global Action Menu

To interact with visualizations, double tap a visualization. It now will fill up the whole screen (Figure 23.13).

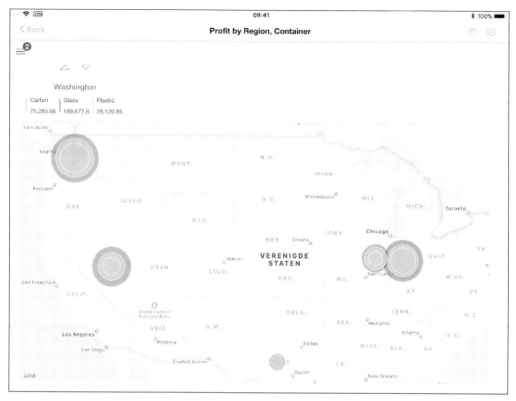

Figure 23.13 Interacting with a Visualization

Depending on the type of visualization you have different interaction options. You can see the individual values for each data point by tapping for example a single bar or data point, swipe the axes to change the sorting order, use the arrows to drill up or down on the data, and pinch to zoom in or out on a chart. You can also use the **Legends** tab   in the **Global Actions** menu to show the legend of the chart, which can be used to select a certain series or data point (Figure 23.14).

23

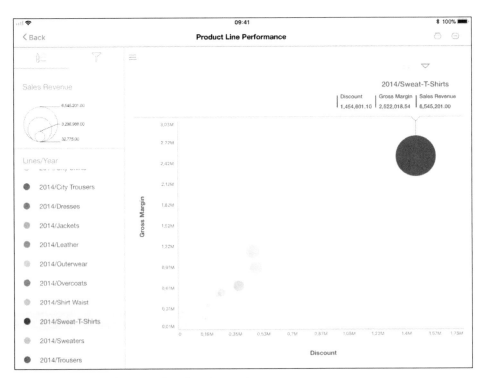

Figure 23.14 Using the Legends Tab to Interact

All these gestures are documented in the mobile app itself, in the **Interactions Guide** (Figure 23.15). You can find this via the **Settings** icon ⊖ (Figure 23.16).

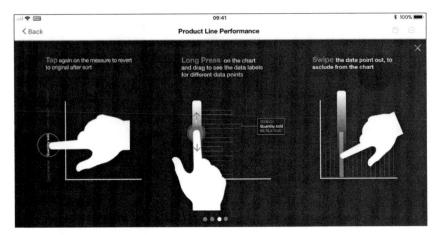

Figure 23.15 Interactions Guide

23.5.2   Collaboration Features

The **Settings toolbar** not only contains the **Interactions Guide**, it also features the **Help Center**, **Information** about the document, and a number of interesting collaboration options (Figure 23.16).

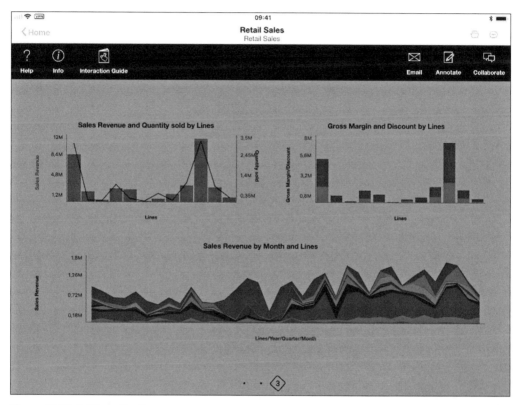

Figure 23.16 Settings Toolbar

The report can be shared and discussed with colleagues over the SAP Jam Collaboration platform. If you want to add some texts, lines, or boxes; blur parts of the content; or crop the output of the content, you can use the **Annotation** option (Figure 23.17). You can even record a **Voice Memo** as an annotation (Figure 23.18). Finally, you can send an **Email** that contains a screenshot of the content (annotations included).

23

Figure 23.17 Annotation Options

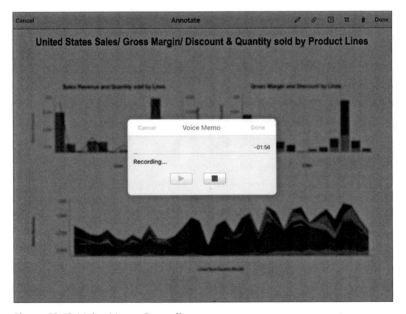

Figure 23.18 Voice Memo Recording

23.6   Summary

This chapter discussed the features and setup specifics for the SAP BusinessObjects Mobile app. As you've seen, the mobile app can bring a lot of value, as it allows you to take your SAP Lumira, discovery edition stories on the road.

After going through the supported devices, we looked at how to set up a connection to the BI platform in the mobile app, and made the SAP Lumira documents mobile-ready by using categories. We discussed the native and HTML modes that SAP Lumira, discovery edition stories can run in. Finally, we explored the native functionalities of the mobile app, when running an SAP Lumira, discovery edition story.

In the next chapter, we cover the topic of interoperability.

23

Chapter 24

Interoperability with SAP Lumira, Designer Edition

With interoperability, SAP Lumira, discovery edition and SAP Lumira, designer edition can work together and extend each other's capabilities.

Interoperability is a term that we hear more and more in SAP's business intelligence ecosphere. You can see it as a container description for all interactions that go beyond the boundaries of an individual BI tool. For example, a user could start in an SAP Lumira, designer edition application, looking at KPIs results at a high aggregation level, let's say a bar chart that shows the total weekly sales numbers per region. From here, he/she could click on one of the bars in a report and jump to a very detailed SAP Crystal Reports document that lists all the individual sales orders for the selected region. The tools are extending each other in this scenario via the use of OpenDocument parameters. In Chapter 22, we gave a short introduction on how to use OpenDocument links and parameters.

This chapter focusses on the exclusive interoperability options between SAP Lumira, discovery edition and SAP Lumira, designer edition. This was one of the major new features in SAP Lumira 2.0. As we have seen earlier in this book, the two SAP Lumira clients (discovery edition and designer edition) now use a common backend add-on for the SAP BusinessObjects BI platform. Also, they are built on the same code base and use the common .lumx file type. This means that a document created in SAP Lumira, discovery edition can be opened (and edited) in SAP Lumira, designer edition and vice versa. Voila, there we have the foundation for interoperability.

In this chapter, we look at possible usage scenarios for SAP Lumira's new interoperability options, and we discuss the current limitations.

The only prerequisite to using interoperability is that you have both the SAP Lumira, discovery edition and SAP Lumira, designer edition client tools installed.

24.1   Adding Advanced Features

In our first scenario we start out with a simple SAP Lumira, discovery edition story, where we have a number of KPIs on top of the story, and a chart placed below them. The KPIs show the results for the full year, where the column chart shows the quarterly trend over the past years (Figure 24.1). We want to be able to click a KPI and have the trend of the selected measure displayed in the chart.

Adding such a functionality is not (yet) included in SAP Lumira, discovery edition. With linked analysis (see Chapter 17), we can only pass filter values between charts. Here we don't want to filter, but show a different measure. For this, we need to go to SAP Lumira, designer edition and a script that adds this feature.

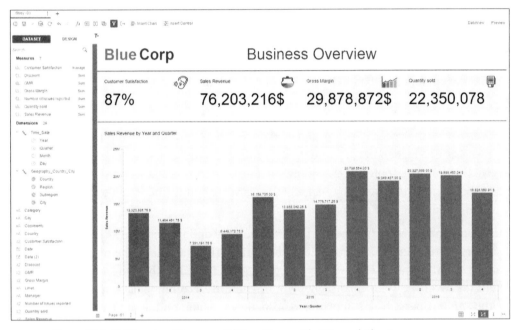

Figure 24.1 SAP Lumira, Discovery Edition Story with KPIs and Chart

After saving the story in SAP Lumira, discovery edition, we can see the same document pop up in SAP Lumira, designer edition as a .lumx file (**BLUE**) in the **Documents** view. This .lumx contains the story as a composite component (Figure 24.2). If your SAP Lumira document contains multiple stories, you will find multiple composites here. In the next section, we take a more detailed look on what we can do with the specific characteristics of these composites.

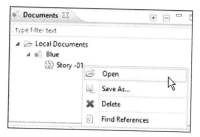

Figure 24.2 .lumx File with Story in SAP Lumira, Designer Edition

When we open the composite, we see that a container component of the type **Story** is used. All the objects that we used to create the story, like the charts, images, and shapes, are now available as components in the **Outline** view (Figure 24.3). We also see all the **Data Sources** that have been used, and some **Technical Components**.

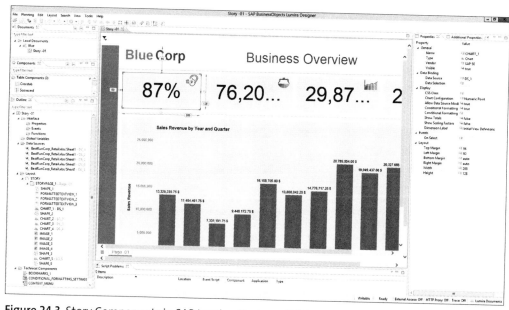

Figure 24.3 Story Components in SAP Lumira, Designer Edition

In this example, we add a simple script to the images in the four KPI blocks (Figure 24.4). In the **On Click** events, we add an event that changes the selected measure in the data source that is used for the column chart (**DS_5**).

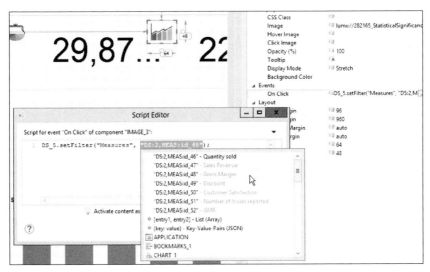

Figure 24.4 Adding a Script in SAP Lumira, Designer Edition

After saving the story in SAP Lumira, designer edition and opening the document in SAP Lumira, discovery edition, we can now click the images and execute the event scripts that we just added to change the displayed measure in the chart (Figure 24.5).

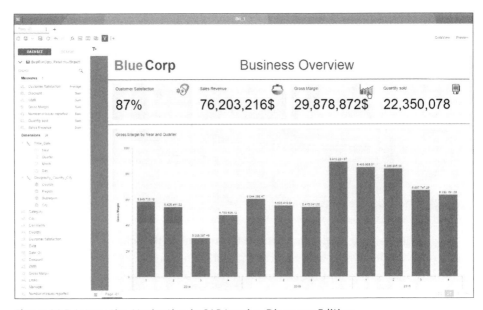

Figure 24.5 Interactive Navigation in SAP Lumira, Discovery Edition

24.2   Combining Multiple Stories

In SAP Lumira, designer edition we can create new applications from scratch, by adding new data sources and adding components to the layout canvas, writing scripts, etc. But, we also have the ability to reuse objects from existing SAP Lumira, designer edition applications and SAP Lumira, discovery edition stories and combine and enrich those in a new story.

With SAP Lumira 2.0, the composites were introduced, which act a bit like an application in an application. Composites are modular blocks of components that can be reused in one or even multiple applications. A great feature of this is that when a change is made in the original composite, this is immediately reflected in all the applications that use this composite.

As we have seen, a complete SAP Lumira, discovery edition story is also represented as a composite, and thus also has these characteristics.

In the following example, we combine two stories that were created in SAP Lumira, discovery edition and saved in separate .lumx document. Next to a BlueCorp story (Figure 24.1), we also created a RedCorp story (Figure 24.6). As good practice, we renamed the stories to **Story – Blue** and **Story – Red**, to make it clear where they came from (Figure 24.7).

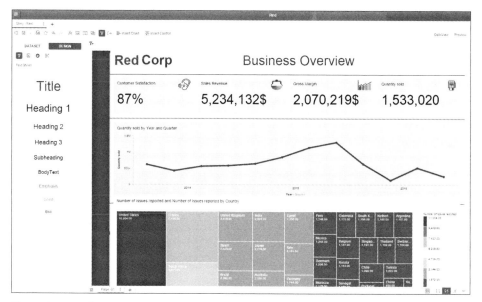

Figure 24.6 RedCorp SAP Lumira, Discovery Edition Story

In SAP Lumira, designer edition, we created a new document in which we added a new application called **BLUE_AND_RED** (Figure 24.7).

Figure 24.7 Blue and Red Stories

In this new application, we add a **Pagebook** component. We then drag and drop the **Story – Blue** composite onto the first page, drop the **Story – Red** composite onto the second page, and rename the stories once more (Figure 24.8).

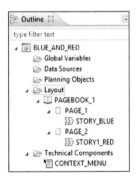

Figure 24.8 Outline with Two Stories

Figure 24.9 shows the output of this application in a browser. With the **Pagebook** controller on the right side of the page, the user can switch to the second page.

As we are using the composites in this SAP Lumira, designer edition application, any changes to these composites will be reflected in the application, without having to change it. We open our RedCorp story once more in SAP Lumira, discovery edition and make some obvious changes to it: everything that was red is now adjusted to yellow, and a filter was added (Figure 24.10). After refreshing the SAP Lumira, designer edition application in the browser, the adjusted story is displayed (Figure 24.11).

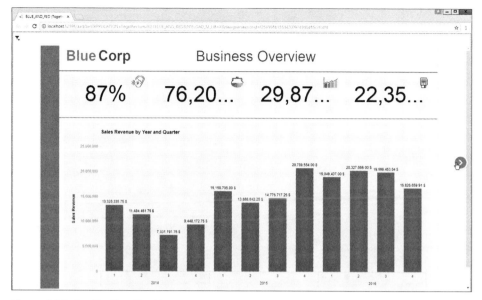

Figure 24.9 Application Runtime

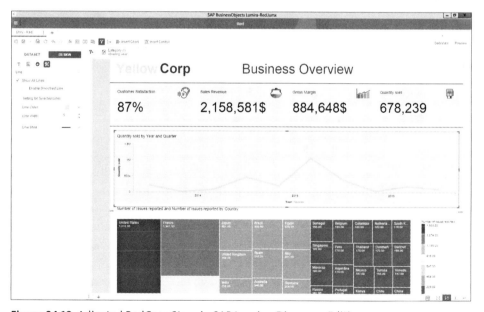

Figure 24.10 Adjusted RedCorp Story in SAP Lumira, Discovery Edition

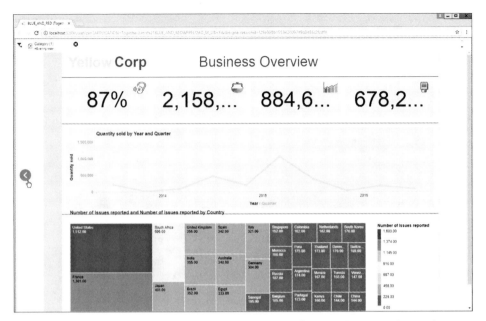

Figure 24.11 SAP Lumira, Designer Edition Application Reflecting the Story Changed in SAP Lumira, Discovery Edition

24.3   Upgrading the Story

In the previous section, we added the composites of the SAP Lumira stories one-on-one to a new application. What we also can do is copy individual objects from a composite into a new application. This gives a different set of possibilities, as we have the option to only use parts of the story that were prepared in SAP Lumira, discovery edition. For example, only the data sources and the charts are used, while all the objects that are relevant to the layout and look and feel of the story are not taken into account.

This approach is extremely useful in the scenario where a business user creates a story with SAP Lumira, discovery edition, is happy about the data and the visualizations, but wants this story to be used by a wide user community. The IT department could then upgrade this story to a standardized governed application or dashboard with SAP Lumira, designer edition. This can be done by using templates and custom CSS classes to improve the layout and apply the corporate reporting standards. They can use the adaptive layout component to make the application more usable on mobile devices and, as we have seen in Section 24.1, additional interactivity features can be added by using scripts.

Let's go through the steps to do this:

1. First, we add a new application in our SAP Lumira document via the **Create Application...** option (Figure 24.12).

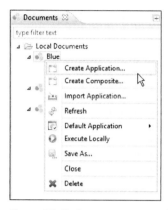

Figure 24.12 Create a New Application

2. In this example, we use the **Standard Basic Layout** template that is included in the SAP Lumira, designer edition installation (Figure 24.13). Of course, you can also use your own templates or select **Blank** to use no template at all.

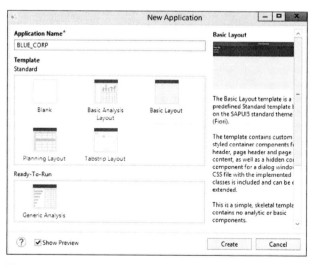

Figure 24.13 New Application Templates

3. As shown in Figure 24.14, we now can copy and paste objects from our story composite (**Story – Blue**) to our new application (**BLUE_CORP**). In this example, we copied the five data sources, and the five charts.

Figure 24.14 New Application with Reused Objects

4. We used a grid layout component to arrange the four KPI tiles on top and adjusted the **Layout** settings in such a way that all the components resize accordingly when the window size of the browser changes (Figure 24.15).

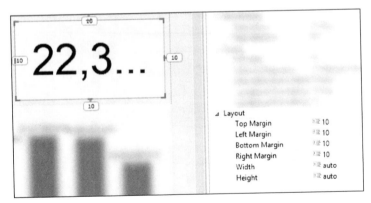

Figure 24.15 Layout Settings

5. Figure 24.16 shows the output of our application in the browser. As you can see, although the browser window is resized in a bit of a strange way, all the charts are still displayed nicely, without any overlap or missing pieces.

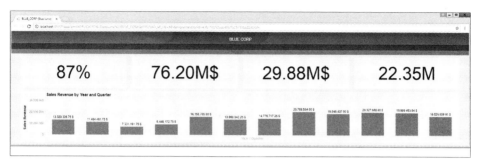

Figure 24.16 Application in Browser

24.4   Data Enrichment

The final interoperability scenario that we discuss here brings a unique feature of SAP Lumira, discovery edition into SAP Lumira, designer edition: data enrichment. In the previous scenario, we already saw that we can copy and paste data sources from the SAP Lumira, discovery edition story composites to SAP Lumira, designer edition applications. In the broadest sense, this means that all the actions available for an acquired dataset in SAP Lumira, discovery edition (in the **DataView** mode) are still usable in SAP Lumira, designer edition. As such, data enrichments like custom hierarchies, custom groupings, trimmed fields, replacements, etc. are available. Custom dimensions and measures that we can create ourselves with the formula editor are also present, as are the built-in calculations to create counters, moving averages, or etc. Finally, merged, appended, and linked datasets are in as well.

As you can imagine, these features provide a lot of possibilities for powerful interoperability scenarios between SAP Lumira, discovery edition and SAP Lumira, designer edition. We are able to use SAP Lumira, discovery edition to prepare our datasets that we want to leverage in SAP Lumira, designer edition applications. We can also bring in local, offline data this way. To make it even more interesting, we can keep using SAP Lumira, discovery edition to maintain the dataset, after the application has been published. Let's look at that scenario in a bit more detail.

24

In our dataset, we create a custom grouping of the countries, dividing them in a **Main**, **Growth**, and **Others** group (Figure 24.17). We do this in the **DataView** mode, using the **Group By Selection** option.

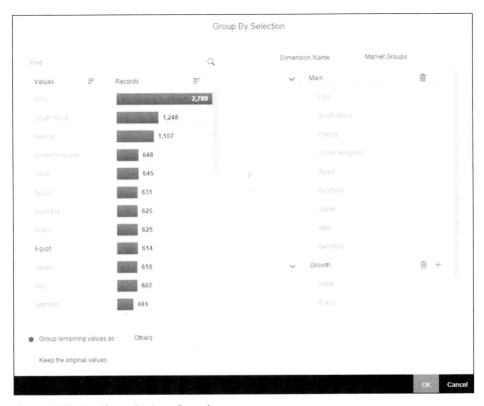

Figure 24.17 Creating a Custom Grouping

Next, we set up a crosstab that shows the number of incidents for these new groups, for each month. In addition, we add a moving average measure via the **Calculations** menu (Figure 24.18).

We save the story and switch over to SAP Lumira, designer edition. Here we add a new application to our SAP Lumira document. We use the **Basic Analysis Layout** template. Now we copy the data source from the composite into the application and link all the visualization and navigation components to this data source. The result is shown in Figure 24.19.

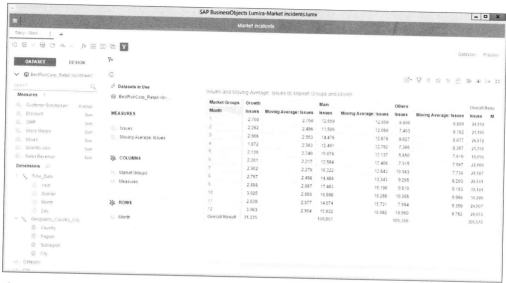

Figure 24.18 Set Up a Crosstab with Moving Average Measure

Figure 24.19 SAP Lumira, Designer Edition Application Using Data Source Created in SAP Lumira, Discovery Edition

When we save this application and then execute it in a browser, we can play around with the dimensions and measures. Figure 24.20 shows the output, after removing the moving average measure and adding the countries. Now we can clearly see the grouping that we set up in the data view of SAP Lumira, discovery edition.

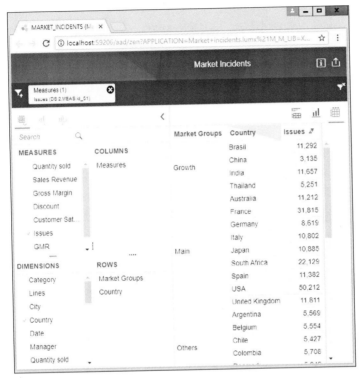

Figure 24.20 Application in Browser

Let's go back to SAP Lumira, discovery edition, where we open our .lumx document once more. We will now make some changes to the setup of the **Market Groups**. For example, we remove a bunch of countries from the **Main** group and move **China** from the **Growth** group to the **Main** group (Figure 24.21). Finally, we save the story again.

If we run the application from SAP Lumira, designer edition again, we will notice that the changes in the **Market Groups** are now reflected in the output of the crosstab (Figure 24.22).

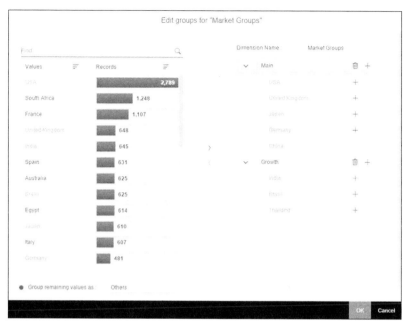

Figure 24.21 Edit Groups

Figure 24.22 Application in Browser After Changing the Dataset

24.5   Limitations

Interoperability between SAP Lumira, discovery edition and SAP Lumira, designer edition comes with a few limitation, which we discuss in this section.

24.5.1   Editing

Most of the actions that we used in the previous sections have a significant impact on the available features in SAP Lumira, discovery edition, after editing a story in SAP Lumira, designer edition. Most importantly, we cannot add any more pages to the story, and we are also not able to add visualizations to a page. We are able to use the context menu actions on a visualization (i.e., a filter) and refresh imported datasets.

To remind you of these limitations, you will get a warning message every time you save a story in SAP Lumira, designer edition that was originally created in SAP Lumira, discovery edition reminding you that you will no longer be able to edit the story in SAP Lumira, discovery edition. When you open this story in SAP Lumira, discovery edition, you will get another warning that the story is now read-only, as it has been modified in SAP Lumira, designer edition.

A good practice is to create a copy of a story before you start editing it in SAP Lumira, designer edition, as there is no option to revert back afterward.

24.5.2   Data Sources

We have seen in the data enrichment scenario that we can keep using imported data sources that were created (and adjusted) in SAP Lumira, discovery edition and in SAP Lumira, designer edition applications. We can also add live data sources in SAP Lumira, designer edition to such an application. A limitation here is that these application with mixed data sources cannot be scheduled on the SAP BusinessObjects BI platform.

24.6   Summary

This chapter demonstrated how SAP Lumira, discovery edition and SAP Lumira, designer edition can work together, where each tool uses its specific features to extend the capabilities of the other tool. This is called interoperability. We looked at four different real-world usage scenarios. Additionally, we discussed the limitations of interoperability.

Appendices

A   Converting SAP Lumira 1.x Documents to SAP Lumira 2.1   473

B   Software Development Kit   483

C   The Authors   489

Appendix A

Converting SAP Lumira 1.x
Documents to SAP Lumira 2.1

For users who have already created SAP Lumira 1.x documents, SAP released an update that enables you to convert and reuse existing stories in SAP Lumira 2.1.

Since the release of SAP Lumira 1.x in May 2012, a lot of visualizations and stories have been created by the SAP Lumira community. Now that SAP Lumira 2.1 has been introduced, we want to leverage and reuse our investments. This chapter lists the prerequisites and explains the steps you need to take to convert existing SAP Lumira 1.x documents to the new SAP Lumira 2.1 .lumx format, stored locally and on the SAP BusinessObjects BI platform.

As per the writing of this book, there are also limitations related to features that work differently. Section A.4 highlights the most important limitations. Let's start by listing the prerequisites.

A.1   Prerequisites

To be able to convert existing SAP Lumira 1.x documents to SAP Lumira 2.1, an update of the SAP Lumira desktop application to version 1.31 patch 8 or higher is required. As of version 1.31 patch 8, a **Save for Migration** option has been added which enables you to set a mandatory flag so that SAP Lumira 1.x documents can be imported into SAP Lumira 2.1.

SAP Lumira 1.31 patch 8 can be downloaded from the SAP Software Download Center on the SAP Support Portal and installed, similarly to the processes described in Chapter 2, Section 2.3 and Section 2.4.

A.2   Convert Local Document

To convert a local SAP Lumira 1.x document to SAP Lumira 2.1, please follow the steps listed here:

1. Open the document you want to convert in SAP Lumira 1.31 patch 8 or higher.

2. Click on **File** · **Save for Migration,** as shown in Figure A.1.

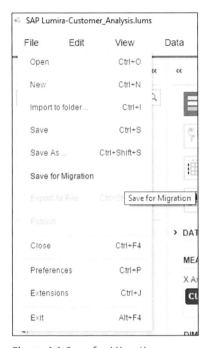

Figure A.1 Save for Migration

3. The **Save Option** dialog box is displayed (Figure A.2). Click on **Save.**

4. A dialog prompts you to confirm whether you want to replace the existing SAP Lumira 1.x document. There is no need to change the name of a document during this step. An SAP Lumira 1.x document that has been saved with the **Save for Migration** option can still be opened and edited in SAP Lumira 1.x. However, it could be helpful during the migration process to add a prefix for reference.

5. A message will be displayed to confirm that the document is saved successfully.

6. Start SAP Lumira, discovery edition and click on **File** · **Import to folder** (Figure A.3) to import the SAP Lumira 1.x document into the local documents folder.

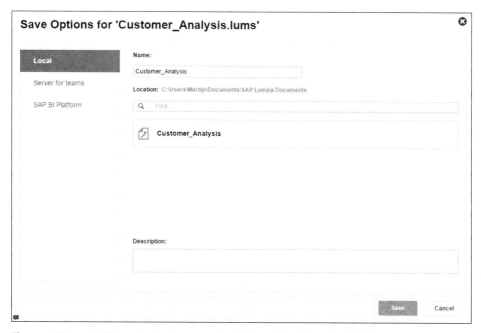

Figure A.2 Save SAP Lumira 1.x Document with Save for Migration Option

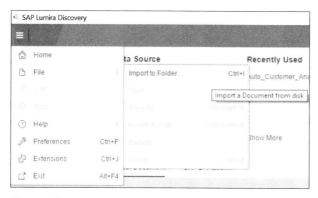

Figure A.3 Import SAP Lumira 1.x Document in SAP Lumira 2.1 Local Folder

7. Select the SAP Lumira 1.x document and click **Open**.

8. A confirmation dialog is displayed that indicates the document is successfully imported. Click on **OK** to open the imported document.

> **Note**
>
> If the SAP Lumira 1.x document was not saved with the **Save For Migration** option before importing it to SAP Lumira, discovery edition, you will receive an error message with the text Unable to open document. Make sure the **Save for Migration** option is selected in SAP Lumira Desktop.

> **Note**
>
> Please note that the SAP Lumira document still has a .lums extension after importing it to the local folder. This is highlighted by a different icon and document type in the **Local Document** section on the home page. Only .lums documents that were saved with the **Save for Migration** option are listed.

9. Next, save the SAP Lumira document in your local folder and automatically convert it to the SAP Lumira 2.1 .lumx format. Click on **File • Save As** to open the **Save Document** dialog box.

10. Click on **Save**. A confirmation dialog, informing you that once the new version is saved, you won't be able to open the document in an earlier version of SAP Lumira, will be displayed.

11. Click **OK** to save the Lumira document into the new (.lumx) version. A message will be displayed to indicate that the document was saved successfully.

12. In the **Local Document** section on the home page, the SAP Lumira document will now be available with **Type** .lumx.

A.3   Convert Document on SAP BusinessObjects BI Platform

After upgrading to the latest version of SAP Lumira, server edition, described in Chapter 21, Section 21.2, none of the existing SAP Lumira 1.x documents published on the SAP BusinessObjects BI platform can be opened from the BI Launchpad. When trying to open an SAP Lumira 1.x document from the BI Launchpad, you will receive an error message reading **Cannot access the document created using older format of Lumira**.

Please follow next steps to open, convert, and re-publish SAP Lumira documents to the SAP BusinessObjects BI platform:

1. Open SAP Lumira 1.31 Patch 8 desktop client and click on **File · Preferences · Network**.

2. Enter the URL of the SAP BusinessObjects BI platform as shown in Figure A.4.

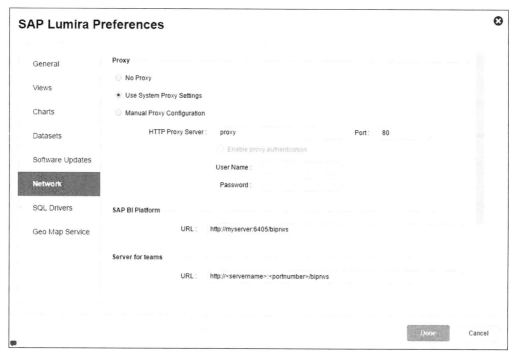

Figure A.4 SAP Lumira Preferences: Network

3. Replace the <servername> with the first part of the BI launch pad URL, for example: *http://***myserver***:8080/BOE/BI*. Replace the <portnumber> with the port number on which the Web Application Container Server (WACS) is running. By default, this is port 6405 for HTTP.

4. To validate the port number, log in to the CMC (Central Management Console) and browse to **Servers · Core Services · <CMS>.WebApplication ContainerServer**. Open the service and scroll down to the properties of the Web Application Container Service. Here you can find the HTTP port defined (Figure A.5). If your WACS is configured to run on HTTPS, please scroll down and recover the HTTPS port from the **HTTPS Configuration** section.

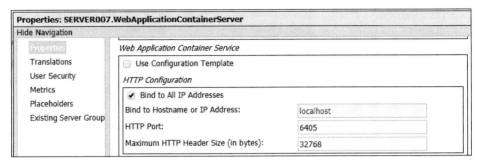

Figure A.5 HTTP Port of the Web Application Container Service

5. Click on **Done** to save the network preferences.

6. Next step is to log in to the SAP BusinessObjects BI platform. Select the **Authentication Type** and enter the **User Name** and **Password**. Please notice that the URL is copied from your network preferences (Figure A.6).

Figure A.6 Connect to SAP BusinessObjects BI Platform

7. Click **Connect**.

8. Browse to the folder where your SAP Lumira 1.x document is stored.

9. Select the SAP Lumira 1.x document and double-click on the document name to open the document (Figure A.7).

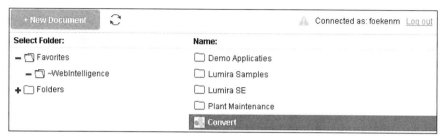

Figure A.7 Browse to the SAP Lumira 1.x Document on the SAP BusinessObjects BI Platform

10. Now repeat steps 2 through 8 from Section A.2 to convert the SAP Lumira 1.x document which was retrieved from the SAP BusinessObjects BI platform using both the SAP Lumira 1.31 patch 8 and SAP Lumira 2.1 desktop clients.

11. Instead of saving the SAP Lumira document locally, we can directly save it to the SAP BusinessObjects BI Platform. Click on **File** · **Save As** to open the **Save Document** dialog box.

12. Switch to SAP BusinessObjects BI platform, as shown in Figure A.8.

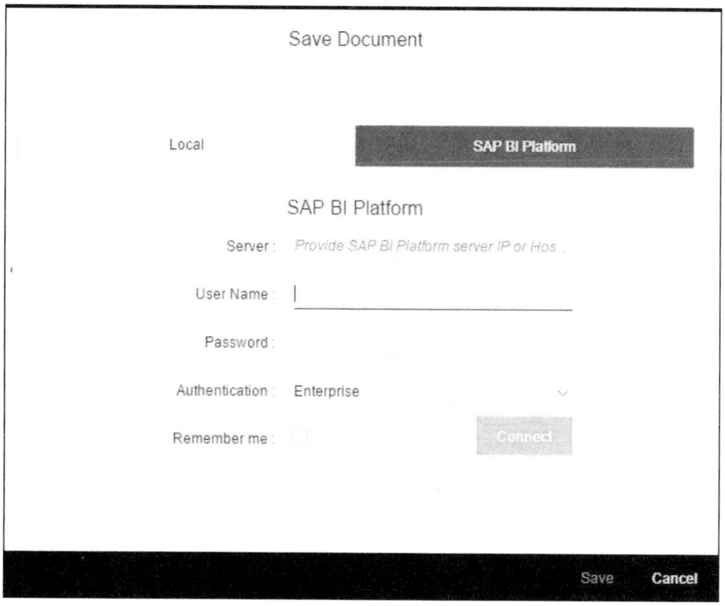

Figure A.8 Save Document to SAP BusinessObjects BI Platform

In SAP Lumira 2.1, all communication to the SAP BusinessObjects BI platform is handled through CORBA. This means that instead of using the URL for the WACS you enter your CMS name only. Internally the WACS is contacted to make calls and display the folders.

SAP Lumira, Discovery Edition 2.1 Logon to SAP BusinessObjects BI Platform Issues

If you run into any issues connecting to the SAP BusinessObjects BI platform, please consult SAP Note 2525751 (*https://launchpad.support.sap.com/#/notes/2525751*). This note contains information on how to troubleshoot and resolve these issues, including how to enable tracing.

13. Enter the **Server**, select the **Authentication**, and submit your **User Name** and **Password**. Click on **Connect**.

14. Browse to the folder and click on **Save**, as shown in Figure A.9.

Figure A.9 Save SAP Lumira 2.1 Document to SAP BusinessObjects BI Platform

15. A **Confirmation** dialog, informing you that once the new version is saved, you won't be able to open the document in an earlier version of SAP Lumira, will be displayed. Please confirm by clicking **OK**.

16. Now log in to the SAP BusinessObjects BI platform through the BI Launchpad and browse to the location where the SAP Lumira document is stored. The document is now visible and you can open it to validate whether all features have been converted properly (Figure A.10).

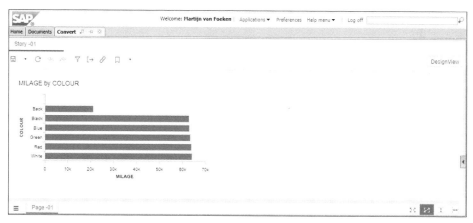

Figure A.10 View Converted SAP Lumira Document on BI Launchpad

A.4   Limitations

As per the writing of this book, the following limitations when converting SAP Lumira 1.x document to SAP Lumira 2.1 are applicable:

- Conversion of SAP Lumira 1.x documents based on SAP HANA online, as a data source is not supported.

- SAP Lumira 1.x documents with SAP BusinessObjects BI universe (.unv) cannot be refreshed.

SAP Lumira 2.1 Conversion Note: List of Features/Limitations

A full list of features that work differently and current limitations when SAP Lumira 1.x documents are converted to SAP Lumira 2.1 is available through SAP Note 2509882 (*https://launchpad.support.sap.com/#/notes/2509882*).

Appendix B
Software Development Kit

Being able to create your own visualization and data access extensions can be extremely valuable. SAP Lumira offers both a Visualization and Data Access SDK that will enable you to keep up with changing visualization demands and available data structures.

SAP Lumira offers a software development kit (SDK) that allows you as a developer to create third-party components, known as SDK extension components or extensions. As mentioned in Chapter 3, Section 3.2.7, these components extend the functionality of SAP Lumira. In the recent years, technologies like d3.js have simplified innovative chart creation. The ability to create data access extensions provides you with a way to quickly connect to new data structures.

Creating an extension requires specific skills and knowledge like HTML, CSS, and JavaScript (including the jQuery framework) and can be performed by using any XML and JavaScript editor. Reading this appendix will not make you a skilled extensions developer. The scope of this appendix is limited to providing you with an overview of different SDKs and explaining which development tools can be used. You'll also learn where to find additional information and samples.

B.1 Development Tools

SAP offers development tools that can help to design and create extensions. In the following sections, we explain how to set up these tools to get you started.

B.1.1 SAP Cloud Platform Web IDE

SAP Cloud Platform Web IDE is a web-based development environment that simplifies the end-to-end application lifecycle: prototyping, development, packaging, deployment, and custom extensions. You can try it for free or log in at *https://cloud-platform.sap.com/capabilities/devops/web-ide.html*.

After completing the sign-up process, select your **Region** and click on your account to access the SAP Cloud Platform Cockpit (Figure B.1).

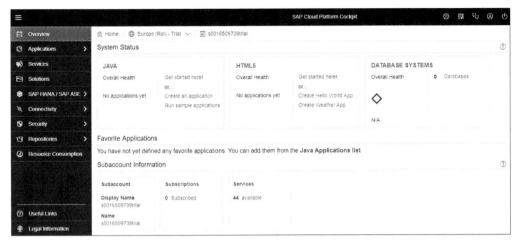

Figure B.1 Overview of the SAP Cloud Platform Cockpit

Select **Services** from the menu, click on **SAP Web IDE** (Figure B.2), and launch the service.

Figure B.2 Select the SAP Web IDE Service

The next step is to enable the VizPacker plugin, which is described in the following section.

B.1.2   VizPacker Plugin

VizPacker provides an extension framework with an API that allows you to customize visualizations or develop your own extensions based on the Visualization SDK. Let's take a look at how to enable the VizPacker plugin in the SAP Web IDE environment.

1. Select **Tools • Preferences** and click on **Plugins** (Figure B.3).

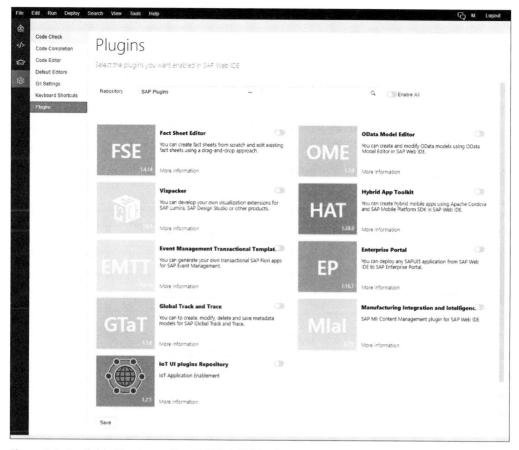

Figure B.3 Available Plugins on the SAP Web IDE Environment

2. Toggle the button next to **VizPacker** and click **Save**.

3. Refresh your browser to activate the plugin.

4. When you select the development icon in the left bar, you will notice a new icon is displayed in the top-right corner indicating that the VizPacker plugin is enabled.

B.2   Visualization SDK

With the Visualization SDK, you can create new chart types, known as Visualization extensions. Now that we have VizPacker plugin installed, let's learn the process of creating a visualization extension:

1. Create a project.
2. Upload a CSV file that acts as the data source.
3. Customize the code and styling options.
4. Prepare the extension to use in SAP Lumira, discovery edition.
5. Extract the content and deploy the extension in SAP Lumira, discovery edition.

To create a new project, click on **File · New · Project from template**. Under **Categories**, choose **Visualization SDK** (Figure B.4) and click **Next**.

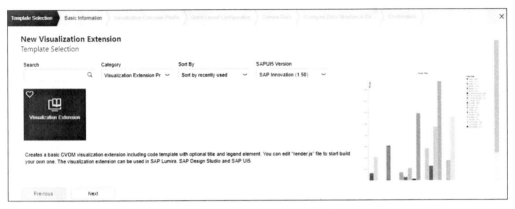

Figure B.4 Select New Visualization Extension as Template

On the **Basic Information** tab, enter a **Project Name** and click **Next**. Complete the requested information on all subsequent tabs depending on the requirements of the visualization extensions that you want to develop.

> **SDK Documentation**
>
> For more information on how to create an extension using the Visualization SDK, please refer to the *Visualization SDK Plugin for SAP Web IDE Guide* on *https:// help.sap.com*. Here you can also find the Visualization API Reference, which lists all the namespaces and methods exposed by all visualizations.

After completing the wizard, your project is created (Figure B.5) and you are now able to customize the code and styling by modifying the *render.js* file. The **VizPacker Quick**

Preview displays how the visualization renders when deployed. Furthermore, you can toggle the **Data Table** and **Data Binding Panel** to view or change the data.

Figure B.5 Project in SAP Web IDE

After finalizing your changes, you have to prepare the file for use in SAP Lumira, discovery edition. Click **Pack**.

A message is displayed to indicate that the Visualization extension has been packed and is successfully downloaded (Figure B.6). You can now install the extension as described in Chapter 3, Section 3.2.7.

Figure B.6 Visualization Extension Packed and Downloaded

In the next section, we describe how to use the Data Access SDK to create Data Access extensions.

B.3   Data Access SDK

Data Access SDK extensions enable you to import additional data sources such as XML files, or other formatted data into SAP Lumira, discovery edition not covered by the default supported data sources that are described in Chapter 5. For example:

- Event log files
- Directory listings
- Online social data sources such as Twitter and Facebook
- Google Analytics

By using a data source extension, users can perform the standard workflow when importing data, like preview, edit and refresh. Furthermore, users can develop their own user interface, including a dialog box to select a file or connect to a remote data source.

SDK Documentation

A step-by-step guide how to create a Data Access extension is beyond the scope of this book. For more information on how to create an extension using the Data Access SDK, please refer to the *Developer Guide: Data Access SDK* on *https://help.sap.com*. Here you can also download Data Access SDK templates and samples to get you started.

Appendix C
The Authors

Xavier Hacking is an SAP business intelligence specialist from the Netherlands, and works as a consultant for Interdobs. He has a master's degree in industrial engineering and management science from the Eindhoven University of Technology. For the past 10 years he has worked with a wide range of products from SAP Business Warehouse and SAP BusinessObjects BI toolset.

Xavier has coauthored numerous books, including *SAP Lumira, Designer Edition—The Comprehensive Guide, 3rd Edition*, *SAP BusinessObjects Design Studio—The Comprehensive Guide, 2nd Edition*, *SAP BusinessObjects Dashboards 4.1 Cookbook*, *Getting Started with SAP BusinessObjects Design Studio* and *SAP BusinessObjects Dashboards 4.0 Cookbook* and is a writer for *SAP BI Expert* magazine. He is also part of the Dutch BI Podcast, and blogs on all sorts of business-intelligence-related topics at *http://www.hackingsap.com*. You can follow him on Twitter at *@xjhacking*.

Martijn van Foeken is an SAP business intelligence specialist working as a consultant for Interdobs in the Netherlands. Martijn has a Master of Science degree in business administration with a specialization in knowledge and information management from Radboud University in Nijmegen.

He has more than 12 years of experience with business intelligence and IT consultancy working with a wide range of SAP BusinessObjects BI products as well as SAP HANA and SAP Analytics Cloud. You can follow him on Twitter at *@mfoeken*.

Index

.lumx file format 36, 365, 455, 456
30-day trial 48

A

Access levels 407
Access rights 422
Ad-hoc data comparison 242
Advanced features 456
Aggregation type 104, 108, 193, 260, 320
AIX 392
Analysis options 259
   drilling 263
   filtering 262
   sorting 260
   swap axes 264
   totals 260, 261
Analytic view 380
Appending data 227
Application authorizations 407
Array bind size 156
Array fetch size 156
Auditing 414
Authentication 172
Authorizations 407
Axis scale 241

B

Bar charts 237, 271, 272, 323
   formatting 273
   pictograms 273
   properties 272
Base map 310
Batch files 63
BI inbox 434
BI Launchpad 37, 38, 109, 383, 421, 428, 440, 445
Bookmarks 411, 413, 430
   dropdown menu 432
   manage 412
   metadata 413

Box plots 302, 303
Bubble charts 292
   for time series 294
   formatting 293
   properties 293
Business intelligence portfolio 38
Business users 42

C

Calculated dimensions 204, 206
Calculated measures 206
Calculated objects 204
   create 204
Canvas 88, 235, 255
   default 236
   limitations 238
   settings 89
Central Management Console
   (CMC) 133, 414, 439, 441
   auditing 415
Chart Builder 238
   chart properties 240
   conditional formatting 252
   reference lines 249
Chart creation 235
Chart picker 105
Chart types 105
   overview 306
Charts 81
Choropleth 310
Choropleth maps 313
Collaboration 451
Color palette 245
   customize/create 246
   default 245
Column charts 274, 359
Combination charts 304
   multiple chart types 305
   two measures 305
Comparison charts 271
Composites 459

Conditional formatting 251
  conflicts 252
  rules 252
  text 253
Connection pool mode 156
Content management system (CMS) ... 387, 391
Controls 338
  adding to canvas 339
  choice 340, 342, 343
  complex filter 340, 344
  control type dialog 340
  date 340, 342, 343
  deleting 345
  dropdown 340, 342
  editing 345
  options 340
  slider 340, 343, 344
  text box 340, 341
Correlation charts 289
Create groups 220
Crosstab 255, 374, 466
  add new 255
  analysis options 259
  context menu 257
  creating 255, 256
  display options 258
  filter bar 262
  formatting 256, 257
  maximize mode 262
  number format 258
CSV file 376
Currencies and units 134
Custom groupings 466

D

Data Access SDK 84
Data acquisition 113
  Microsoft Excel 114
  query with SQL 149
  SAP BW 124
  SAP HANA 136
  text files 117
  universe 144
  Windows clipboard 121

Data actions 219
  for strings 222
  live data 219
Data analysis 97, 181
Data enrichment 465
Data manipulation 189
Data preparation 99, 465
Data refresh 426
Data sources 32, 68, 96, 159, 264, 425,
  457, 470
  editing 77
  recently used 68
Data summary 99
Data type 322
Data view 86, 98, 182, 220, 377, 466
  facet view 182
  grid view 182
  sorting icons 182
  summary tab 183
Database middeware 149
Dataset links 356
  defining 356
Datasets 81
  auto-enrichmentauto-enrichment 229
  combine 78
  create from clipboard 121
  create from Excel 115
  create new 144
  creation with SQL 154
  edit acquisition details 162
  edit connection parameters 160
  enrichments 81
  export 373, 376
  export as file 376
  export to PDF 373
  filtering 318
  limitations 113
  linking 77, 353
  linking v. merging 353
  menu 237
  merging 223
  primary 357
  publish 74, 110
  publish to SAP HANA 377
  refresh 159
  republish 380

Datasets (Cont.)
restore 354
secondary 361
size 132
Date data type 100
Date/time hierarchies 100, 201
Delegated search 135
Design view 87, 104, 424
grid 89
Device-specific category 441
Dimensions ... 102, 128, 142, 173, 183, 190, 239, 266, 357
actions 191
date data type 100
hierarchies 128
linked 359
matched 358
palette 245
selection 226
Document rights 409
Donut charts 283
formatting 284
properties 284
Drill by 328, 329
X-axis dimensions 331
Drill down 328, 329
Drill up 328
Dynamic calculations 268

E

Edit rights 431
Enrichment files 230
Esri 310
Esri ArcGIS 311
Esri ArcGIS Online service 83
Esri base maps 310, 312
Event scripts 458
Export records 375
Export types 375
Extensions 84, 418

F

Facet view 98, 185
change measures 186

Feeding panel 239, 361
adding measures 239
Filter bar 325
Filter by measure 262
Filter operators 322
Filtering data in visualizations 320
adding filters 320
alternative workflow 324
bar charts 320
data picker 323
dimensions 320
drill options 328
filter dialog 321
hierarchies 328, 329
interacting with filters 325
maximum members 323
operators 322
ranking 331, 333
selecting data points 326, 327
Filtering story data 336
applying filters 336
interacting with filters 338
tokens 325
Filters 262, 317, 355, 448
add 324
apply 319
datasets 318
display 374
editing 326
icons 325
ranking 332
using controls 338
Formulas 205
character string functions 207
data and time 209
expression functions 213
miscellaneous functions 216
numeric functions 217
operator functions 218
syntax 207
Functions 205
Funnel charts 287

G

Geo maps 83, 173
   bubbles 313
   choropleth 313
   markers 314
   pie charts 315
   setting up 312
Geographic hierarchies 194
   latitude/longitude 198
   names 195
   solved/unsolved 197
   validation 196
Geographic visualizations 309
Global bookmarks 431
Grid layout 464
Grid view 183
   cell width 185
   rearranging 184
   sorting 185

H

Heap size 355
Heat map 107, 278, 279
Help menu 78
Hierarchies 134, 194, 381
   custom 202
   live data 194
Hierarchy levels 264
Highlight outliers 255
Home page 67

I

InfoProvider 126, 168
Inner join 225
Input controls 448
Input parameters 139, 176
Input variables 126
Installation 47
Installation logs 59
Installation Manager 55, 56, 60
Interoperability 44

J

JavaScript Object Notation (JSON) 230
Join operator 225, 354
Join types 354, 355, 360

K

KPI blocks 457

L

Language setting 80
Latitude/longitude 198
Layer types 312
Left outer join 225
License agreement 56
License model 47
Lifecycle management 384, 416
Line charts 107, 297, 298
   for time series 299
   formatting 299
   properties 298
   time series 299
Linked analysis 334
   considerations 336
   editing 335
Linking datasets 353, 361
   limitations 355
   terminology 354
   terms 354
Linux 392
Live data 167
Local documents 69, 365
Log files 63, 65

M

Managed connections 409
Mapping adjustments 164
Marimekko charts 274
   context menu 275
   properties 275
   stacking 276
Measures 128, 134, 183, 193, 239, 359
   actions 193

Measures (Cont.)
   combined 361
   create 102, 103
   options 239
   sorting 187
Menu 71
   data 76
   edit 76
   homepage 72
   preferences 80
Microsoft Excel 97, 114, 427
   merged cells 117
   multiple sheets 116
Mobile category 439
   generic 439
Moving average measure 468
Multi-dimensional analysis service (MDAS) 394

N

Network charts 294, 295
Numeric point 279

O

Object dependencies 191
Objects 190
Offline maps 309, 311, 315
   formatting 315
OLAP connection ... 130, 143, 168, 171, 173, 177
   SAP HANA 142
Online maps 309, 310
   customized 312
OpenDocument 371
   generating links 428
   link syntax 429
   syntax 429

P

Package structure 379
Pagebook 460
Parallel coordinates charts 303
Parent level objects 200
Percentage charts 281

Pictograms 273
Pie charts 281
   formatting 283
   properties 282
Pool timeout 156
Preview mode 109
Privileges 64
Product Availability Matrix (PAM) 51, 168
Promotion Management 416, 418

Q

Query with SQL 149, 154, 428
Quick Sizer 400
   template 402

R

Radar charts 276, 277
   line formatting 276
Ranking 331
   limitations 333
Reference lines 249, 251
   dynamic 249, 250
   fixed 249
RESTful web services (RWS) 387

S

SAP Analysis for Microsoft Office 41, 45, 259
SAP Analytics Cloud 39, 42
SAP BEx Analyzer 39
SAP BEx conditions 135
SAP BEx query 126, 168, 170, 427
SAP Business Warehouse (SAP BW) 96, 124, 168, 425, 427
   create document 169
   data acquisition 124
   direct connection 125, 168
   limitations 132, 173
   support versions 124
   versions 168
SAP BusinessObjects BI
   analysis options 259
   portfolio 39
   tools 43

SAP BusinessObjects BI platform 35, 37, 70,
    109, 130, 168, 174, 368, 400, 422, 426, 438
    HTML mode 444
    managed connection 380
    managing content 406
    opening documents 371
    SAP Lumira integration 383
    server 371
    share stories 369
    sharing documents 370
    version 387
SAP BusinessObjects BI universe 144
    limitations 148
SAP BusinessObjects Design Studio 37, 386
SAP BusinessObjects Live Office 40
SAP BusinessObjects Mobile 38, 43, 437
    categories 441
    collaboration 451
    connectivity 438
    grouping 441
    mobile category 439
    server 438
    supported components 443
    supported devices 437
    using content 445
SAP BusinessObjects Web Intelligence . 41, 421
SAP BW live data 264
    attributes 266
    compact display 266
    dynamic calculations 267
    hierarchies 265
    suppress zeros 266
SAP Crystal Reports 40–42, 45, 421, 455
SAP HANA 96, 136, 143, 173, 378, 427
    connectivity 175
    dataset publishing 380
    direct connection 137
    direction connection 173
    HTTP connection 394, 395
    server 138
    supported versions 137, 174
SAP HANA Info Access Service 174, 395
SAP HANA Live 174, 380, 394
SAP HANA online discovery 75
SAP HANA Studio 381

SAP HANA view 75, 138, 176
    limitations 76
SAP HANA XS 174
SAP Jam Collaboration 451
SAP Java Connector 64
SAP Lumira
    documents folder 368
    extensions 410
    rooms 94
    SDK administrators 410
    web applications 385
SAP Lumira 2.0 455
    vs. SAP Lumira 1.0 92
SAP Lumira document 365
    appending 227
    bookmarks 430
    import 72
    interactions 424
    multiple users 426
    save locally 365
    save without data 367
    saving 73, 369
    share 368
    sharing and scheduling 432
SAP Lumira integration 383
SAP Lumira server 389
SAP Lumira server 1.x 386
SAP Lumira suite 36, 40
    scope 42
SAP Lumira, designer edition 37
    composites 460
    data preparation 465
    editing 470
    interoperability 455
    limitations 470
    script 456
SAP Lumira, discovery edition 36
    analysis options 259
    BI Launchpad UI 422
    chart comparison 306
    client tool 425
    creating charts 235
    download 51
    mobile 437
    SAP BEx features 264
    system requirements 50

SAP Lumira, discovery edition (Cont.)
   toolbar 90
   uninstall 59
   updating 61
SAP Lumira, server edition 38, 383, 404
   application maintenance 393
   deployment scenarios 385
   download 387
   installation 387
   installation wizard 391
   modify/remove 393
   system requirements 386
   Windows install 390
SAP ONE Support Launchpad 51
SAP Roambi Analytics 42
SAP Support Portal 388
Scatter plots 289
   animation 290
   for time series 291, 292
   formatting 291
   measures 290
   properties 290
Scatters 291
Scheduling 434
   reoccurance 435
Schemas 378
Secure Login Client 405
Security 384
Separation formats 117
Sharing 35, 432
Single sign-on 404
Sizing 399
   backend systems 403
   users 399
Solaris 392
Source time format 101
SQL databases 149
SQL drivers 83, 149
   install/uninstall 152
Stacked area charts 300
   properties 300
Stacked bar charts 284
   properties 285, 286
Stacked column charts 286
Stories 33, 95, 347, 424
   actions 422

Stories (Cont.)
   combining 459
   composites 456
   create new 96, 435
   filter 337
   finalize 107
   formatting 347
   mobile navigation 446
   mode 445
   native and HTML modes 443
   opening 422
   page settings 348
   pages 347
   running on mobile 446
   saving 426
   sharing 109, 365
   upgrading 462
Story formatting
   background 351
   images 350, 351
   text boxes 349
String objects 192
Structures 134
System requirements 50

T

Tag cloud 277
Templates 463
Text boxes 349
   styles 349
Text files 117, 427
   create dataset 118
   parameters 120
Time dimension 291
Toolbar buttons 91
Tracing 63, 64
Trees 295, 296
Trend charts 297
Troubleshooting 63

U

Universe query panel 147
Universes 427
User interface 67

User rights 408
User types 399

V

Variables 176
Visualization properties, generic 247
Visualization SDK 84
Visualizations 33
    creation 104, 359
    formatting 245
    interaction options 449
    mobile app 448
    picker 236
    properties 246, 247
    sharing 373

W

Waterfall charts 301
    formatting 302
    properties 301
Windows clipboard 121
    edits 162

X

X.509 certificate 405

Z

Zero suppression 135

- Install and configure SAP Lumira

- Build full-scale applications for planning, OLAP analysis, and more

- Learn how to use and develop SDK extensions

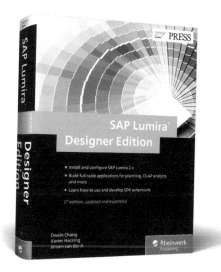

Dwain Chang, Xavier Hacking, Jeroen van der A

SAP Lumira, Designer Edition

The Comprehensive Guide

If building top-of-the-line analytical applications and dashboards is on your to-do list, you'll find everything you need in this guide to SAP Lumira, designer edition! Explore the IDE, understand the application design process, and take an in-depth look at component properties. Then enhance your applications with CSS, scripting for interactivity, and performance tuning. From installation to working with the SDK, this book is your one-stop shop!

approx 775 pages, 3rd edition, avail. 05/2018
E-Book: $69.99 | **Print:** $79.95 | **Bundle:** $89.99

www.sap-press.com/4512

- Your one-stop reference for all things WebI

- From report creation to publication, and everything in between

- Updated for release 4.2, SAP HANA, and more

Christian Ah-Soon, Jim Brogden, Dallas Marks, Gabriel Orthous, Heather Sinkwitz

SAP BusinessObjects Web Intelligence

The Comprehensive Guide

Bring your data presentations into focus with this comprehensive guide to SAP BusinessObjects Web Intelligence. Updated for WebI 4.2, this book will teach you to create, design, and share your reports, while exploring the fundamentals of WebI and its extended capabilities. This fourth edition includes information on data source options for building new documents and queries, and a new HTML5-based viewing interface. Punch up your reporting and analysis!

814 pages, 4th edition, pub. 09/2017
E-Book: $69.99 | **Print:** $79.95 | **Bundle:** $89.99

www.sap-press.com/4412

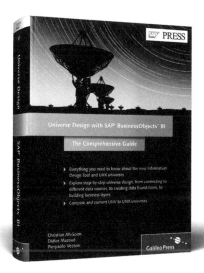

- Everything you need to know about the new Information Design Tool and UNX universes

- Explore step-by-step universe design, from connecting to different data sources, to creating data foundations, to building business layers

- Compare and convert UNV to UNX universes

Christian Ah-Soon, Didier Mazoué, Pierpaolo Vezzosi

Universe Design with SAP BusinessObjects BI

The Comprehensive Guide

Are you the master of your UNX universes? This comprehensive resource spans universe creation to universe publication. You'll learn to build single- and multisource data foundations and business layers and to convert UNV to UNX using the Information Design Tool. Get the step-by-step instructions and screenshots you need to design universes for the BOBJ galaxy!

729 pages, pub. 11/2013
E-Book: $69.99 | **Print:** $79.95 | **Bundle:** $89.99

www.sap-press.com/3412

- Everything you need to know about the new Information Design Tool and UNX universes

- Explore step-by-step universe design, from connecting to different data sources, to creating data foundations, to building business layers

- Compare and convert UNV to UNX universes

Christian Ah-Soon, Didier Mazoué, Pierpaolo Vezzosi

Universe Design with SAP BusinessObjects BI

The Comprehensive Guide

Are you the master of your UNX universes? This comprehensive resource spans universe creation to universe publication. You'll learn to build single- and multisource data foundations and business layers and to convert UNV to UNX using the Information Design Tool. Get the step-by-step instructions and screenshots you need to design universes for the BOBJ galaxy!

729 pages, pub. 11/2013
E-Book: $69.99 | **Print:** $79.95 | **Bundle:** $89.99

www.sap-press.com/3412

Interested in reading more?

Please visit our website for all new book
and e-book releases from SAP PRESS.

www.sap-press.com